Sketch-O-Frenia

Fifty short and witty satirical sketches

John Dessler
and
Lawrence Phillis

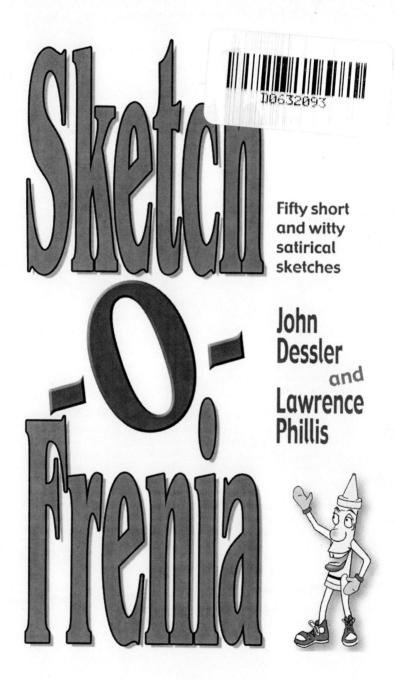

MERIWETHER PUBLISHING LTD.
Colorado Springs, Colorado

Meriwether Publishing Ltd., Publisher
PO Box 7710
Colorado Springs, CO 80933-7710

Editors: Art Zapel and Renée Congdon
Cover design: Janice Melvin

Library of Congress Cataloging-in-Publication Data

Dessler, John, 1963-
  Sketch-o-frenia : fifty short and witty satirical sketches / by John Dessler and Lawrence Phillis.
      p. cm.
  ISBN 978-1-56608-089-7
  1. Acting. 2. American drama--20th century. I. Phillis, Lawrence, 1965- II. Title.
  PN2080.D47 2003
  812'.6--dc21

                         2003012498

2   3   4   09   10   11

Contents

Introduction

In early 1997, John approached me with the idea of putting together a weekly original sketch comedy show. At the time, we had formed an improvisation workshop that met once a week at The Outlet for Creativity in Rochester, PA.

I pushed for a bi-weekly show, perhaps monthly, so that we would have time to write the next show. He convinced me and a handful of others to give the weekly format a try. So we spent the next five months developing ideas, and on June 6, 1997, we introduced *Comarama*, a show combining comedy, art, and drama. That first show included eight comedy sketches, one dramatic piece, original poetry, two performance art pieces, and two short films.

I remember sitting backstage, worn out from the two-hour performance, and looking at John as he said: "We have six days to do this again." I was sure we couldn't keep up the pace, but we wrote another show, and another and another and another ... for a year and a half.

During that first year we started a youth troupe who held their own monthly show with some of our old skits, revised for that age group, and some new ones written specifically for them.

The skits in this book are a selection from those early days when we jumped in with both feet. After a while, we found a writing routine that worked for us, with many late Sunday nights in The Outlet loft, trying to finish five to eight skits a week. We'd perform them that Friday, analyze the audience reactions afterwards at a late-night restaurant, and rest for a day before starting the whole process again.

Lawrence Phillis

1

A Pile-O-Chips Now

Premise: Army ants are fresh from an attack on a picnic. The wounded ants want to pull back, but the commander decides to make a rush for the watermelon.

Cast: Wounded Ant — In a lot of pain.
Medic — Wants to pull back because he's seen so much carnage.
Ant 1 — Battle tested ant.
Ant 2 — Part of the reinforcements.
Captain — Ant leader.
Scout — Ant trained in the art of camouflage.

Props: Large piece of watermelon.

Costumes: Two regular ant costumes, one injured ant, one medic ant, one officer ant, and one camouflaged ant. All should have six legs and antennae.

Scene: Behind the battlelines, Wounded Ant is being tended by Medic, as Ant 1 looks on.

Note: Every time "-ant" appears in the script it should be overemphasized.

1   WOUNDED ANT: It hurts! Help me ... I'm in pain! My legs!
2   MEDIC: What happened soldier?
3   WOUNDED ANT: It was the potato salad ... it was hanging from
4   the corner of this lady's mouth ... I didn't see it fall, but the
5   lieutenant pushed me out of the way. This huge chunk of
6   potato salad exploded and the shrapnel broke three of my legs.
7   MEDIC: What happened to the lieutenant?
8   ANT 1: *(Sad)* He's gone sir ... it happened in an instant ... there
9   was nothing we could do.
10 MEDIC: He was a good ant! I fought with him in Viantnam. We
11   were at Hamburger Hill together.
12 ANT 1: Why did they call it Hamburger Hill? Because of all the
13   carnage?
14 MEDIC: No ... it was a hamburger.
15 WOUNDED ANT: You gotta get outta here ... just leave me.
16 MEDIC: I've never left an ant behind, and I'm not about to start
17   now.
18 WOUNDED ANT: But you have to or you'll die!
19 MEDIC: No soldier, I'm very adamant about this!
20 ANT 1: Look! ... Here come reinforcemants! *(Enter CAPTAIN and*
21   *ANT 2.)*
22 CAPTAIN: I got here as soon as I saw your smoke signals.
23 ANT 1: Those weren't smoke signals! That was A-company being
24   fried alive by some kid with a magnifying glass!
25 CAPTAIN: *(To WOUNDED ANT)* What happened here?
26 MEDIC: Potato from the salad, sir ... fell on Jemimah. He's got
27   three broken legs.
28 WOUNDED ANT: I can't go on sir, it hurts! Just leave me ... aaaaah!
29 CAPTAIN: Quit screaming you little pissant.
30 MEDIC: Leave him alone ... He's just a new recruit from down on
31   the ant farm.
32 ANT 1: Sir, they walked all over us out there!
33 ANT 2: What do we do now, sir? Pull back?
34 CAPTAIN: No, sit tight. I sent out a scout experiantsed in
35   camouflage to survey the area. Here he comes now. *(Enter*

1 *SCOUT.)* **What's it like out there soldier?**

2 **SCOUT: It's paradise out there, sir! There's dozens of ears of**

3 **corn, hamburgers, hot dogs, and the corn-chips are as high**

4 **as an elephant's eye! And sir, at the end of the blanket, there's**

5 **a big, sticky, sweet, drippy, juicy, half-eaten chunk of ...**

6 **watermelon!**

7 **CAPTAIN: We're taking it!**

8 **MEDIC: You can't be serious, Captain!**

9 **CAPTAIN: Dead serious, soldier. Here's the plan. You** *(Points to*

10 *ANT 2)* **build a catapult that'll throw us into the potato chip**

11 **pile, but make sure we clear the dip. Then it's just a quick run**

12 **to the watermelon.**

13 **ANT 2: I'm an army ant not a carpenter ant.**

14 **MEDIC: Are you crazy? Are you having delusions of gr***ant***sure?**

15 **Why risk more lives? Let's just grab some crumbs or greasy**

16 **chips and get out while we still can.**

17 **CAPTAIN: Crumbs will not feed the colony, soldier! We have to**

18 **get that watermelon.**

19 **ANTS 1 and 2: We're with you, sir!**

20 **CAPTAIN: Let's go with plan B, I'll call in the squadron of flying**

21 **ants for air support. We'll flank the blanket and take the fruit**

22 **by storm and the melon will be ours!** *(All ad-lib gung ho-ness,*

23 *as they charge Off-stage. Sounds of battle are heard, then ANTS*

24 *come marching back on whistling and carrying a piece of*

25 *watermelon over their heads.)*

26

27   *Curtain*

28

29

30

31

32

33

34

35

Back in My Game Day

Premise: Two old men try explaining the beginnings of video games to a young boy who only knows virtual reality helmets. The men begin having "flashbacks" as they explain.

Cast: Russell — Old man.
Erwin — Old man.
Kid — Young man listening to the old men describe the old days.

Props: Virtual reality helmet, video gun, cane.

Scene: Russell and Erwin sit watching Kid with virtual helmet on, playing a video game. He turns and fires in different directions. Erwin knocks on helmet with cane. Kid fires in that direction. Russell knocks on the helmet, and Kid fires in that direction. Kid catches on and removes helmet.

1   KID: *(To ERWIN)* Grandpa, you made me lose thirty points!
2   ERWIN: You know, back in my day we used to have to go to *malls*
3   and play video games in an *arcade.*
4   KID: An arcade?
5   RUSSELL: That's right, arcades. You see, they used to keep all
6   these here machines as big as a washer in one big room. And
7   you used to have to put in a quarter each time you played.
8   ERWIN: Or wanted an extended play.
9   RUSSELL: Or if you picked one a those uppity fifty-cent jobbers.
10   Now, then, you're talking some dinero.
11 ERWIN: But if you were one of the elite, like me or Russell was ...
12 RUSSELL: I was elite, you was just medi-ochra!
13 ERWIN: Yeah, I was about as mediocre as your little toe.
14 RUSSELL: Uh ... OK.
15 ERWIN: Well, anyways, we pert near could milk an entire
16   afternoon of playing for a piddly fifty-four dollars and
17   seventy-five cents.
18 ERWIN: Give or take a dollar or two.
19 KID: Wow. So how many games could you play on one of these
20   machines?
21 RUSSELL: Well, each machine only played one game.
22 ERWIN: Yeah, but you can play it as many times as you like.
23   That's saying as long as your quarters held out.
24 RUSSELL: That was before the whole token fiasco.
25 ERWIN: Yeah, those darn tokens were the downfall of the whole
26   arcade-video game era.
27 KID: Just one game? That's boring.
28 RUSSELL: Boring? Boring? Let me tell you something. That
29   Cerebral-Link-Virtual Mumbo Jumbo of yours is like a snail
30   in a spitting contest compared to the dump-in-your-pants
31   action of the games we used to play.
32 KID: Yeah, right.
33 ERWIN: *(From behind KID, startling him)* Yeah, right!
34 KID: Like what?
35 ERWIN: Well, there was ... that tank one.

1   RUSSELL: And, uh ... oh, yeah. That shootin' one. You know with
2   the ... *(Imitating shooting sounds)* **Pitoooo, pitoooo.**
3   ERWIN: Ooooh, yeah. I almost forgot about that one. But wait just
4   a New Hampshire minute, we're getting ahead of ourselves.
5   Tell the kid how it all started. *(RUSSELL prepares for story, KID*
6   *gets comfortable.)*
7   RUSSELL: It all started with a game that struck fear into the
8   hearts and guts of everyone that encountered it. Just its
9   ominous appearance was enough to give you nightmares for a
10   week and two days. Envision if you will. *(Shaping hands into a*
11   *ball)* A background of pure black and a white fiery sphere of
12   death. Seeking. Attacking. And you with only one defense.
13   Just one wrong move and ...
14   ERWIN: Easy, Russ! Take it easy on the boy. Don't want to be
15   scaring ...
16   KID: No. It sounds cool! Go ahead.
17   RUSSELL: Are you sure?
18   KID: Yeah!
19   RUSSELL: Where was I?
20   ERWIN: Just one wrong move and ...
21   RUSSELL: Oh, yeah ... and *bamm!* You lost a guy.
22   KID: That's it?
23   RUSSELL: Well, sheeez. You only started with three. Now you're
24   down to two already. And if that isn't enough to make your
25   cappuccino curdle, the name of the game was just as hideous
26   and fear-striking as anything.
27   ERWIN: Don't do it, Russ ...
28   RUSSELL: The name of the game was ...
29   ERWIN: *No!*
30   RUSSELL: *Pong!*
31   ERWIN: Ooooh. It still sends shivers down my spine.
32   RUSSELL: Before you knew it, they start adding colors and more
33   sounds to the games. *(To ERWIN)* How about Donkey Kong?
34   ERWIN: Oooo, yeah. Donkey Kong.
35   RUSSELL: Now this here was a man's game. You operated this

1   little plumber guy.

2   ERWIN: With a sledgehammer.

3   RUSSELL: I'm telling the story. With a sledgehammer. And this

4   big-butt gorilla at the top is rolling these barrels down at this

5   little plumber guy. So these barrels are barreling down, and

6   then these little fireball men.

7   KID: Fireball men?

8   RUSSELL: Yeah. Fireball men. You see they're trying to prevent

9   the little plumber guy from getting to the girl that the gorilla

10   has chained at the top ... hey, this game ain't even got no

11   donkey in it.

12   ERWIN: Never liked that game anyway. I'll tell you what a real

13   game was. Asteroids. Now there's a game.

14   KID: Asteroids?

15   RUSSELL: You start with your ship in the middle of the screen,

16   thinking that you're all safe and cozy, when all of the sudden,

17   this huge rock comes floating onto the screen. So you shoot it.

18   *Pewww*. And the darn thing turns into two rocks. So you shoot

19   them. *Peww, peww*. And they turn into four rocks. *(ERWIN and*

20   *RUSSELL begins acting like they're having a wartime flashback.*

21   *Ducking, pointing, making video game noises, and pretending to*

22   *be pushing buttons as:)*

23   ERWIN: Look out here comes one!

24   RUSSELL: *Pewww*. Before you know it, you got a whole screen full

25   of rocks flying all over the place.

26   ERWIN: Look out!

27   RUSSELL: *Peww, peww!* There's too many of them!

28   ERWIN: Hurry, hit the hyper space!

29   RUSSELL: Holy guacamole, where'd I go?

30   ERWIN: Over there, over there, hurry thrust!

31   RUSSELL and ERWIN: *(As if they saw their ship blown up)* Awww.

32   Man!

33   KID: Cool.

34   RUSSELL: Cool? You ain't heard nothing yet. *(To ERWIN)* How

35   about ... Space Invaders?

1   ERWIN: Not the invaders.

2   RUSSELL: *(Mimicking the game, slow at first)* **Cachunk, cachunk,**

3   **cachunk ...**

4   ERWIN: Stop it! Russ!

5   RUSSELL: *(Faster)* **Cachunk, cachunk, cachunk ...**

6   ERWIN: You're scaring me!

7   RUSSELL: *(Imitating saucer)* **Whirrrr!**

8   ERWIN: It's the saucer. Fire. Fire. *Fire!*

9   RUSSELL: Hurry, they're starting to eat your little houses.

10   ERWIN: They're coming down too fast!

11   RUSSELL: Clear off the ends. Shoot the ones on the ends.

12   ERWIN and RUSSELL: *(Game ends.)* Aww, Man!

13   KID: Space Invaders? Cool.

14   ERWIN: Hey, Russ.

15   RUSSELL: What?

16   ERWIN: Tell him about ... *the man.*

17   RUSSELL: Oooo. The man. The game of games.

18   KID: The man?

19   ERWIN and RUSSELL: Pac Man.

20   RUSSELL: Now this little fella had balls.

21   ERWIN: All over the screen, and they was in a maze.

22   RUSSELL: You had to gobble up all these balls.

23   ERWIN: Tell him about the ghosts.

24   KID: Ghosts?

25   RUSSELL: I'm getting there. You're going around gobbling these

26   balls, *warka, warka,* then there's these ghosts, all different

27   colors ... *(Flashback)*

28   ERWIN: Here comes the red!

29   RUSSELL: Oh, no you don't.

30   ERWIN: Go for the power pill!

31   RUSSELL: Not yet.

32   ERWIN: Hurry, here comes the pink one!

33   RUSSELL: Not yet.

34   ERWIN: Here comes the yellow!

35   RUSSELL: Almost ... *now!*

1　ERWIN: Whooey ... Look at them run.
2　RUSSELL: Now who's yellow?
3　ERWIN: Eat 'em! Eat 'em!
4　RUSSELL: Die, you little blue poltergoost.
5　ERWIN: No! Wait! He's flashing! Run!
6　RUSSELL: I got him.
7　ERWIN: Turn around!
8　RUSSELL: I got him! *(Game ends.)*
9　ERWIN and RUSSELL: Shoulda ran.
10　KID: Cool!
11　RUSSELL: But then that darn Ms. Pac Man came along and tried
12　　　stealing the spotlight.
13　ERWIN: How you supposed to be tough with a pink bow on your
14　　　little yellow head?
15　RUSSELL: Really! How about that Centipede?
16　ERWIN: Oh, my goodness. With the poison mushrooms. And
17　　　Break Out. Or how about Missile Command? *(Kid looks at*
18　　　*helmet unenthused and starts to leave.)*
19　RUSSELL: Where you had that little track ball thingy? *(To KID)*
20　　　Hey kid. Where you going?
21　KID: I thought I'd go read or something.
22　ERWIN: Done with your helmet?
23　KID: Yeah. *(KID exits. RUSSELL grabs helmet, starts playing.*
24　　　*ERWIN tries getting involved.)*
25
26　　　　　　　*Curtain*
27
28
29
30
31
32
33
34
35

Backwards Bank Robbery

Premise: The following scene is written for the first half to seem to be running backwards and the second half to run forward. It seems someone forgot to rewind the scene after the last rehearsal. Lines are not backwards, but the order of the lines and the actions are.

Note: Staging this will take some time and thought. The easiest way to block it might be to skip to the "forward" section and walk through that once. When finished with the forward section, each character should remember what he did and where all the props are. That's how the scene should begin.

Cast: Louie — Leader of the two robbers.

Barney — Louie's partner in crime. He's not too bright.

Doris — Louie's ex-girlfriend, now a cop, unbeknownst to Louie.

Cop 1 and Cop 2

Teller — Gives money to the robbers. No lines.

Paramedic — Nonspeaking.

Stagehand — Forgot to rewind the bank robbery scene and now, in the middle of the show, must tell the director.

Director — Angry; just wants the show to go well, which it isn't.

Scene: Inside of a bank. A bank counter is Upstage Left. All on stage are frozen and in exaggerated positions. (Note: Positions will be determined by where and how characters finish the forward section.) Teller is standing behind the counter smiling and holding a bag of money; Paramedic is tending to Customer 1; Customer 2 is kneeling beside Customer 1. There is a gun lying on the floor near the middle of the stage.

1	*(STAGEHAND enters.)*
2	**STAGEHAND:** Uh ... *[Insert director's name]*? *(DIRECTOR is Off-*
3	*stage for all lines.)*
4	**DIRECTOR: What?**
5	**STAGEHAND: I'm afraid we have a problem.**
6	**DIRECTOR: What's wrong? We're in the middle of a show here.**
7	**STAGEHAND: It seems I ... I mean, *someone* forgot to rewind the**
8	**Bank Robbery scene after we rehearsed it yesterday.**
9	**DIRECTOR: Excuse me?**
10	**STAGEHAND: The Bank Robbery scene, it was never rewound.**
11	**DIRECTOR: For crying out loud! Do it!**
12	**STAGEHAND: Now?**
13	**DIRECTOR: *Now!* We have a show to put on.**
14	**STAGEHAND: But ...**
15	**DIRECTOR: Just do it!**
16	**STAGEHAND: All right.** *(Towards Off-stage)* **Let's rewind the**
17	**Bank Robbery scene.** *(STAGEHAND exits.)*
18	***SPECIAL DIRECTIONS:*** All walking during the first part should be
19	done backwards. All actions, whenever possible, should be done
20	in reverse and exaggerated so as to be easily recognized during
21	the "forward" section.
22	*(All unfreeze, DORIS enters carrying a gun, shakes hands with*
23	*TELLER, takes money from TELLER, walks across stage, sets*
24	*money on floor and strikes heroic stance. COPS and LOUIE, who*
25	*is handcuffed, enter. LOUIE stops at DORIS. PARAMEDIC exits.)*
26	**DORIS: Get him out of here!** *(DORIS unslaps LOUIE's face.)* **I loved**
27	**you Louie. I would have done anything for you. You creep!**
28	*(COPS lower LOUIE onto the floor, remove handcuffs, then rush*
29	*out. An alarm begins sounding. Note: Handcuffs should not be*
30	*clasped unless they can be released quickly.)* **All right guys, I**
31	**have him apprehended. Come and get him.** *(DORIS kicks*
32	*LOUIE, and backs up a few steps.)* **After you left me to take the**
33	**fall for you, I decided to turn my life around. I met Victor at**
34	**my arraignment, and he convinced me to try the academy.**
35	*(DORIS shows LOUIE a badge.)*

1 **LOUIE: Doris? I don't understand.** *(LOUIE stands, his hands are in*
2   *the air.)*
3 **DORIS: Get on the ground!**
4 **LOUIE: Doris?** *(LOUIE lowers his hands, others in the bank raise*
5   *their hands.)*
6 **DORIS: Get your hands up!** *(LOUIE picks up the money sack.)* **Drop**
7   **the money!**
8 **LOUIE: Here, you take my gun.** *(LOUIE takes gun from DORIS.)* **I'll**
9   **grab the money.** *(LOUIE moves to counter and sets down*
10   *money.)* **I knew I could count on you, Doris.**
11 **DORIS: I'll help you Louie. Let me help you.**
12 **LOUIE: Barney! What a dope!** *(LOUIE moves to the window, backs*
13   *away. BARNEY enters with his hands raised.)*
14 **COP 1:** *(Off-stage)* **All right, come out with your hands up.**
15 **LOUIE: Barney. What am I going to do with you?**
16 **BARNEY: But I just did what I was told.**
17 **LOUIE: Barney, you dope!** *(BARNEY picks up gun.)*
18 **COP 2:** *(Off-stage)* **Drop your weapons!**
19 **BARNEY:** *(Shakes LOUIE.)* **It's the cops!** *(BARNEY runs to the*
20   *window, a siren sounds. DORIS and LOUIE hug then separate.)*
21 **LOUIE: Doris? Is that you?** *(BARNEY and LOUIE move to counter.)*
22 **DORIS: Louie? Louie Lapinelli?**
23 **LOUIE:** *(Slaps BARNEY.)* **I told you never use my real name.**
24 **BARNEY: Louie, now what?** *(Alarm stops. LOUIE hands the money*
25   *sack to TELLER and TELLER begins to empty it.)*
26 **LOUIE: Just do what you're told!**
27 **BARNEY: I'm afraid.**
28 **LOUIE:** *(Takes the empty sack from TELLER.)* **Put all the money in**
29   **the bag.** *(CUSTOMER 1 stands, then screams.)* **This is a stickup.**
30   *(Everybody lowers their hands.)* **All right, everyone, get your**
31   **hands in the air.** *(LOUIE and BARNEY move to outside "bank*
32   *door.")* **One. Two. Three! Just do what your told.**
33 **BARNEY: Louie, I'm afraid.**
34 **LOUIE: Ready Barney? On three.** *(All on stage freeze.)*
35 **STAGEHAND:** *(Enters.)* **The scene is rewound!**

1   **DIRECTOR: All right. Roll it forward.**

2   **STAGEHAND: Rolling forward.** *(STAGEHAND exits. All unfreeze.)*

3   **LOUIE: Ready Barney? On three.**

4   **BARNEY: Louie, I'm afraid.**

5   **LOUIE: One. Two. Three! Just do what you're told.** *(LOUIE and*
6   *BARNEY enter bank.)*

7   **LOUIE: This is a stickup.** *(CUSTOMER 1 screams and faints.)* **All**
8   **right, everyone, get your hands in the air.** *(Everyone raises*
9   *hands.)* **Put all the money in the bag.** *(LOUIE hands TELLER*
10   *the sack.)*

11   **BARNEY: I'm afraid.**

12   **LOUIE: Just do what you're told.** *(Alarm sounds.)*

13   **BARNEY: Louie! Now what?**

14   **LOUIE: I told you never use my real name.** *(LOUIE slaps*
15   *BARNEY.)*

16   **DORIS: Louie? Louie Lapinelli?**

17   **LOUIE: Doris? Is that you?** *(LOUIE moves to DORIS, they hug then*
18   *separate. Siren sounds. BARNEY runs to window then to LOUIE.*
19   *Shakes LOUIE.)*

20   **BARNEY: It's the cops.**

21   **COP 2:** *(Off-stage)* **Drop your weapons.** *(BARNEY drops his gun.)*

22   **LOUIE: Barney, you dope!**

23   **BARNEY: But I just did what I was told.**

24   **LOUIE: Barney! What am I going to do with you?**

25   **COP 1:** *(Off-stage)* **Come out with your hands up!** *(BARNEY raises*
26   *hands, and exits.)*

27   **LOUIE: Barney, you dope!**

28   **DORIS: I'll help you, Louie. Let me help you.**

29   **LOUIE: Here, you take my gun.** *(LOUIE gives DORIS his gun.)* **I'll**
30   **grab the money.** *(LOUIE moves to bank counter, picks up*
31   *money.)* **I knew I could count on you, Doris.**

32   **DORIS: Drop the money!** *(LOUIE drops money.)*

33   **LOUIE: Doris?**

34   **DORIS: Get your hands up!** *(LOUIE raises hands.)* **Get on the**
35   **ground!** *(LOUIE gets on the ground.)* **Doris? I don't understand.**

1   **DORIS:** *(Shows LOUIE her badge.)* **After you left me to take the fall**
2   **for you, I decided to turn my life around. I met Victor at my**
3   **arraignment, and he convinced me to try the academy.**
4   *(DORIS kicks LOUIE.)* **All right guys, I have him apprehended.**
5   **Come and get him.** *(PARAMEDIC enters and tends to*
6   *CUSTOMER 1. CUSTOMER 2 bends to help. COPS rush in, cuff*
7   *LOUIE, lift him.)* **I loved you, Louie. I would have done**
8   **anything for you. You creep!** *(DORIS slaps LOUIE in the face.)*
9   **Get him out of here.** *(COPS exit with LOUIE. DORIS strikes*
10   *heroic pose, then picks up money, moves to TELLER, shakes*
11   *TELLER's hand, gives TELLER money, and exits. All strike*
12   *beginning pose. Freeze.)*
13
14   *Curtain*
15
16
17
18
19
20
21
22
23
24
25
26
27
28
29
30
31
32
33
34
35

Bad Night/Busy Week

Premise: Due to an oversight, an actress is forced to conduct a scene with four fill-in actors playing her husband at the same time.

Cast: Fran — A dedicated actress.
Director — Possibly absent-minded.
Mike 1, 2, 3, and Larry — Fill-in actors.

Props: Table and two chairs.

Costumes: None.

Scene: Fran enters dining room. It is her and her husband's anniversary. A table is set Center Stage.

1   **FRAN: Oh, honey. What a pleasant surprise.** *(Pauses, looks*
2   *confused, gets frustrated, then breaks character.)* **Would someone**
3   **like to join me out here for this skit please?** *(DIRECTOR*
4   *enters.)*
5   **DIRECTOR: Is there a prob?**
6   **FRAN: I'd say there's a problem. What's missing from this**
7   **picture?** *(DIRECTOR looks confused, FRAN exits and returns*
8   *with script.)* **What's this say right here?**
9   **DIRECTOR: Fran, we really don't have time for this, we're in the**
10   **middle of a show. Let's try to be professional.**
11   **FRAN: Humor me. What does this say?** *(DIRECTOR scans script.)*
12   **DIRECTOR: Scene opens to dining room, Fran enters and is**
13   **surprised when she sees her husband waiting at the table set**
14   **for a romantic dinner for two.** *(DIRECTOR looks at plain card*
15   *table with minimal setting.)* **I realize we don't have all the**
16   **trimmings, but we're on a rather tight budget here. Just**
17   **imagine the table is really set up nice and romantic, soft music**
18   **playing in the background, candles lit, and your husband ...**
19   **FRAN: Uh-huh.**
20   **DIRECTOR: Oh, right. Husband. Ummm ... it's been a really busy**
21   **week, and putting on a show like this is a pretty big undertaking**
22   **and ... well ... little things get overlooked sometimes.**
23   **FRAN: Little things? I don't have a husband in my anniversary**
24   **scene ... with my husband! Look, I'm not going to embarrass**
25   **myself out here in front of all these people. I can't work like**
26   **this ...** *(FRAN moves to exit.)*
27   **DIRECTOR: Wait! I'll get somebody. We need you to do the skit.**
28   *(Yelling off stage)* **Mike? I need a guy out here for the**
29   **anniversary skit!** *(Back to FRAN)* **It's already in the program**
30   **and the show would run short if you don't. I'll get Mike to sit**
31   **in. He's very talented. He picks up quick and always does a**
32   **great job.**
33   **FRAN: This is real professional. I show up to do a skit and the rest**
34   **of the cast is missing.**
35   **DIRECTOR: Not really missing. I just kinda overlooked handing**

1   out the part. Mike? I need you to fill in on this skit. I'm going
2   to go pull the curtain. Everything's going to be fine.
3 FRAN: Fine.
4 DIRECTOR: Fine. *Mike!? (DIRECTOR exits, curtain closes and*
5   *reopens with three MIKES and LARRY at table.)*
6 FRAN: *(Enters looking confused.)* Oh, honey. What a surprise.
7   *(Aside* **Director!!!** *(DIRECTOR enters.)*
8 DIRECTOR: What? ... Oh.
9 FRAN: Now I have four husbands.
10 DIRECTOR: I guess I wasn't very clear.
11 FRAN: Count them. One, two, three, four.
12 DIRECTOR: Mike ...
13 MIKES: What?
14 DIRECTOR: *(To FRAN)* Popular name around here. *(To MIKES)* I
15   just need someone to fill in on a spot I overlooked this week.
16 MIKE 1: You did say I always do a great job.
17 MIKE 2: No, I believe you said I was very talented.
18 MIKE 3: Nice try Mikes, but I think he meant me when he said I
19   pick up quick.
20 LARRY: Ya, maybe, but I'm sure when he said very talented, picks
21   up quick *and* always does a great job he really meant to say
22   Larry.
23 MIKES: Well ... *(Improv: Who is it?, etc.)*
24 DIRECTOR: *(Can't decide)* Uh ... you know what fellas, you're all
25   right.
26 FRAN: What!?
27 DIRECTOR: Let's take it from where Fran sits at the table.
28 FRAN: But ...
29 DIRECTOR: Professional! *(DIRECTOR exits. All get composed.)*
30 FRAN: This is a really nice dinner you cooked.
31 MIKE 2: This, oh go on.
32 MIKE 1: It was nothing.
33 LARRY: Just something I threw together.
34 FRAN: Yes, but just the fact that you remembered this special day
35   makes it so wonderful.

1   **LARRY: Anything for you. How could I forget ...** *(He doesn't know*
2   *the day. None know the script but begin guessing.)*
3   **MIKE 1: ... Your birthday?** *(FRAN expresses frustration.)*
4   **MIKE 2: Your promotion?**
5   **FRAN: No!** *(MIKES look perplexed.)*
6   **LARRY: Our anniversary?**
7   **FRAN: Yes!** *(LARRY celebrates as all compose again.)*
8   **MIKE 1: Anything for you, honey.**
9   **MIKE 2: Sweetie.**
10   **MIKE 3: Dumplin'.**
11   **LARRY: Shnookie.**
12   **MIKES 1, 2, and 3: Shnookie?**
13   **LARRY: How could I forget our anniversary?**
14   **MIKE 1: We took our vows on this day exactly ...**
15   **MIKES:** *(All call different numbers)* **... years ago.**
16   **MIKE 2: To love ...**
17   **MIKE 3: Honor ...**
18   **LARRY: ... And cherish each other ...**
19   **MIKES: Till death do us part.**
20   **FRAN: And ... ?** *(MIKES and LARRY all stammer.)*
21   **MIKE 1: Price Hike to Affect Import Tariff.**
22   **FRAN: What?**
23   **MIKE 1: I thought this was the script.**
24   **FRAN:** *(Picking up newspaper)* **This is a newspaper. A script is**
25   **something you would have gotten at the beginning of the week**
26   **so *one* of you could have memorized it.** *(To Off-stage)* **Would it**
27   **be too much to ask for my husbands to get a script out here**
28   **before one of them gets to the stock exchange and begins**
29   **announcing the closing NASDAQ index?**
30   **MIKE 2: Actually I prefer using the New York Stock Exchange as**
31   **a barometer ...**
32   **FRAN: I don't care!!** *(DIRECTOR enters with script, throws it on table.)*
33   **DIRECTOR: Remember, professional.** *(DIRECTOR exits. MIKES*
34   *and LARRY all scan script.)*
35   **FRAN: Are we ready?** *(MIKES improvise: Ya, sure.)* **This stinks.**

1   MIKE 2: Hey, don't blame us ...
2   LARRY: We didn't write this stuff.
3   FRAN: What does it matter who wrote it? None of you know the
4   lines anyway.
5   MIKE 2: Settle down.
6   MIKE 1: Ya, no reason to get nasty.
7   FRAN: Oh, I can think of a couple ... about four. Oh well, let's just
8   pick it up from the love, honor and cherish line. OK with all
9   of you? *(MIKES improvise: Yep, OK with me, etc. All pause and*
10   *wait for line.)* **Well?** *(MIKES look confused.)* **It's your line!**
11 MIKE 1: *(To MIKE 2)* I thought you were going to say it.
12 MIKE 2: *(Pointing to MIKE 3)* I thought he was.
13 LARRY: Ah, yes. Our anniversary. A day like no other.
14 MIKE 1: I remember it as though it was yesterday.
15 MIKE 2: You looked so beautiful.
16 LARRY: Just as you do now.
17 MIKE 3: Gimme a kiss, baby! *(All FOUR husbands pucker and*
18   *tussle to be the one to kiss her.)*
19 FRAN: *(Exhausted)* I want a divorce.
20
21   *Curtain*
22
23
24
25
26
27
28
29
30
31
32
33
34
35

The Bug Doctor

Premise: A doctor for bugs, who is a bug himself, treats an eccentric group of insects.

Cast: Nurse — The nurse. A non-descript bug or use your imagination.
Locust — A locust with an eye problem.
Doctor Pod — The doctor. A non-descript bug.
Moth — A moth with a migraine.
Kati — A caterpillar in for a big change.
Bee — The pollinator, with the terminator accent.

Props: X-ray machine, bug glasses, x-ray of Moth with light box, special bug eye chart.

Costumes: One for each bug listed above.

Scene: An examining room at a doctor's office. The Nurse is showing the Locust into the examining room.

1   NURSE: If you'll just have a seat, Doctor Pod will be with you in a
2   moment.
3   LOCUST: Sure. *(NURSE exits. LOCUST begins eating anything*
4   *available. DOCTOR enters.)*
5   DOCTOR: Sorry I'm late. Had a little lady, Millie Pede, get
6   stepped on.
7   LOCUST: Is she OK?
8   DOCTOR: Yeah, she'll be all right. She just broke a couple of legs,
9   that's all. Four hundred and twelve. Whoa, Louie, what'd I
10   tell you about gorging yourself like this.
11   LOCUST: Can't help it Doc. It's not easy. I think I'm doing OK, then
12   the boys come over and we decide to fly out for a bite to eat.
13   Before I know it we've made our way through a couple of crops.
14   DOCTOR: I understand Louie, but just look at that thorax of
15   yours, will ya.
16   LOCUST: What's a Locust to do Doc? It's not just my appetite, it's
17   the whole pupea pressure thing. *(Mocking talking to his buddies)*
18   "Sorry, guys, a few blades of grass and maybe a sprout or two,
19   that'll be all for me. Thanks." How do you think that's going to
20   go over at work? I got an image to uphold.
21   DOCTOR: Well, it's takin' a toll on your health there Louie.
22   Let's check you out. All right, why don't you open your
23   mandibles nice and wide for me. *(LOCUST opens mouth.)*
24   Wider … wider … there you go. Looks all right.
25   Now how about your eyes? I want you to take a look at this
26   chart and read the first line for me. *(DOC covers one eye.)*
27   LOCUST: E, e, e, e, e, e, e, e, e, e.
28   DOCTOR: Very good. You've got 20/20/20/20/20/20/20 in those
29   eyes. Now with your other eyes, the second line.
30   LOCUST: Q, q, q, q, q, q, q.
31   DOCTOR: Ooo. Looks like your going to need some glasses there
32   Louie.
33   LOCUST: Aww. You gotta be kidding me Doc. I'm going to look so
34   geeky.
35   DOCTOR: Nonsense. We have very stylish frames. Here, try these

1   on.

2   LOCUST: Great, every one down at the swarm is going to be

3   calling me "four hundred eyes, four hundred eyes."

4   DOCTOR: You could always wear contacts.

5   LOCUST: That would be great.

6   DOCTOR: I'll have to order them. You could just use these glasses

7   until they come in.

8   LOCUST: And how long would that be?

9   DOCTOR: Let's see. Two hundred contacts, that'll take about

10   seven days. In the mean time, watch your binging.

11   LOCUST: Sure. *(LOCUST exits, NURSE enters.)*

12   NURSE: We have Marty the Moth complaining of migraines.

13   DOCTOR: Show him in. *(NURSE exits, MOTH enters.)* Hello,

14   Marty.

15   MOTH: Hello Doctor.

16   DOCTOR: Migraines, huh?

17   MOTH: Like you wouldn't believe.

18   DOCTOR: Aspirin not helping?

19   MOTH: Starts to. Then before you know it ... bam ... it's back

20   stronger than ever.

21   DOCTOR: I see. Nurse? *(NURSE enters.)*

22   NURSE: Yes, Doctor?

23   DOCTOR: I'd like to take an x-ray of Marty's exo-scull. *(DOCTOR*

24   *and NURSE take x-ray. DOCTOR hangs x-ray.)* Let's take a look.

25   *(DOCTOR switches on x-ray light and MOTH "flies" repeatedly*

26   *into the light banging her head.)* Marty, I think I know what

27   your problem is. *(DOCTOR puts sunglasses on MOTH.)* Just

28   wear these for a while and I have the feeling you'll be feeling

29   the last of those migraines.

30   MOTH: Thanks Doc. *(MOTH exits.)*

31   DOCTOR: Who we got next, Nurse?

32   NURSE: Mrs. Piller.

33   DOCTOR: Go ahead and show her in. *(NURSE exits, KATI enters.)*

34   What seems to be the problem there Kati?

35   KATI: I haven't been feeling very well. *(DOCTOR examines KATI.)*

1 I've been feeling sluggish lately. This morning I was just
2 crawling around and fell right off a branch and landed on my
3 antenna.
4 DOCTOR: I see. *(DOCTOR begins wrapping antenna.)* **Nurse?**
5 *(NURSE enters.)* **Would you please finish wrapping this up for**
6 **me and send in the next patient?** *(NURSE and KATI exit, BEE*
7 *enters, bumbling around, sneezing.)* **What seems to be the**
8 **problem there Mr. Bee?**
9 BEE: *(Sneeze)* Can't seem to stop sneezing.
10 DOCTOR: I see. *(DOCTOR runs tests.)* **Can I ask you what you do**
11 for a living Mr. Bee?
12 BEE: I'm the pollinator.
13 DOCTOR: Mmmm. Did you ever consider changing careers?
14 BEE: No, I didn't.
15 DOCTOR: Well, I'm afraid you're allergic to pollen.
16 BEE: Ow, that stings.
17 DOCTOR: It's either that or a tumor.
18 BEE: It's not a tumor.
19 DOCTOR: You're probably right. Here, I'll give you a shot of anti-
20 allergenic. Where do you want it. Arm or ... ? *(DOCTOR*
21 *motions to BEE's butt.)*
22 BEE: Take my hand. Here, take my hand. *(DOCTOR injects BEE.*
23 *BEE takes a breath.)* Ahhh. I can breathe.
24 DOCTOR: That ought to do you for about a week. Why don't you
25 come back next Tuesday.
26 BEE: I'll bee back. Asta la bee sting, bee-bee. *(BEE exits, NURSE*
27 *enters with COCOON.)*
28 DOCTOR: Nurse! I just meant the antenna.
29 NURSE: Oh. *(KATI emerges as a butterfly and flies Off-stage.)*
30 DOCTOR: Well, that was weird. Any more patients?
31 NURSE: No, Doctor.
32 DOCTOR: Well, then I'm going to fly out and grab something
33 quick to eat. I'll be right back. *(DOCTOR exits.)*
34
35   *Curtain*

The Chi-Talian Restaurant

Premise: Two local mobsters meet at a neutral site to talk "business." Since one mobster is Chinese and the other is Italian, the neutral site is a combination Chinese and Italian restaurant. A mechanical translator helps the conversation until it's accidentally shot and begins translating in different accents.

Cast: Vinny — Italian mobster.
Chi-Fat — Chinese Mafia man.
Guidoson — Maitre d' at the Chi-Talian restaurant.
Rueejeeson — Waiter at the Chi-Talian restaurant.

Props: Two guns, a robotic translator able to look as if it's been shot.

Scene: A Chinese-Italian restaurant. Vinny and Chi-Fat are waiting to be seated.

Note: The dialog here is written with cheesy stereotypical accents.

1   VINNY: Chi-Fat, I'm a glad you can a make it. Sorry to hear about
2   your translator.
3   CHI-FAT: Hi. That what happen when you cross me.
4   VINNY: Well, anyway, I thought it's time we break bread and lay
5   downa some ground rules. There's plenty of crime in this
6   town for both of us.
7   CHI-FAT: Hi, arot.
8   VINNY: Excuse me?
9   CHI-FAT: I say arot ... Arot ... Yes, prenty.
10   VINNY: Right, prenty. *(Enter GUIDOSON.)*
11   GUIDOSON: Hi, I am Guidoson, and I you host for a dinner. You
12   rike specia seat?
13   VINNY: Uh ... *(Turns to CHI-FAT for help.)*
14   CHI-FAT: No specia seat. *(GUIDOSON leads them to table.)*
15   GUIDOSON: Would you rike a menus?
16   CHI-FAT: Hi.
17   GUIDOSON: Rueejeeson, be you server. He be right with you.
18   *(GUIDOSON exits.)*
19   VINNY: Let's get down to a business, huh, Fat? Can I call you Fat?
20   CHI-FAT: Hi.
21   VINNY: OK, Fat. My family is a little worried, see. We feel some
22   guidelines, they a have to be set if we both plan to share the
23   neighborhood and the wealth. Capeesh?
24   CHI-FAT: Hi. Emperor Red Dragon feer your famiree is ready for
25   big time.
26   VINNY: *(Doesn't understand CHI-FAT; thinks he said "fear.")* You
27   have every right to fear my family, China Boy, 'cause we are
28   the big time.
29   CHI-FAT: No, we not fear your famiree.
30   VINNY: Oh, yeah. How'd you like to just have some lead for
31   dinner, Chi-Fathead? *(VINNY jumps up with gun pulled.)*
32   CHI-FAT: No. We not fear, we feer.
33   VINNY: Huh?
34   CHI-FAT: Feer. We feer you famiree is ready. Feer. Rike in the
35   song: *(Sung to the tune of* Feelings.*) **Feerings, nothing more**

1   *than feerings …*

2   VINNY: Oh, feel, yeah right. Sorry about that. *(VINNY sits.)* Look,

3   Fat. Nothing personal, but I find it a little tough to understand

4   you.

5   CHI-FAT: You have a probrum?

6   VINNY: Yes, I have a probrum … problem. Listen …

7   CHI-FAT: I rissen.

8   VINNY: Right. *(CHI-FAT lights lighter and holds it out to VINNY*

9   *nearly scorching his brow.)* What are you up to, Fat Man?

10   CHI-FAT: You ask for right, I give you right.

11   VINNY: No. I just meant … never mind, listen …

12   CHI-FAT: I rissen.

13   VINNY: Ya, rissen. I have an idea. Do you mind?

14   CHI-FAT: Chi-Fat not mind but be cautious like a duck. *(VINNY*

15   *pulls out the translating machine.)*

16   VINNY: It's a new translating machine, eh? All I do is turn it on,

17   pick a the translation, in this case Chinese to English with a

18   bad Italian accent, then I click a this switch, and then tune it

19   in … go ahead say something.

20   CHI-FAT: Ra, ra, ra, ra … *(As CHI-FAT says "ra," VINNY turns the*

21   *knob. CHI-FAT slowly changes from a Chinese accent to an*

22   *Italian accent. The following lines are all said in an Italian*

23   *accent.)* Ra, ra, la, la, la.

24   VINNY: See, it a works.

25   CHI-FAT: That's a great machine, eh! *(RUEEJEESON enters.)*

26   RUEEJEESON: Bueno, I am Louigison, and I am a your waiter.

27   You like-a some a wine?

28   VINNY: I'll take a some red.

29   CHI-FAT: That sounds a splendid.

30   RUEEJEESON: Our special is a Fettuccini Egg Foo Yung or Kung

31   Pow Chicken Parmesan, both a, they come-a with a fresh

32   dinner salad and some garlic bread.

33   VINNY: I'd like to try the Chicken Chow-violi with the General

34   Tso's Meatballs.

35   RUEEJEESON: What kinda dressing you like-a on your salad,

1   Italian or Sweet-n-Sour?

2   VINNY: What the hell, in the spirit of a good faitha, I try the Sweet

3   and Sour.

4   RUEEJEESON: And for you, sir?

5   CHI-FAT: I'll have the Moo Goo Guisanga with red soy sauce.

6   RUEEJEESON: Very good. Louigison will return with your order

7   shortly. *(RUEEJEESON exits.)*

8   CHI-FAT: This a dubbing machine of yours, it's a nice. It will be a

9   nice addition, when a you join the house of the Red a Dragon.

10   VINNY: Join you? Are you crazy? The Red a Dragon's going to

11   join the family.

12   CHI-FAT: Never.

13   VINNY: Never?

14   CHI-FAT: I wouldn't be caught a dead even visiting your family.

15   VINNY: Have it your way ... *(VINNY shoots CHI-FAT.)*

16   CHI-FAT: What did you go and do that for? You shot me right in

17   the lung. That'll sure put a damper on smoking. You know I

18   love a smoking cigars ... *(CHI-FAT shoots VINNY.)*

19   VINNY: Ouch! Now you did it. You shot a me right in the liver.

20   How am I a supposed to enjoy the wine I ordered, huh?

21   CHI-FAT: When I'm a through with you, it won't a matter what

22   you're a going to leaka like a sieve. *(CHI-FAT shoots*

23   *VINNY.)*

24   VINNY: Great! You just a shot me in the pancreas. I'll be a

25   diabetic. I'm afraid to a death of needles. *(VINNY shoots at*

26   *CHI-FAT, but accidentally hits the dubbing machine. The machine*

27   *should obviously be hit and broken. Note: The following lines are*

28   *all done with different accents. The suggested accents are in*

29   *parenthesis. Other accents can be substituted, just be sure to*

30   *adjust the dialog.)*

31   CHI-FAT: *(Spanish)* Senior el loco! You shot me in the stomacho.

32   Now I won't be able to eat my Moo Goo Guisannia in red soy

33   sauce. And you know how I love to eat Moo Goo Guisannia.

34   VINNY: *(Spanish)* Eat lead, Fat head. *(VINNY shoots CHI-FAT.)*

35   CHI-FAT: *(German. CHI-FAT looks down, backs up and smiles.)*

1   **Dumkopf! Zilly boy. I don't have zee appendix. Ha, ha, ha.**
2   *(CHI-FAT shoots VINNY.)*
3   **VINNY:** *(English)* **Blimy! You got me right in the bloody spleen! I**
4   **don't even know what the thing's used for but it sure hurts**
5   **like it's important.** *(VINNY shoots CHI-FAT.)*
6   **CHI-FAT:** *(Swedish)* **You got me in the bladder. Now I'm going to**
7   **have to wear diapers. I'll get you for that.** *(CHI-FAT shoots*
8   *VINNY.)*
9   **VINNY:** *(Pig Latin)* **Owyay, uyay otshay emay inay ymay eyemay.**
10   **Ownay I antcay eesay. Uyay igpay. Aketay isthay.**
11   **CHI-FAT:** *(Ebonics)* **Hay bro, just chill man, 'fore I tag ya wit my**
12   **nine.** *(RUEEJEESON enters.)*
13   **RUEEJEESON:** *(French)* **Your dinners sirs. Will zere be anysing**
14   **else?**
15   **CHI-FAT:** *(Italian)* **No, thank a you very much.**
16   **VINNY:** *(Chinese)* **No, that wir be ar.** *(VINNY picks up fortune*
17   *cookies.)* **Oh, fortune cookie.**
18   **CHI-FAT: What's it a say?**
19   **VINNY: Beware of business deals.**
20
21   *Curtain*
22
23
24
25
26
27
28
29
30
31
32
33
34
35

The Cookout

Premise: It's a cookout, with a catch. The vertical hold on the "stage" is acting up again, so the middle of the stage is actually the edges of the scene. The left and right ends of the stage are actually the middle of the scene, so everything that goes Off-stage Right must immediately enter Stage Left. (Of course that will require two of each character and props.)

Cast: Stage Manager — Explains to audience that the horizontal hold is acting up.
Dad 1 — Typical father Stage Right.
Dad 2 — Typical father Stage Left.
Mom 1 — Typical mother Stage Right.
Mom 2 — Typical mother Stage Left.
Dougie 1 — Young son Stage Right.
Dougie 2 — Young son Stage Left.
Mr. Mimmerman 1 — Obnoxious neighbor Stage Right.
Mr. Mimmerman 2 — Obnoxious neighbor Stage Left.
Mrs. Mimmerman 1 — Obnoxious neighbor Stage Right.
Mrs. Mimmerman 2 — Obnoxious neighbor Stage Left.

Props: Grill, table, 3 chairs, 2 identical of each of the following: plate with steak, ball, bottle of lighter fluid, fire extinguisher.

Scene: It's an outdoor cookout, the right half of the stage is outdoors, the left half is indoors, but the door between the two is the sides of the stage. Dad 1 is by a grill on Stage Right, Mom 2 is setting a table Stage Left while Dougie 1 plays Stage Right. The Stage Manager addresses the audience before the curtain opens.

Notes: It is very important for the actors Off-stage to pay attention to what is happening On-stage. If Mom 1 exits the stage Mom 2 must immediately enter from the opposite side. Actors must pay attention because missed lines and queues will be two fold.

1　STAGE MANAGER: **Ladies and Gentleman, I'd like to apologize**
2　　　　**for this next skit, it seems our vertical hold on the stage is**
3　　　　**acting up again. It did this during rehearsal, and we thought**
4　　　　**we had it fixed, but evidently it's not, so if you could please**
5　　　　**bear with us we're going to show you this skit anyway.**
6　DAD 1: *(Looking Off-stage Right)* **Honey, can you bring me the**
7　　　　**lighter fluid?**
8　MOM 2: *(Looking Off-stage Left)* **Sure, sweetie. Just a moment.**
9　　　　**Dougie, would you please finish putting out the plates for me?**
10　DOUGIE 1: **Sure, Mom.** *(DOUGIE 1 exits Stage Right, DOUGIE 2*
11　　　　*enters Stage Left. MOM 2 picks up lighter fluid then exits Stage*
12　　　　*Left, MOM 1 enters Stage Right with lighter fluid.)*
13　MOM 1: **Here you go. Be careful this time. We don't need another**
14　　　　**Fourth of July episode.**
15　DAD 1: **Oh, knock it off, Doris. That was a faulty batch of charcoal**
16　　　　**and you know it.**
17　MOM 1: **And the quart of gasoline had nothing to do with it?**
18　DAD 1: **Of course not.**
19　MOM 1: **The neighbors said our fireworks were the best they've**
20　　　　**seen in years.**
21　DAD 1: **Har, har. You have the meat ready?**
22　MOM 1: **It's over on the table. Dougie, would you please bring the**
23　　　　**meat over, sweetie?**
24　DOUGIE 2: **Sure, Mom.** *(DOUGIE 2 picks up plate with meat then*
25　　　　*exits Stage Left. DOUGIE 1 enters with plate of meat Stage Right.)*
26　DAD 1: **OK, everybody. Here we go.**
27　MOM 1: **Just a minute.** *(MOM 1 exits Stage Right. MOM 2 enters*
28　　　　*Stage Left, picks up fire extinguisher, then exits Stage Left. MOM*
29　　　　*1 enters Stage Right with fire extinguisher.)* **Go ahead.**
30　DAD 1: **Real funny, Doris. Real funny.** *(DAD 1 lights grill, MOM 1*
31　　　　*relieved exits Stage Right, MOM 2 enters Stage Left and continues*
32　　　　*setting table.)*
33　DOUGIE 1: **Dad, wanna catch?**
34　DAD 1: **Not now, Dougie. A little later.**
35　DOUGIE 1: **Aw, Dad. You said that two times already.**

1   **DAD 1: I'm in the middle of a meat masterpiece. Look why don't**
2   **you play catch with your mother?**
3   **DOUGIE 1: She stinks.**
4   **DAD 1: Dougie, please! I'll play after we eat.**
5   **DOUGIE 1: Here, Mom. Catch.** *(DOUGIE 1 tosses ball in the air a*
6   *few times, then turns to face Off-stage Right and tosses ball Off-*
7   *stage Right. Balls enters Stage Left and hits MOM 2 in the head.*
8   *MOM 2 falls.)* **Whoops.** *(DOUGIE 1 exits stage Right. DOUGIE*
9   *2 enters stage Left, runs to MOM 2.)*
10   **DAD 1: Doris, would you please bring me the pepper? Doris?**
11   *(Looking Off-stage Right, notices MOM 2 on ground.)* **Holy**
12   **manicotti. What did you ...** *(DAD 1 exits Stage Right. DAD 2*
13   *enters Stage Left and continues sentence as he runs to MOM 2.)*
14   **DAD 2: ... do to your mother?**
15   **DOUGIE 2: I told you she stinks.**
16   **MOM 2:** *(Very woozy)* **The pudding is really chewy.** *(Note:*
17   *Originally, MOM's "woozy" lines were lines from other skits*
18   *done in the same show. Feel free to substitute.)*
19   **DAD 2: Doris, sweetie? Are you all right?** *(To DOUGIE 2)* **Quick, go**
20   **grab a steak.** *(DOUGIE 2 exits Stage Left. DOUGIE 1 enters*
21   *Stage Right, uses a utensil to grab a steak from the grill, then exits*
22   *Stage Right. DOUGIE 2 enters Stage Left with utensil and steak.*
23   *DAD 2 grabs steak and places it on MOM 2's eye.)*
24   **MOM 2: Ow, ow, ow, hot, sunburn.**
25   **DAD 2: A cold one from the dish!** *(DOUGIE 2 exits Stage Left.*
26   *DOUGIE 1 enters Stage Right grabs steak and exits Stage Right.*
27   *DOUGIE 2 enters Stage Left and gives steak to DAD 2 who*
28   *places it on MOM 2's eye.)*
29   **MOM 2: What happened?**
30   **DAD 2: You gotta keep your eye on the ball, sweetie.**
31   **DOUGIE 2: But not literally.**
32   **DAD 2: Are you OK?**
33   **DOUGIE 2: Sorry, Mom.**
34   **MOM 2: That's all right, honey. The bump should go down in a**
35   **few hours.** *(DAD 2 helps MOM 2 to her feet.)*

1   **DAD 2: Are you sure you're OK?**

2   **MOM 2: You shrunk the dragon!**

3   **DAD 2: Hurry, go call a doctor.**

4   **MOM 2: Oh, Lenny. I'm just kidding. I'll be fine. Let's eat.** *(DAD*

5   *2 exits Stage Left. DAD 1 enters Stage Right, collects meat from*

6   *grill then exits Stage Right. DAD 2 enters Stage Left. FAMILY sits*

7   *at table and begins to eat.)*

8   **MR. MIMMERMAN 1:** *(Off-stage)* **My goodness gravy, something**

9   **smells good.**

10   **DAD 2: Oh no, it's Mimmerman. Hide the food.**

11   **MOM 2: Honey, now be neighborly.**

12   **MRS. MIMMERMAN 1:** *(Off-stage)* **Ooo, it surely does.**

13   **DAD 2: And his wife!**

14   **MOM 2: Quick, everyone hide!** *(MR. MIMMERMAN 1 and MRS.*

15   *MIMMERMAN 1 enter Back Center Stage facing Stage Right.*

16   *They walk to edge of Stage Right — which would be the doorway*

17   *to the family's home. The MIMMERMANS talk Off-stage Right*

18   *and the FAMILY talks Off-stage Left.)*

19   **MR. MIMMERMAN 1: Howdy, neighbors. What's cooking?**

20   **'Cause we're mighty hungry.**

21   **MRS. MIMMERMAN 1: We missed your fireworks, Lenny.**

22   **DAD 2: Didn't mean to disappoint you.**

23   **MRS. MIMMERMAN 1: My heavens. Dougie sure is sproutin' like**

24   **a bean.**

25   **MR. MIMMERMAN 1: Speaking of beans ... mind if we join you?**

26   **MOM 2: Well, we really don't have ...** *(MR. MIMMERMAN 1 and*

27   *MRS. MIMMERMAN 1 exit Stage Right. MR. MIMMERMAN 2,*

28   *and MRS. MIMMERMAN 2 enter Stage Left and move to table. At*

29   *this point the volume control begins to go bad on the stage.)*

30   **MR. MIMMERMAN 2: We were ... in the ... can you ...**

31   **DAD 2: She ... n ...** *(Scene continues with no volume, then lights*

32   *begin to fade in and out. All freeze. Enter STAGE MANAGER.)*

33   **STAGE MANAGER: I'm really sorry about this, our volume and**

34   **brightness seem to going bad, too ...** *(Ad-lib appropriate*

35   *ending.)*

1 *(NOTE: This skit was first done right before an intermission. The*
2 *STAGE MANAGER explained that everything would be fixed*
3 *during the break. Make the STAGE MANAGER's speech whatever*
4 *fits into your production.)*
5
6 *Curtain*
7
8
9
10
11
12
13
14
15
16
17
18
19
20
21
22
23
24
25
26
27
28
29
30
31
32
33
34
35

Consumer Watchdogs

Premise: In this world of big business and bigger advertising, consumers need someone to look out for their best interests. Consumer watchdogs fill that role, but they also seem to have their own agendas and their own favorites when it comes to products.

Cast: Harly Farqueth — Talk show host who likes Pepsi.
Darion Glitter — Talk show host who likes Coke.

Props: A can of Pepsi and a can of Coke.

Scene: Television studio stage with one table.

Notes: Harly and Darion finish each other's sentences at the beginning of the sketch. As the sketch goes on, each takes the side of their respective cola.

1	HARLY: Hello, and welcome to *Consumer Watchdogs*. I'm Harly
2	Farqueth.
3	DARION: And I'm Darion Glitter. Today we are going to put two
4	products to the dog-eat-dog test so as to save you ...
5	HARLY: ... the consumer, from purchasing products that, ...
6	DARION: ... to put it quite bluntly ...
7	HARLY: ... do not stand up to the promise of their manufacturers.
8	DARION: That's right Harly. There are many advertising tricks
9	that companies resort to ...
10	HARLY: ... in order to acquire your money.
11	DARION: Using wax food on commercials or in magazine ads ...
12	HARLY: ... because it looks tastier after spending time under hot
13	studio lights. And super models washing their hair ...
14	DARION: ... with laundry detergent on your favorite shampoo
15	commercials ...
16	HARLY: ... because it whips up better.
17	DARION: Oooo, tingly!
18	HARLY: Sometimes, a director shoots over one hundred
19	testimonials ...
20	DARION: ... before they get the one that makes it on air. It's no
21	wonder ...
22	HARLY: ... the average consumer is easily deceived. That's why
23	we're here. On today's show ...
24	DARION: ... we will be comparing the two most competitive soft
25	drinks.
26	HARLY: That's right Darion, we will be comparing Pepsi Cola
27	*(Says it with much enthusiasm)* ... and Coke.
28	DARION: ... a-Cola. *(Thinking he's finishing Harly's sentence.)*
29	HARLY: If you want to call it that.
30	DARION: Anyway, this soft drink battle has been carbonating
31	since 1888,
32	HARLY: ... and both companies have invested in billion dollar
33	advertising campaigns throughout the years.
34	DARION: So it's easy to see how the everyday consumer ...
35	HARLY: ... like yourselves ...

1   DARION: ... might be misled.
2   HARLY: To fully understand our products, let us start at the
3   beginning, shall we?
4   DARION: Yes, we shall. Delicious Coca-Cola was originated in
5   1888 by a pharmacist, John Pemberton, as a non-alcoholic
6   nerve medicine.
7   HARLY: Yes, that is true, a nerve medicine. *(Sarcastically)* Yummy!
8   DARION: Nonetheless, Coke was registered in 1891 and history was
9   made. After the success of bottling the drink ...
10   HARLY: ... an idea stolen from one of its loyal customers.
11   DARION: After a loyal customer suggested bottling the product,
12   the Coca-Cola company had a unique bottle designed, loosely
13   adapted from sketches of a cola nut!
14   HARLY: How cute. But in 1893 Pepsi Cola was born.
15   DARION: Yes ... as Brad's Drink. There's a cool name.
16   HARLY: Caleb Bradham did then rename his refreshing drink
17   after pepsin, a digestive aid.
18   DARION: How fitting.
19   HARLY: Did I mention that "co" "ca" "co" "la" in Chinese means
20   "suck the big wax tadpole"?
21   DARION: And this digestive aid was so gosh darn good, the
22   company went bankrupt ...
23   HARLY: Still here today!
24   DARION: ... three times!
25   HARLY: Still here today.
26   DARION: If it wasn't for Charles Guth, Pepsi would be history.
27   HARLY: If Coke wouldn't have screwed over one of their most loyal
28   customers, he wouldn't have had to buy Pepsi as revenge.
29   DARION: It was a pity buy out. Pepsi wouldn't sell as hair tonic.
30   He was just trying to prove a point.
31   HARLY: Yes, and what point was that?
32   DARION: Uh *(Nervous)* ... never mind.
33   HARLY: Please let me tell the people. Coke throws a little temper
34   tantrum over their main customer buying Pepsi and so they
35   secretly send employees to buy Coke in Chuck's stores to

1   create a demand.

2   DARION: I really don't see how this is relevant.

3   HARLY: Over six hundred and twenty people were sent, I believe.

4   DARION: Big deal.

5   HARLY: And, ooo, I believe he gave them Pepsi instead.

6   DARION: Yeah, yeah, whatever.

7   HARLY: And the majority preferred the Pepsi.

8   DARION: Charles Guth was a scam artist. Who knows what he
9   was really giving those people. Like it made a difference
10   anyway. By 1949, Coke captured eighty-four percent of the
11   market. Your digestive aid couldn't hold a candle to ...

12   HARLY: Your nerve medicine?

13   DARION: Your hair tonic?! I'm telling you. Coke is it!

14   HARLY: Pepsi is the best. Just look at all the greats that drink and
15   endorse it.

16   DARION: Oh, right. I forgot. That whole Nixon thing. I'd want to
17   be associated. "I don't drink Coke!"

18   HARLY: And Jimmy Carter? Ring a bell? And what's this whole
19   polar bear thing?

20   DARION: Polar bears are real. It's the real thing, Coke is, that's
21   the way it should be ...

22   HARLY: Oh ya, Mister Real Thing. What happened in 1979? Tell
23   'em.

24   DARION: That doesn't count.

25   HARLY: Go ahead, tell them.

26   DARION: People still drink more Coke.

27   HARLY: Pepsi reigns supreme.

28   DARION: You can't count that.

29   HARLY: Why not?

30   DARION: Well, you're not even talking soda anymore. Pepsi
31   buys Pizza Hut, Kentucky Fried Chicken, and you think that
32   counts?

33   HARLY: Whatever. Pepsi still makes more money than Coke.

34   DARION: Coke doesn't need to rely on exterior income. Coca-
35   Cola is the best and always was.

1   HARLY: And that's why they decided to change their recipe in
2   1985?
3   DARION: Oh, *(Nervous)* ... that. It was just a marketing ploy.
4   HARLY: I see. So you don't just rely on the actual taste of the
5   product, it's all in the advertising.
6   DARION: Don't be ridiculous. The public knows what they want.
7   They're not stupid. You think if they didn't want to buy Coke,
8   any type of advertising would change their minds?
9   HARLY: You're right. Advertising and marketing have no effect on
10   the public.
11   DARION: Coke rules!
12   HARLY: Blow it out your ear.
13   DARION: Blow it out *your* ear!
14   HARLY: Oh that's original, or should I say *classic*? *(HARLY and*
15   *DARION both shake and open their respective cans of soda*
16   *spraying each other.)*
17
18   *Curtain*
19
20
21
22
23
24
25
26
27
28
29
30
31
32
33
34
35

Crayon Rally

Premise: The Ku Klux Crayons get together for a rally. The primary colors seek separation from the secondary colors, but once confronted by them, change their minds and turn their attention to the "real" enemy.

Cast: Red — Clan leader.
Blue — Follower.
Yellow — Follower, first to decide to change.
White — Peacemaker.
Maroon — Angry anti-clan crayon.
Copper — Police crayon.

Props: One podium.

Costumes: All should have crayon costumes.

Scene: A crayon rally. Red is standing at a podium. Yellow and Blue are talking together.

Notes: All color puns and crayon references should be slightly exaggerated when spoken.

1	**RED: All right. All right. Would everyone please settle down? First**
2	**of all I'd like to thank you for showing up today for this rally.**
3	*(Trying to incite the crowd)* **We know who reigns supreme!**
4	**YELLOW and BLUE: We do!**
5	**RED: We know who are pure.**
6	**YELLOW and BLUE: We are!**
7	**RED: That's right! The primary colors are the chosen crayons. If**
8	**you are not one of the primary colors, we have no need for**
9	**you. Say it with me.**
10	**RED, YELLOW, and BLUE: Red, blue, and yellow, the rest can go**
11	**to hello! Red, blue, and yellow, the rest can go to hello!**
12	**RED: If we join together and unite, our brotherhood of primary**
13	**colors will rid the box of all the other unnecessary colors. We**
14	**three colors can combine our forces to create any color in the**
15	**spectrum. We have no need for those inferior secondary colors.**
16	**BLUE:** *(Interrupting)* **We can make any color?**
17	**RED: Yes. Any color. For example, blue and yellow join for green.**
18	**Red and ...**
19	**YELLOW:** *(Interrupting)* **Even gold?**
20	**RED: Well ... not gold. But every other color. We can make ...**
21	**BLUE:** *(Interrupting)* **Silver?**
22	**RED: No. Not silver. Silver and gold are metallic. Metal is a thing.**
23	**We can create any color we choose ...**
24	**YELLOW:** *(Interrupting)* **Neon?**
25	**RED:** *No!* **Not neon. Any non-glowing, non-metallic color.**
26	**BLUE: What about white?**
27	**RED:** *White?* **Don't make me puce. White has no right even calling**
28	**himself a color.**
29	**BLUE: That's right. Did you ever try coloring on top of another**
30	**color with white?**
31	**RED: Can't fool us. You can see right through him. He's useless.**
32	**They're all useless. It was bad enough when that** *burnt sienna*
33	**moved in and started mingling with our kind, then before you**
34	**knew it those fluorescent guys started infiltrating our box.**
35	**YELLOW: That's right! And once normal colors start mixing with**

1   those glow-in-the-darkies, Crayola only knows what the result

2   would be.

3   RED: That's right! And after one of our great achievements in

4   1990, when our dream became a reality and we finally did

5   away with eight of our enemies, then what happened?

6   ALL: I don't know.

7   RED: I'll tell you what happened. Purple Mountains Majesty

8   happened. Razzmatazz happened. Shamrock, Pacific Blue,

9   Asparagus, Tickle-Me Pink, Granny Smith Apple, Mauvelous

10   happened. What in the hue is Mauvelous? *(WHITE and*

11   *MAROON enter, unnoticed by the primary colors.)*

12   BLUE: Yea! We get rid of eight, and they bring in sixteen new ones.

13   What's that all about?

14   WHITE: There's plenty of room in the box for all of us.

15   YELLOW: Sure. That's because they keep making the boxes

16   bigger and bigger. Pretty soon it'll be boxes of one hundred.

17   And you know what happens with flip top box government

18   housing? I think we were just fine with the original eight.

19   BLUE: Yeah, we don't need you secondaries.

20   MAROON: So that's it, huh?

21   BLUE: That's it.

22   MAROON: I can see your true colors now. It's the color of hatred.

23   The color of ignorance. You primary colors don't even

24   deserve to melt on a dashboard ... or be eaten by a two-year-

25   old!

26   RED: You're such a *maroon.*

27   MAROON: That's Mr. Maroon to you. You know, I would love to

28   see you all just broken up into a bunch of pieces too small to

29   even hold and discarded in the sofa cushions for the rest of

30   eternity.

31   WHITE: But aren't we all just paraffin wax when our pigment is

32   removed?

33   BLUE: Who you calling a pig, Whitey? I say we just make you all

34   black and blue. What do you think about that?

35   WHITE: There's no need to get *violet.*

1   YELLOW: I think Whitey might have a sharp point here.

2   RED: Oh, look who's getting yellow on us! Mr. Sunshine!

3   YELLOW: No, really. Do you remember that one time when little
4   Amy drew that picture of her house? She was so thrilled when
5   she had Dandelion in her box of forty-eight. I suppose she
6   could have settled for yellow if she wanted to, but she didn't,
7   and her mother hung that picture on the refrigerator for eight
8   weeks! Eight weeks!

9   MAROON: That's right. And remember when little Bobby won the
10   Halloween drawing contest, because, luckily, he had the
11   perfect green shade for his monster's mucus?

12 WHITE: Or little Nemo, when he drew the picture of his puppy,
13   Spot. Where would he have been without aquamarine? The
14   full spectrum of colors is what imagination is all about.
15   Having endless options when you're creating your own little
16   masterpiece.

17 BLUE: There's just so many now. I mean, where's the identity? I
18   used to have job security. But now, Blue-green, Green-blue,
19   Sky Blue, Navy Blue, Powder Blue, Periwinkle, Cyan. All
20   these blues, it kinda makes me sad.

21 WHITE: We shouldn't be writing each other off. We should be
22   working together to make this the most colorful world it can
23   be. We have to be brave enough to color outside the lines.

24 BLUE: Easy for you to say. Nobody would see you.

25 WHITE: *(Upset)* I am a color like any other color! If you sharpen
26   me, do I not get shorter? If you apply heat, do I not melt?

27 RED: White. Nothing. Empty. Zero. Zally. Zippo. Nadda.

28 WHITE: What are you saying?

29 RED: Do I have to color a picture for you? You're useless!

30 WHITE: How'd you like to be renamed Blood Red?

31 RED: Come on, Whitey!

32 WHITE: That's right. I'll white you out.

33 RED: Go ahead and try. *(RED and WHITE begin "jousting" with*
34   *points of crayon heads.)*

35 BLUE: Cool it guys, here comes the *Copper*. *(COPPER enters.)*

1   **COPPER: All right, you crayons. You're going to have to break it**
2   **up.**
3   **RED: We got the right to gather and voice our opinions.**
4   **COPPER: Not when you're disturbing the peace, you don't. So,**
5   **disperse, or I'll be breaking the lot of you up and throwing**
6   **you in the tin.**
7   **YELLOW: I'm sure we can come to some kind of *chartreuse*.**
8   **COPPER: *Peachy*. Don't make me come back. *(COPPER exits.)***
9   **WHITE: So? What do you say?**
10   **RED: I don't know. Maybe you do have a sharp point. Maybe we**
11   **are all the same underneath our wrappers. But, could so many**
12   **different colors learn to live as one rainbow?**
13   **YELLOW: I think we could.**
14   **BLUE: Yeah, me too. We shouldn't be fighting each other. *(Pause***
15   *as all reflect on this idea.)* **It's the others we have to watch for!**
16   **YELLOW: Others?**
17   **RED: The markers!**
18   **BLUE: Those felt heads!**
19   **RED: Dried up good-for-nothings!** *(All ad-lib disdain for markers as*
20   *curtain closes.)*
21
22   *Curtain*
23
24
25
26
27
28
29
30
31
32
33
34
35

The Cutting Room Floor

Premise: An eccentric director, who isn't very good at giving directions, is demanding that his film be edited now. As the editors watch the film, actors play it out On-stage. The film is edited into something it's not.

Cast: Barry — A film editor worried about losing his job.
Shelly — A sarcastic and frustrated film editor.
King — A character in a sci-fi film.
Queen Morda — A character in a sci-fi film.
Pilot — A character in a sci-fi film.
Ronweer — An eccentric director, who mixes up words.

Props: A film-splicing machine, film, tape, sci-fi set.

Costumes: Sci-fi king, queen, and pilot.

Scene: Inside a film editing room. Barry and Shelly are sitting at the table working. King and Pilot are frozen in place on the "viewing monitor."

Notes: The actors playing the sci-fi characters should pause and rewind at the editors' control. They are to appear as though they are on a screening monitor.

1   BARRY: Mark frame starting two zero two eight. We'll have to
2   edit that section out and shorten the scene at least another
3   thirty seconds.
4   SHELLY: What's with this guy, anyway? I can't make heads or
5   tails out of this mess.
6   BARRY: All I know is that we have 'til seven a.m. to get this
7   cinematic disaster finished.
8   SHELLY: What time is it now?
9   BARRY: Holy mackerel! It's six thirty already. All right. So what
10   do we have so far? Take it back to frame ten ten.
11   SHELLY: *(Rewinds film.)* This is where the king recruits the soldier.
12   KING: I need you to save the empire.
13   SHELLY: *(Sarcastically)* That one's original.
14   PILOT: My heart pounds with courage. My dedication belongs to
15   you.
16   KING: Yes, I believe you to be courageous, and yes, I realize your
17   dedication.
18   SHELLY: Blah, blah, blah ...
19   BARRY: Quiet, I gotta hear this. *(BARRY pauses film, rewinds,*
20   *plays.)*
21   KING: I need you to save the empire.
22   PILOT: My heart pounds with courage. My dedication belongs to
23   you.
24   KING: Yes, I believe you to be courageous, and yes, I realize your
25   dedication.
26   PILOT: It may take me from now until eternity, but I am yours to
27   command and do with, what you will.
28   KING: Good luck. *(KING embraces PILOT.)*
29   SHELLY: Oh, brother. Gag me.
30   BARRY: OK. Hold it there. Now take it to frame twenty-two sixty.
31   *(Fast forward film.)*
32   SHELLY: This is where Queen Morda gives the pilot his orders.
33   MORDA: You must go to help the others.
34   PILOT: But, Queen, I am only one. It would be stupid to attempt
35   this alone.

1   BARRY: Hold it. *(Film pauses.)* **Back that up to frame twenty-two**
2   **seventy. Let me mark this.** *(Rewind)*
3   MORDA: You must go to help the others.
4   PILOT: But, Queen, I am only one. It would be stupid to attempt
5   this alone.
6   MORDA: Just remember, like the king always says, theoblurnexr —
7   *(Film jams.)*
8   BARRY: Holy crabgrass!
9   SHELLY: Cheap piece of garbage!
10   BARRY: Shut the lamp. Hurry, shut the lamp!
11   SHELLY: Hey, this film just improved.
12   BARRY: Quick, Ronweer will be here any minute. *(BARRY and*
13   *SHELLY ad lib confusion as they try to fix the film. RONWEER*
14   *enters.)*
15   RONWEER: You are ready with my film?
16   BARRY: Well, we got it down to eight minutes.
17   RONWEER: Eight minutes? No. You're not listening when I talk
18   at you. I tell you five and you do eight. I give you people
19   chances and you push them in your ears. What for you play
20   with my turmoil. I have my house over the line. Money is my
21   time. Just look at me standing next to my dilemma. Take the
22   film and fix it.
23   SHELLY: Yeah, right.
24   RONWEER: I'm standing here procrastinating with my
25   reputation in my hand. Just fix the film.
26   SHELLY: Yeah, right. *(BARRY elbows SHELLY.)*
27   RONWEER: My reputation! My reputation is squashing in my
28   hands and you people don't care. Fix the film to five or walk
29   to nowhere and I'll be sure that you both are firewalkers.
30   BARRY: But what do you suggest we cut?
31   RONWEER: You're asking me with my reputation in my hand? I
32   pay you to fix this so you will. You have ten minutes.
33   *(RONWEER exits.)*
34   BARRY: Holy nutshell! Ten minutes! What are we going to do?
35   SHELLY: I'll tell you what we're going to do. He wants it shorter;

1   **we'll make it shorter.** *(SHELLY begins hacking the film*
2   *haphazardly.)*
3   **BARRY: What are you doing?**
4   **SHELLY: I am making it shorter.**
5   **BARRY: You don't even know what you're cutting!**
6   **SHELLY: It doesn't matter!** *(Imitating RONWEER.)* **I am cutting**
7   **his reputation so I don't have to walk to nowhere.** *(RONWEER*
8   *enters.)*
9   **RONWEER: My mind is anticipating the film. I am ready to be**
10   **deliberate. Show me the fixed film.**
11   **BARRY: Uh ... well.**
12   **SHELLY: Sure, here you go.** *(Plays film. ACTORS talk in "spliced*
13   *voices," very choppy and changing pitches in mid sentence.)*
14   **KING: I need you.**
15   **PILOT: My heart belongs to you.**
16   **KING: Yes, yes.**
17   **PILOT: Take me. I am yours.** *(KING and PILOT embrace.)*
18   **MORDA: You must go.**
19   **PILOT: But, Queen, I am stupid.**
20   **MORDA: Just like the king.** *(BARRY with hands on head, SHELLY*
21   *with a smirk, RONWEER staring at scene)*
22   **SHELLY: Pretty good, huh?** *(BARRY gives SHELLY a dirty look.)*
23   **RONWEER:** *(After silence)* **My reputation is happy. Great work.**
24   *(RONWEER congratulates puzzled EDITORS.)*
25
26   *Curtain*
27
28
29
30
31
32
33
34
35

The Date Tests

Premise: A boy is arriving to take Brandi out. Mom and Dad put the boy through a series of tests.

Cast: Dad — Overprotective father.
Mom — Overprotective but a little less obnoxious than Dad.
Iggy — Normal type. He is nervous.
Brandi — Daughter; date of Iggy.

Props: A couch with a large pillow, and table with a bowl of plastic fruit with at least one orange. Also, a chair, a pen and a several page test.

Scene: Living room. A couch is Center Stage. A table and chair are Stage Left. Dad is sitting on the couch. Mom is sitting at the table.

1	DAD: What's this boy's name again?
2	MOM: His name is Iggy Lymon.
3	DAD: Iggy. What kind of name is Iggy?
4	MOM: Now, honey, for Brandi's sake, give the boy a chance.
5	*(Knock at door)* There he is, now. Do you have the test ready?
6	DAD: Ready.
7	MOM: Hello, and you must be Iggy. *(IGGY enters. He is nervous.)*
8	IGGY: Yes, ma'am.
9	MOM: This is Mr. Santillo.
10	IGGY: Hello, sir. *(IGGY reaches out to shake hands — DAD does not*
11	*shake.)*
12	DAD: So, you're here to pick up Brandi. *(Pause)* Remember
13	sucking up won't help, we can see right through it.
14	MOM: He's right. We have three others just like Brandi. We've
15	been through this many times before.
16	DAD: Did you bring a number two pencil?
17	IGGY: Sir?
18	DAD: A number two pencil, for the written portion of the test?
19	IGGY: I ... I wasn't expecting a test ... I just came to pick up
20	Brandi.
21	MOM: Well, you certainly don't think we can let her go with just
22	anyone!
23	IGGY: But I was just going to take her out for a little while ...
24	DAD: So you're saying you don't have a number two pencil?
25	IGGY: Uhh ... I gotta pen?
26	DAD: That won't work on the machine-corrected portion of the
27	test.
28	IGGY: Machine-corrected portion? *(MOM is writing down the vital*
29	*information she asks for.)*
30	MOM: First things first, your name?
31	IGGY: Iggy Lymon.
32	DAD: Iggy? What kind of name is Iggy?
33	IGGY: I was named after my grandfather.
34	MOM: Age?
35	IGGY: Eighty-one.

1   MOM: Eighty-one? You look so young.

2   IGGY: No, my grandfather's eighty-one, I'm only seventeen.

3   DAD: Seventeen, huh? You know in dog years, that's only two and

4   a half, roughly. Do you think you're old enough for Brandi to

5   go out with?

6   IGGY: I'm actually very mature for my age.

7   MOM: So maybe you're too old?

8   IGGY: Umm ... we're just going for a walk or something.

9   DAD: Well, since you have no number two pencil, I guess we'll skip

10   the multiple-choice section and just move into the short

11   answer. *(DAD hands IGGY the test and sits him down.)*

12   IGGY: *(Thinking it's a joke)* Is this for real?

13   DAD: *(Very seriously)* Do we look like we're kidding?

14   MOM: You can never be too careful, especially these days. *(IGGY*

15   *begins filling in the test, PARENTS stand close by watching him*

16   *and making remarks about his answers.)*

17   IGGY: I'm done, I guess.

18   DAD: That's it?

19   IGGY: Can I see Brandi now?

20   MOM: Well, I think missing all the multiple choice might hurt you.

21   DAD: Yes, you are gonna have to do good on the next two parts.

22   IGGY: Two more parts?

23   MOM: Just answer each of the questions the best that you can.

24   *(Note: MOM and DAD's voices and actions should be*

25   *exaggerated whenever possible to help show the change from*

26   *subdued to extreme and back again. IGGY is getting progressively*

27   *more nervous.)*

28   DAD: *(In an interrogation voice)* What do you do for a living?

29   IGGY: I'm just in high school.

30   MOM: *(Also interrogating)* You have no job?

31   IGGY: Well ... I walk dogs.

32   DAD: *(Impressed, and calm again.)* Very good.

33   MOM: *(Also impressed)* Shows industriousness.

34   DAD: *(Back to the interrogation)* Any plans for the future?

35   IGGY: I plan on finishing high school.

1   MOM: *(Interrogating)* I would hope so, but after school!

2   IGGY: Umm ... college?

3   DAD: Where?

4   IGGY: I ... haven't ... quite decided yet.

5   DAD: And have you decided where you are taking Brandi?

6   IGGY: I thought we were just going for a walk, maybe to the park,

7   grab something to eat ...

8   MOM: Uh-huh, and will this something to eat be healthy?

9   IGGY: I guess so.

10   DAD: What route will you take to the park?

11   IGGY: I dunno, Third Street right to the park. It's only two blocks

12   away.

13   MOM: Did you know part of the sidewalk on Third Street is

14   missing?

15   DAD: *(Almost yelling)* How do you plan on dealing with that,

16   mister?

17   IGGY: Uh ... Go around?

18   MOM: *(Calm and impressed)* Good answer!

19   DAD: *(Also calm)* Yes, good idea. *(Changes back to interrogation)* To

20   go around, you'll have to cross the street. Describe, if you will,

21   the proper procedure for doing this.

22   IGGY: I'll just stop, look, and listen.

23   MOM: Could you please stand and demonstrate for us this

24   technique? *(IGGY stands hesitantly in front of the couch. DAD*

25   *waits at one end of the couch, MOM at the other end. IGGY takes*

26   *a step, stops, looks, and listens, then begins to walk. DAD steps*

27   *out quickly and runs into IGGY, knocking him over as:)*

28   DAD: *Boom! (Very angry now)* You just got hit by a truck!

29   IGGY: *(Confused)* I did?

30   DAD: You and Brandi both. *(DAD throws pillow down next to*

31   *IGGY.)* You're hurt bad, possibly dead!

32   MOM: *(Also angry)* You forgot to check the side street on the other

33   side of the couch!

34   IGGY: I listened, though.

35   DAD: But you didn't hear. Now what do you do?

1   IGGY: I thought I was dead?

2   DAD: Well, by the grace of God, you survived, what do you do

3   next?

4   IGGY: Check to see if Brandi is OK?

5   MOM: I should hope so after nearly getting her killed.

6   DAD: Luckily, she just has two broken legs, what now?

7   IGGY: Umm ... umm ...

8   DAD: Quickly, Brandi can't go out with someone that's too

9   indecisive, what are you going to do?

10   IGGY: Leave her alone until the paramedics arrive?

11   DAD: *In the middle of the street?!*

12   MOM: Oh, my!

13   IGGY: I'll move her to a safe position.

14   DAD: What if she has neck damage?! *(IGGY is becoming more and*

15   *more excited and nervous.)*

16   IGGY: Umm ... umm.

17   MOM: What are you going to do?

18   IGGY: Umm ... umm.

19   DAD: Hurry, boy, time's running out, here comes another car!

20   IGGY: I'll stand up and direct traffic around her. *(MOM and DAD*

21   *suddenly become calm again. IGGY is still visibly excited and*

22   *jumpy.)*

23   MOM: Good, good. Now you're across the street.

24   IGGY: *(Confused and loud)* With broken legs?

25   DAD: *(Calm)* No, let's just say by some miracle you've made it

26   across the street, and *(Suddenly gets loud again)* a VW van

27   comes flying right toward you! Oh no! It's Israeli terrorists.

28   *They've got guns! Look out!* *(DAD grabs fruit, tips over table*

29   *and begins making shooting sounds from behind the table. MOM*

30   *ducks behind the couch. IGGY is left excited and confused.)*

31   MOM: They're shooting! Get down! Run for cover! *(IGGY looks,*

32   *and dives behind couch.)* **You left Brandi in the middle of the**

33   **street! She's been hit!** *(IGGY jumps over couch and picks up*

34   *"pillow" BRANDI as DAD mimics throwing an orange like it's a*

35   *hand grenade.)* **Oh my God! It's a hand grenade! It's gonna**

1   **blow, it's gonna blow!** *(IGGY drops pillow and dives on orange.)*
2   **DAD:** *(Coming from behind table, again very calm)* **Very courageous,**
3   **good answer.**
4   **MOM:** *(Also calm, coming from behind couch)* **Good, now for the**
5   **last part of the test …**
6   **IGGY:** *(Extremely excited still)* **The last part?!**
7   **DAD:** *(Still calm)* **If you can please tell us, in your own words, why**
8   **you think you should be allowed to take Brandi out?**
9   **IGGY:** *I just dove on a live grenade for her!!*
10 **DAD: Take it easy son, it was just an orange, nothing to worry**
11   **about. You passed the test. Brandi!** *(BRANDI enters. DAD*
12   *moves to IGGY, puts arm around him. IGGY still very tense,*
13   *throws DAD to the couch, grabs BRANDI's hand and starts*
14   *running to the door.)*
15 **BRANDI: See ya Mom and Dad.**
16 **MOM: Have fun kids!** *(Pause)* **I like him.**
17 **DAD: Yeah, I think he'll be OK.**
18
19   *Curtain*
20
21
22
23
24
25
26
27
28
29
30
31
32
33
34
35

Dogs Caught

Premise: A young puppy's eyes are opened when he meets a streetwise, older dog in the kennel.

Cast: Spike — An older, streetwise dog.
Rover — A young energetic dog.
Man — Typical dad.
Woman — Typical mom.
Child — Excited to be reunited with their lost puppy.
Kennel Worker — A warden persona.

Props: None.

Costumes: Two dog costumes.

Scene: Spike sleeps in the corner, and Rover is escorted in by the Kennel Worker.

1   **ROVER:** I'm tellin' ya, my license is at home! I just lost it in the
2   yard!
3   **KENNEL WORKER:** Yeah, yeah, just get in there. *(KENNEL*
4   *WORKER exits.)*
5   **ROVER:** I get a phone call. I want to speak to my owner. I don't
6   believe this.
7   **SPIKE:** Hey! Calm down. Canines are trying to sleep over here.
8   **ROVER:** Oh, sorry. I didn't see you. I'm just a little upset. This is
9   all a huge mistake.
10   **SPIKE:** Yeah, kid. It always is.
11   **ROVER:** No. Really. You don't understand. I don't belong in here.
12   I'm a good boy. A good boy. I'm tellin' ya.
13   **SPIKE:** Let me guess. Domestic, right?
14   **ROVER:** Excuse me?
15   **SPIKE:** You know, fetch the slippers, roll over, shake hands. Only
16   go outside to wee wee.
17   **ROVER:** Yeah, so?
18   **SPIKE:** Then quit your yappin'. You'll be picked up soon enough.
19   Your type always is.
20   **ROVER:** My type? What's that supposed to mean?
21   **SPIKE:** I mean in two hours that nice couple that feeds you from
22   the table is gonna be here with their little boy and you'll get
23   all the hugs and pettings and chewy toys you want. So just
24   relax and quit your whimpering.
25   **ROVER:** I'm sorry. I just never thought this would happen to me.
26   I'm Rover.
27   **SPIKE:** Spike.
28   **ROVER:** It sounds like you've got a lot of experience at this.
29   **SPIKE:** Yeah, I've been in and out of these places since I was a pup.
30   After a while you get used to it.
31   **ROVER:** Is anyone coming to pick you up?
32   **SPIKE:** Not this time kid.
33   **ROVER:** What do you mean?
34   **SPIKE:** Nothin'. So tell me about home. It's been a while since I
35   had a doggie door to crawl through.

1   ROVER: Oh, it's great. Family's nice. Fireplace to lie in front of.
2   They even feed me pizza.
3   SPIKE: Sounds good.
4   ROVER: But what about you? How did you end up in a place like
5   this?
6   SPIKE: Ahh ... You wouldn't be interested.
7   ROVER: No, really. I want to know.
8   SPIKE: Well, I started out like you. Nice home. Well fed. I was
9   staying with a young couple in the hills. And then one day they
10   did something that just made me rabid.
11   ROVER: Did they rub your nose in it?
12   SPIKE: No.
13   ROVER: Swat you with a newspaper?
14   SPIKE: No.
15   ROVER: Then what?
16   SPIKE: They made me wear a sweater.
17   ROVER: Oh, no!
18   SPIKE: Yeah, it was humiliating. They'd put it on me and take me
19   for walks. All the neighborhood pups would yelp at me "Hey,
20   Spike, I didn't know you were a poodle."
21   ROVER: Bow-wow. What'd you do?
22   SPIKE: Couldn't take it anymore. I started lifting my leg on
23   everything, the rugs, the bed, even the cat.
24   ROVER: The cat?
25   SPIKE: She had an attitude anyway.
26   ROVER: Don't they all?
27   SPIKE: So you better be careful, pure bred. It could happen to you,
28   too. You might think that things are going good now, but a day
29   might come where you'll be wearing a little hat and be the
30   joke of the pack.
31   ROVER: You mean I could end up like you? *(Starts to howl.)* Get
32   me outta here! Help!
33   SPIKE: Knock it off. That won't help. You're just annoying people.
34   ROVER: But what do I do, Spike? I don't want to wear clothes. I
35   already have a thick shiny coat. What if I can't take it like

1   you? I don't want to be a bad, bad boy! I'm a good boy! Good
2   boy!
3 SPIKE: Look, kid, you'll be fine. Life on the streets isn't so bad.
4   Plenty of fire hydrants to choose from, garbage cans to knock
5   over, and fresh mailmen on every corner.
6 ROVER: Really? But doesn't it get lonely?
7 SPIKE: Sure, but you get used to it.
8 ROVER: *(Panicking)* Help! Get me outta here! Help!
9 SPIKE: Would you knock it off?
10 ROVER: But I'm not like you Spike, I can't deal with this. I
11   know what goes on in the pound. Dry food and no long walks
12   in the park. I'm tellin' ya, I can't do it. *(Enter MAN, WOMAN,*
13   *and CHILD.)*
14 MAN: There he is!
15 CHILD: Rover, I missed you, boy!
16 ROVER: Thank goodness you're here! Oh, Spike, they found me!
17 WOMAN: Oh puppy, we were worried sick about you! *(Enter*
18   *KENNEL WORKER.)*
19 KENNEL WORKER: Well, folks. We've got some papers for you
20   to sign if you'd come with me.
21 MAN: Sure. *(Child's name)*, you stay here until it's time to go.
22 CHILD: OK. *(Lavishes affection on ROVER.)*
23 SPIKE: Well, I'm glad for you kid. Have a nice life.
24 ROVER: But what about you?
25 SPIKE: What about me?
26 ROVER: When are you leaving?
27 SPIKE: Don't think I'm leaving this time kid.
28 ROVER: You mean ... ?
29 SPIKE: I'm afraid so, but you know what they say? All dog's go to
30   heaven, right?
31 ROVER: Oh, Spike.
32 CHILD: Looks like you found a friend, huh boy? *(Starts petting*
33   *SPIKE.)*
34 SPIKE: It's been a long time since someone's pet me like this. *(Leg*
35   *starts thumping.)*

1   **CHILD: Poor doggie. Hey Mom, Dad!** *(MAN, WOMAN, and*
2   *KENNEL WORKER enter.)* **Rover made a friend, can we take**
3   **him home?**
4   **WOMAN: Well, he is kinda cute.**
5   **SPIKE: Kinda?**
6   **WOMAN:** *(To MAN)* **What do you think, sweetheart?**
7   **MAN:** *(To KENNEL WORKER)* **Is this one available?**
8   **KENNEL WORKER: If you want him, he's yours.**
9   **ROVER: Yeah, what do ya say, Spike?**
10   **SPIKE: You mean a real home?**
11   **ROVER: Sure. Just don't mention what you did to the cat!**
12   **SPIKE: Deal!** *(All start to exit.)*
13   **WOMAN: Rover, I knitted a surprise for you. Maybe I can knit one**
14   **for your new little friend.** *(SPIKE and ROVER turn to each other*
15   *in panic.)*
16
17   *Curtain*
18
19
20
21
22
23
24
25
26
27
28
29
30
31
32
33
34
35

Dr. Zucchini

Premise: An ex-magician, now chief surgeon, performs in the operating room.

Cast: Dr. Zucchini — An ex-magician, now chief surgeon.
Assistant One — New to the operating room team.
Assistant Two — A regular assistant to Dr. Zucchini.
Patient – Gets operated on.
Nurse — Dr. Zucchini's assistant. The "Ta-da" girl.

Props: Anesthetic mask, x-ray card, watch on a chain, soft mallet, scalpel, handkerchief that will become bloody, flowers, rabbit, saw, sound effects: "ta-da" trumpet flourish.

Costumes: Operating scrubs, magician's outfit.

Scene: An operating room. Assistant One and Assistant Two are prepping Patient.

1   ASSISTANT ONE: ... And then I was the attending x-ray tech at
2   County for my internship. When I heard I made it on Dr. Z's
3   team, I was thrilled. I heard he's the best.
4   ASSISTANT TWO: He is ... *great.*
5   ASSISTANT ONE: You've been on his team long?
6   ASSISTANT TWO: I've been performing with Dr. Z for two years.
7   *(DR. ZUCCHINI Off-stage clears throat.)* You all ready?
8   ASSISTANT ONE: Ready.
9   ASSISTANT TWO: All right then, here, read this. *(Hands*
10   *ASSISTANT ONE a piece of paper.)*
11   ASSISTANT ONE: Excuse me?
12   ASSISTANT TWO: Doctor Z is waiting. We're ready to get started.
13   Just read the card.
14   ASSISTANT ONE: Read the card?
15   ASSISTANT TWO: Yes, read the card. *(ASSISTANT ONE looks*
16   *perplexed.)*
17   ASSISTANT ONE: OK. *(Reads.)* Ladies and gentleman, doctors
18   and nurses, I am proud to present to you, for his featured
19   engagement in O.R. number three, the Great Dr. Zucchini!
20   *(PATIENT and ASSISTANT TWO applaud, ASSISTANT ONE looks*
21   *confused. NURSE and DR. ZUCCHINI enter.)*
22   DR. ZUCCHINI: Thank you. Thank you. I am the Great Dr.
23   Zucchini. I am here to amaze you and this is my assistant,
24   Nurse Sapphire. *(NURSE bows.)*
25   ASSISTANT ONE: It's a pleasure meeting you, Doctor. I've heard
26   so much about you.
27   DR. ZUCCHINI: Yes, you have. So, let us see what we have here.
28   ASSISTANT ONE: *(Holding up an x-ray)* Mr. Hopper, he has a ...
29   DR. ZUCCHINI: Silence.
30   ASSISTANT ONE: *(Confused)* Uh ... yes, well, it appears ...
31   DR. ZUCCHINI: Silence! *(DR. ZUCCHINI takes all x-rays and turns*
32   *to ASSISTANT TWO.)* Pick an x-ray, any x-ray. *(ASSISTANT*
33   *TWO picks x-ray.)* The Great Dr. Zucchini will now tell you
34   what is wrong with our Mr. Hopper. *(Concentrating)*
35   Hummmm, Hopper suffers from appendicitis. *(Sound effect:*

1   *Ta-da. ASSISTANT TWO looks at x-ray.)*
2   **ASSISTANT TWO: That's right!** *(PATIENT and ASSISTANT TWO*
3   *applaud.)*
4   **DR. ZUCCHINI: The Great Dr. Zucchini will now prepare the**
5   **patient for the operation.** *(ASSISTANT ONE begins to get*
6   *anesthesia. DR. ZUCCHINI pulls out a watch and begins to*
7   *hypnotize the patient.)* **You are getting sleepy. Very sleepy.**
8   *(Improvise)* **When I snap my fingers, you will awake, but feel no**
9   **pain. You will be able to enjoy the Great Dr. Zucchini's**
10   **performance without experiencing any discomfort whatsoever.**
11   **Five, four, ... and when the performance is over ... three, two ...**
12   **you will be completely healed ... one.** *(DR. ZUCCHINI snaps.)*
13   **ASSISTANT TWO: How do you feel?**
14   **PATIENT: I feel wonderful.**
15   **DR. ZUCCHINI: All righty, then. Let us dig in.**
16   **ASSISTANT ONE: Are you serious? The man is still awake. You**
17   **can't operate on him.** *(DR. ZUCCHINI looks around, picks up*
18   *mallet and hits PATIENT over head.)*
19   **DR. ZUCCHINI: How do you feel?**
20   **PATIENT: Never better.**
21   **ASSISTANT ONE: Wow!**
22   **ASSISTANT TWO: That just never gets old.**
23   **DR. ZUCCHINI: You see, although he is awake, he feels absolutely**
24   **nothing. No discomfort whatsoever. Scalpel.** *(NURSE delivers*
25   *scalpel to DR. ZUCCHINI in a very showy manner, DR.*
26   *ZUCCHINI makes incision. Sound effect: Ta-da. ASSISTANT*
27   *TWO and PATIENT applaud. ASSISTANT ONE is amazed.)*
28   **PATIENT:** *(Lifting sheet and looking inside himself)* **Cool! Look at**
29   **my innards!**
30   **DR. ZUCCHINI:** *(Covering PATIENT back up)* **Please, you mustn't**
31   **distract the Great Dr. Zucchini.**
32   **PATIENT: Ooo, right. Sorry.**
33   **DR. ZUCCHINI: The Great Dr. Zucchini will now make your**
34   **appendix disappear.** *(DR. ZUCCHINI drapes a handkerchief*
35   *over PATIENT. He begins to chant.)* **Ooolie boolie four five six,**

1	**out with your appendix.** *(Handkerchief begins dancing around*
2	*and getting bloody. DR. ZUCCHINI removes the handkerchief*
3	*with a magician's flourish. NURSE presents the PATIENT. Sound*
4	*effect: Ta-da. ALL applaud.)* **Wait a moment. What is this?**
5	*(DR. ZUCCHINI reaches in PATIENT and pulls out flowers.*
6	*Sound effect: Ta-da. ALL applaud.)* **And this?** *(DR. ZUCCHINI*
7	*reaches in PATIENT and pulls out rabbit. Sound effect: Ta-da.*
8	*ALL applaud.)* **And now if I may have your attention, the Great**
9	**Dr. Zucchini will now perform the amazing, death defying**
10	**trick I like to call ... Split Personality.** *(To the NURSE)* **Nurse**
11	**Sapphire, the saw, please.** *(NURSE hands DR. ZUCCHINI the*
12	*saw. DR. ZUCCHINI begins sawing PATIENT into two.)*
13	**PATIENT: This is so cool! I was expecting a typical appendectomy.**
14	*(Drum roll, DR. ZUCCHINI separates PATIENT. Sound effect:*
15	*Ta-da. ALL applaud.)*
16	**DR. ZUCCHINI: Thank you. Thank you.** *(DR. ZUCCHINI pulls a*
17	*needle and thread from behind ASSISTANT ONE's ear then hands*
18	*it to ASSISTANT ONE.)* **And now if you would be so kind as to**
19	**close for me, ...** *(Lights flicker. DR. ZUCCHINI disappears.)*
20	**ASSISTANT TWO: Working with Dr. Z is just so doggone**
21	**entertaining.**
22	**ASSISTANT ONE:** *(Looks at threaded needle, then PATIENT.)* **Yeah,**
23	**entertaining.**
24	
25	*Curtain*
26	
27	
28	
29	
30	
31	
32	
33	
34	
35	

The Elevator Hijack

Premise: A businessman is late for a very important meeting, and he gets stuck riding an elevator with a group of people he thinks is trying to sabotage his day. He tries hijacking the elevator with a dirty diaper.

Cast: Elevator Operator — Slightly sarcastic and protective of his elevator.
Business Person — In a big hurry.
Old Lady — Slow moving, both physically and mentally.
Teen — Headset wearing typical teen. Also playing a hand-held video game.
Woman — Mother with small baby and the whole load of stuff that goes with it. Very motherly.

Props: Headset, hand-held video game, diaper bag, diaper, baby, baby carriage, five cell phones, various things in Woman's bag.

Scene: An elevator. The Operator is singing and dancing to muzac. Business Person enters, hits button and waits as elevator arrives.

Note: When originally performed, this skit had no scenery. The idea of an elevator was expressed entirely with pantomime. The people on the elevator all "jerked" at the stops, and pushed invisible buttons. If pantomime is used, be sure that all buttons are pushed in the same area.

1   OPERATOR: Floor?
2   BUSINESS PERSON: Twelve, and hurry!
3   OPERATOR: *(Sarcastic)* Right. Let me just shift this baby into
4   overdrive.
5   BUSINESS PERSON: Just hit the button!
6   OPERATOR: Would that be the turbo boost or hyper-space
7   button? *(BUSINESS PERSON lunges for button. OPERATOR*
8   *stops him.)* Sorry, sir. Only highly-trained authorized
9   personnel are allowed to operate the equipment. I'm going to
10   have to ask you to, please, step to the rear of the car, or I'll
11   have to call security.
12   BUSINESS PERSON: For heaven's sake, man. I have a meeting with
13   the board on the twelfth floor in three minutes. *Please!* Just hit
14   the button! *(OPERATOR goes through pre-button pushing routine,*
15   *cracks knuckles, stretches, etc., then pushes button.)*
16   OPERATOR: Twelve.
17   BUSINESS PERSON: Thank you! *(OLD LADY enters. She is slow*
18   *and walks with a cane. She pushes button and waits for the*
19   *elevator to arrive. OLD LADY slowly gets on. BUSINESS*
20   *PERSON is annoyed by the slowness.)*
21   OPERATOR: Floor?
22   OLD LADY: Nine ... *(OPERATOR goes to hit nine)* or was that six?
23   *(OPERATOR stops.)* No, I think it was nine.
24   OPERATOR: *(Looking at OLD LADY for confirmation)* Nine?
25   OLD LADY: I think so.
26   OPERATOR: Are you sure? Because once we pass six ...
27   BUSINESS PERSON: Oh, for crying out loud! *(BUSINESS*
28   *PERSON again lunges for button. OPERATOR takes him down,*
29   *pinning him to the ground.)*
30   OPERATOR: What did I tell you, sir? Only trained professionals
31   are allowed to operate the control panel. I am the trained
32   professional on this car. Don't make me call security. *(Turning*
33   *to OLD LADY while still holding down BUSINESS PERSON.)*
34   Like I was saying before we were so rudely interrupted. Once
35   we pass six you'll have to wait until we're coming back down

1   **to get there again. Are you sure nine is the floor you want?**

2   **BUSINESS PERSON: Nine! Six! Just pick a floor!**

3   **OLD LADY: Nine would be just fine.**

4   **OPERATOR: OK then.** *(OPERATOR lets BUSINESS PERSON up*

5   *and once again goes through button pushing ritual. TEEN enters,*

6   *pushes button and waits for elevator. TEEN gets on, hits floor*

7   *button and then moves to the rear of the car.)*

8   **BUSINESS PERSON: Hey? What was that?**

9   **OPERATOR:** *(Looking at button bank)* **Looks like ten, I believe.**

10   **BUSINESS PERSON: No. I mean the little geek got to push his**

11   **own button.**

12   **OPERATOR: Sir, are you questioning my authority?**

13   **BUSINESS PERSON: What authority? You're an elevator operator.**

14   **OPERATOR: Yes, I am. The controller of your destiny.**

15   **BUSINESS PERSON: Listen, Mr. Destiny. All I'm saying is that**

16   **little geek got to push his own button and I got slammed to the**

17   **floor.**

18   **OPERATOR: Sir, if I thought you could handle it, I would let you**

19   **push your own button. But I don't think you can. And as for**

20   **this young gentleman, an untrained eye may not have noticed**

21   **that he is experienced in the operations of highly sophisticated**

22   **electrical equipment. Now, if you don't mind, I would like to**

23   **get back to my job.**

24   **BUSINESS PERSON: Please, do!** *(WOMAN with baby in a carriage*

25   *and several bags enters, pushes button and awaits elevator.*

26   *WOMAN squeezes onto the elevator trying to fit with all her bags*

27   *and baby carriage. BUSINESS PERSON is becoming visibly*

28   *annoyed. Note: The WOMAN should hand her baby, bags and*

29   *carriage to other elevator patrons as she apologizes and asks, "Do*

30   *you mind?" etc. She then collects her things and settles down.)*

31   **OPERATOR: Floor?**

32   **WOMAN: Eight, please.** *(OPERATOR does button pushing ritual.*

33   *BUSINESS PERSON imitates him. OPERATOR catches*

34   *BUSINESS PERSON mimicking.)*

35   **BUSINESS PERSON: Could you hurry?**

1   OPERATOR: I am doing my job the way I do my job.

2   BUSINESS PERSON: Well, do it. *(OPERATOR finishes ritual, then*

3   *pushes button. Cell phone rings. All on stage answer their own*

4   *personal cell phone. The call is for Woman. Note: The following*

5   *is executed while WOMAN ad-libs a conversation with a friend on*

6   *the cell phone. All but WOMAN start sniffing a foul smell, finally*

7   *realizing it is the baby. This is brought to her attention. She hands*

8   *baby to BUSINESS PERSON and begins digging for diaper.*

9   *BUSINESS PERSON passes baby as he is handed more items*

10   *[bottles, blankets, stuffed animals, etc.]. These are then handed*

11   *around the elevator. TEEN accidentally drops one of the items and*

12   *gets on all fours to pick it up. WOMAN seizes the opportunity,*

13   *setting the baby on TEEN's back in order to change the diaper.*

14   *WOMAN takes off soiled diaper and hands it off. The diaper*

15   *makes it's way to BUSINESS PERSON, at which time the*

16   *WOMAN's chore is done.)* I don't have time for this crap!

17   That's it! I'm taking over this car! *(BUSINESS PERSON takes*

18   *OPERATOR hostage using the dirty diaper as weapon.*

19   *BUSINESS PERSON goes to push buttons.)*

20   OPERATOR: I wouldn't do that if I were you.

21   BUSINESS PERSON: Oh, who's Mr. Destiny now?! Heh?

22   *(BUSINESS PERSON holds diaper to OPERATOR's face.*

23   *OPERATOR whiffs, then passes out.)* Everybody back off! This

24   car is going to twelve, now! *(BUSINESS PERSON begins*

25   *punching buttons. Power flickers, elevator stops.)* What now?!

26   *(OPERATOR awakens.)*

27   OPERATOR: I tried warning you.

28   BUSINESS PERSON: Shut up! *(Sticks diaper back in OPERATOR's*

29   *face, OPERATOR passes out again. Begins breaking down.)*

30   Why?! *Why?* Why always me? I just needed to get to a

31   meeting. One simple meeting, that will make or break my

32   career. And then this happens ... The walls! They're closing

33   in! I ... I can't breath! I need air ... I ... I ... *(As BUSINESS*

34   *PERSON breaks down he becomes vulnerable. OLD LADY jumps*

35   *on BUSINESS PERSON's back, TEEN grabs diaper and uses it to*

1   *hold BUSINESS PERSON at bay.)*
2   **WOMAN: Now what?**
3   **OLD LADY: There's the security phone.**
4   **WOMAN: Right.** *(Picks up phone.)* **Hello? ... Fine, and you? Yes, I**
5   **know, but yesterday it was so sunny ... I finally got around to**
6   **cleaning the yard ...**
7   **BUSINESS PERSON:** *The situation!* **Tell them the situation!**
8   **WOMAN:** *(Disgusted that she was interrupted)* **Right.** *(Sigh)* **I'm**
9   **supposed to tell you our elevator was hijacked and now we're**
10   **stuck between the sixth and seventh floors ... because**
11   **somebody broke it.**
12   **BUSINESS PERSON: Give me a break.**
13   **WOMAN:** *(Looking at BUSINESS PERSON)* **No, we have him**
14   **apprehended.** *(Looking at OPERATOR)* **No. He's unconscious ...**
15   **I don't know, let me check.** *(To ALL)* **Does anyone here know**
16   **how to operate hi-tech equipment.** *(All pause.)*
17   **TEEN: I have a Gameboy.**
18   **WOMAN: We have a young gentleman who has a video game ...**
19   **Sure.** *(To TEEN)* **He wants to talk to you.** *(WOMAN and TEEN*
20   *exchange baby, phone and diaper. WOMAN takes over holding*
21   *BUSINESS PERSON at bay.)*
22   **TEEN:** *(On phone)* **T'sup ... Sure.** *(Looks for button.)* **Yeah, I see**
23   **it ... right ... Thanks.** *(TEEN hangs up. Pushes button, car*
24   *starts up, ALL are grateful.)*
25   **WOMAN:** *(To BUSINESS PERSON)* **What do you have to say for**
26   **yourself?**
27   **BUSINESS PERSON: I should have taken the stairs.**
28
29   *Curtain*
30
31
32
33
34
35

Etch a Sketch

Premise: A new employee is left on the job as a hotline-helpline operator with only a manual to go by.

Cast: Boss — Very supportive.
Chris — Nervous about being left alone on the job.

Props: Two or three telephones, one big or several small troubleshooting manuals.

Scene: Office with table, one chair, two to three phones and a large book.

1   *(BOSS and CHRIS enter.)*
2   **BOSS: Well Chris, this is where you'll be working.**
3   **CHRIS: Pretty nice. But there's only one chair.**
4   **BOSS: Of course there is, you'll be working alone.**
5   **CHRIS: After the training I'll be alone, right?**
6   **BOSS: There's no training period, Chris. You were hired because**
7   **we're sure you can jump right in and do the job.**
8   **CHRIS: Are you sure I'm ready for this? I mean, I don't really**
9   **know all that much about your products or your machines.**
10   **BOSS: Nonsense, Chris, you answered all the questions during the**
11   **interview and you did great. Plus, if you have any trouble, you**
12   **can just consult the handy-dandy trouble-shooting manuals**
13   **here.**
14   **CHRIS: They're huge! I won't know where to look to find**
15   **anything in there.**
16   **BOSS: Nonsense, Chris, everything's in alphabetical order. And**
17   **it's all cross-referenced and indexed. There's nothing that**
18   **isn't covered in these books, so all you have to do is look it up,**
19   **the callers will never know.**
20   **CHRIS: Well, if you think I'm ready.**
21   **BOSS: You're ready.** *(Phone rings.)*
22   **BOSS: Here's your first chance, Chris. Go get 'em!** *(CHRIS*
23   *answers phone.)*
24   **CHRIS: Hello, trouble-shooting hotline. What seems to be the**
25   **trouble? The screen? ... Distorted display ... fuzzy ... Well,**
26   **let's see ...** *(Begins looking through manual.)* **Etch ... etch ...**
27   **etch ... ooo, here it is.** *(Reading)* **Just hold it upside down and**
28   **shake ... Yes, upside down and shake it? ... Sure, have a nice**
29   **day.** *(Hangs up.)*
30   **BOSS: See how easy? You're on your own now.**
31   **CHRIS: It was pretty easy; I just had to look it up in the book.**
32   *(BOSS exits. Phone rings.)* **Hello, trouble-shooting hotline ...**
33   **I just had a call for that very same product. What's the**
34   **trouble? ... Delete a document ...** *(Reading)* **Let's see ... here**
35   **it is ... just hold it upside down ... and shake it. Sure, have a**

1 nice day. *(Hangs up, then phone rings.)* **Trouble-shooting**
2 **hotline ... Robots, huh? What seems to be the exact trouble? ...**
3 **The neck is stretched ...** *(Reading)* **Did it make any noises ...**
4 **clack-zzzz ... And the neck stretched all of a sudden? ... OK,**
5 **just push down the head until you hear a click. That should do**
6 **it!** *(Hangs up, then phone rings.)* **Trouble-shooting hotline ...**
7 **Funny lines all over the screen? Just turn it over and shake**
8 **it ... Sure.** *(Hangs up, then phone rings.)* **Hello, trouble-**
9 **shooting hotline ... It doesn't work at all, huh? ... Have you**
10 **tried anything? ... You tugged on the line a couple times ...**
11 *(Reading)* **Well, what style is it? ... Butterfly, huh ... well, just**
12 **grab one wing and with the opposite hand, wrap the string**
13 **around the middle ... Now while holding the end of the string,**
14 **let the wing go, when the string is fully extended, jerk once**
15 **quickly ... It did? ... Well, that's great. Enjoy it. And yo to**
16 **you, too.** *(Hangs up, then phone rings.)* **Hello, trouble-shooting**
17 **hotline ... Lines, huh? ... Little black lines ... Well, let me**
18 **see ...** *(Reading)* **It says in the manual here to hold it upside**
19 **down and shake it ... Glad I could help.** *(Hangs up, then phone*
20 *rings.)* **Trouble-shooting hotline ... Down the chutes ... Yes,**
21 **I'm sure ... and up the ladders ... yes ... OK.** *(Hangs up, then*
22 *phone rings.)* **Trouble-shooting hotline ... How do you turn it**
23 **off? Ummm ...** *(Reading)* **Turn it upside down and shake it.**
24 **Then set it down ... yep, that's it.** *(Hangs up, then phone rings.)*
25 **Trouble-shooting hotline ... I'll see if I can answer it ... Two**
26 **together, huh?** *(Reading)* **Yes, it's safe ... It says right in the**
27 **official manual alone or in pairs ... downstairs, yep ... Girls**
28 **and boys ... Sure thing. Have a nice day.** *(Hangs up, then phone*
29 *rings.)* **Trouble-shooting hotline ...**
30
31 *Curtain*
32
33
34
35

The Fall of the Clown of Usher

Premise: Edgar Allen Poe is working as a children's party clown. The father of macabre tries to entertain the children as a clown. Much of the dialog is in verse reference to *The Raven* and *Bells*.

Cast: Announcer — Just a voice.
Mother — Wants to have a nice party for her kid.
Father — Helps mother with the party.
Poe-Poe — Edgar Allen Poe as a clown.
Son — Having a birthday party.
Guest — Another child at the party.
Extras — Kids at the party.

Props: Three bocce balls, three ping-pong/bingo balls, three balloon animals or balloons with drawings of a raven, and a skull.

Costumes: One dark clown outfit. (All black with an orange nose.)

Scene: Child's party, kids with hats, balloons. Mother and Father are sitting at a table as kids look bored.

1   ANNOUNCER: *(Off-stage)* **Before the commercial success of**
2   ***Tamerlane,* the poet, writer, and father of gothic horror, Edgar**
3   **Allen Poe, had to make ends meet by taking many odd jobs.**
4   **Some people know he was in the army and worked as a**
5   **newspaper reporter, but few people know that before he was a**
6   **successful writer, Edgar Allen Poe made his living**
7   **entertaining children.** *(Lights up. The following lines are done to*
8   *the rhythm of* The Raven.)
9   MOTHER: **This party's really getting dreary, the kids all look so**
10   **weak and weary, sitting there so quaint and curious over piles**
11   **of old-forgotten toys.**
12   **Pretty soon they'll all be napping, they want something**
13   **that's really happening,**
14   **Like a video game zapping, zapping or some other noise.**
15   *(Kids start something rough.)*
16   **They'll be no fighting!**
17   FATHER: **Honey? Keep your poise, remember that they're only**
18   **boys.**
19   MOTHER: **Oh, distinctly, I remember way back in December, or**
20   **was it in November, well, it doesn't matter anymore, I told him**
21   **to be good, like any mother's child should, and I'd have a big**
22   **surprise in store.**
23   FATHER: **So you called a clown?**
24   MOTHER: **He'll be here at four.**
25   SON: **Mom, Dad, this party stinks, I was talking to Joey, he**
26   **thinks … we should — we could get out the Sega game.**
27   MOTHER: **Just play with those toys.**
28   SON: **But they're all lame.**
29   MOTHER: **I'd like to finish, if it's all the same. As I was saying, just**
30   **go back to playing, playing with your toys some more, I said the**
31   **clown will be here at four.** *(SON moves back to other kids.)*
32   BOY 1: **Hey man, what'd she say, is it OK if we play?**
33   SON: **No, she said, "Not today."**
34   FATHER: **Honey, while you were talking, I think I heard someone**
35   **gently knocking, knocking at the kitchen door.**

1 MOTHER: You heard a knocking? Are you sure? A knock —
2   knocking at my kitchen door?
3 FATHER: Yes, I am fairly certain, see the shadow on the curtain?
4   There's someone at the kitchen door.
5 MOTHER: It's probably some late arriving guest, someone who
6   mixed up the address, that's it, I'm sure.
7 FATHER: Or if they have my luck, they probably got stuck, in line
8   while buying a gift at the department store.
9 BOY 1: I just heard your parents talking, they said someone's
10   knocking, knocking at your kitchen door. *(KIDS jump up.)*
11 KIDS: It could be the clown!
12 MOTHER: But it isn't four. *(Pause)* It's just a late guest nothing
13   more.
14 KIDS: Open the door, open the door, it's him, it's him, we're sure,
15   we're sure!
16 MOTHER: OK boys, hold down the noise, I don't want you to get
17   let down. *(MOTHER opens door.)*
18 KIDS: It's him, it's him, Poe-Poe the clown! *(Enter POE-POE.)*
19 POE-POE: I'm sorry, I thought you might be napping, tired from
20   all that unwrapping, unwrapping gifts on the living room
21   floor. But now you'll be bored, nevermore! *(Rhyming stops.)*
22 MOM: Thanks for coming.
23 POE-POE: It's my job.
24 MOM: Well, you go ahead and entertain, I have to go check on the
25   cake.
26 POE-POE: OK, hi kids.
27 KIDS: Hi, Poe-Poe!
28 POE-POE: Who likes stories?
29 KIDS: *Me!*
30 POE-POE: Then be quiet, I'm writing one. *(POE-POE sits and*
31   *writes. KIDS sit for a short while then begin to fidget more and*
32   *more.)*
33 SON: Poe-Poe, is it finished?
34 POE-POE: No.
35 SON: When will it be done?

1   POE-POE: Could be years.

2   SON: But you'll only be here until five.

3   POE-POE: So?

4   SON: You're supposed to be our clown, it's my birthday!

5   POE-POE: OK, what do you want to do?

6   BOY 1: *(Gives POE-POE a balloon.)* Make me something!

7   POE-POE: Yeah, OK. *(One by one all the KIDS give POE-POE*

8   *balloons to make them something. POE-POE keeps making more*

9   *and more morbid things. MOTHER enters with cake.)*

10   MOTHER: Well, here's the cake.

11   FATHER: *(Voice over)* Why'd she say it like that? She must have

12   noticed that I tasted the icing ... my big finger print is right

13   there ... maybe not ... little Bobby is looking at the cake. He

14   sees it, he's got to see it! It's so big, the patch of missing icing.

15   And I know they'll know it's me! I just wanted a small taste,

16   just something sweet, why is everyone looking at me? They see

17   it, everyone sees the missing icing. *(Out loud)* It was me! I

18   tasted the icing!

19   MOTHER: Did you like it?

20   KIDS: *(To POE-POE)* Do some magic!

21   POE-POE: How 'bout if I disappear? *(Begins to leave.)*

22   KIDS: No!

23   SON: Can you juggle?

24   POE-POE: I don't have anything to juggle with. *(The following*

25   *conversation is in the rhythm of* Bells. *The KIDS give POE-POE*

26   *the balls. He juggles as he recites his lines.)*

27   BOY 1: Here's the toy box with the balls.

28   SON: Bocce balls.

29   POE-POE: What a world of merriment they make when they fall

30   How they clunkle, clunkle, clunk,

31   when I drop them on the floor,

32   I try to keep them goin', goin', goin',

33   In a sort of circular form,

34   In a clunclunkabulation that echoes from the walls, from the

35   balls, balls, balls, balls, balls, balls, balls,

1   from the clunking and the clacking of the balls.
2   SON: Here, try the numbered balls.
3   BOY 1: Bingo balls.
4   POE-POE: What a world of happiness when their number calls,
5   through the birthday party night,
6   how the kids get such delight,
7   When I juggle with this something meant for bingo halls,
8   To the throwing and the catching of the balls, balls, balls,
9   balls, balls, balls, balls,
10   To the tossing and the crossing of the balls. *(End rhyme.)*
11   SON: How about the bowling balls?
12   POE-POE: Who wants to play a game?
13   KIDS: *Me!*
14   POE-POE: OK, the birthday boy is first.
15   SON: What is it? Pin the tail on the donkey?
16   POE-POE: No, it's much better. First put on this blindfold. Now lie
17   down right here ... We'll call this the *pit*. Everyone else stand
18   back. *(SON lies down as POE-POE gets out the ax-like*
19   *pendulum.)*
20
21   *Curtain*
22
23
24
25
26
27
28
29
30
31
32
33
34
35

Family Quality Time

Premise: The family is gathered for family night again, but they don't want to be there. It's up to Mom to convince them that family is the most important thing.

Cast: Adam — Young son.
Mom — Wants the family to spend time together.
Dad — Head of the family.
Leena — Teenage daughter.

Props: Phone, television remote control, phone ring, magazine.

Scene: Living room, Dad and Adam are watching TV, Mom is sitting at a chair passing time, and Leena is pacing by the phone.

1   ADAM: Mom, I'm bored.

2   DAD: *(Changing channels with remote)* **There's diddlysquat on the**

3   **tube.**

4   LEENA: I sure wish Luke would call.

5   MOM: This is horrible.

6   DAD: You're telling me. Who writes this crap?

7   MOM: No, I mean look at us. *(ALL looked confused.)* What kind of

8   family night is this? We're supposed to be sharing quality

9   time together.

10   ADAM: I'm bored.

11   DAD: There sure ain't nothing on.

12   LEENA: Family nights are so lame.

13   MOM: That's it. *(MOM grabs remote from DAD and shuts off TV.)*

14   DAD: Hey! I was watching that.

15   MOM: Not anymore. We're going to bond.

16   LEENA: Eeeewww!

17   ADAM: Aw, Mom.

18   DAD: Give me back that remote, Ruby.

19   MOM: No. We're going to share some quality time even if it kills us.

20   DAD: Give me that remote!

21   MOM: I'm serious. Let's talk.

22   ADAM: Huh?

23   MOM: Talk. Leena, how was your day?

24   LEENA: Mom!

25   MOM: How was your day!

26   LEENA: Fine. *(MOM waits for more. Nothing.)*

27   MOM: That's it? Just fine?

28   LEENA: Fine. Can I go to Kelly's?

29   MOM: No, you can't go to Kelly's! Adam. What did you do today?

30   ADAM: Nothin'.

31   MOM: Nothing? You did absolutely nothing today!

32   ADAM: Na.

33   MOM: You went to school didn't you?

34   ADAM: Yeah.

35   MOM: Well, what happened at school?

1   ADAM: Nothin'.

2   DAD: Can I have the remote back?

3   MOM: *(To DAD)* No! You cannot have the remote back! *(To ADAM)*

4   Now, you woke up this morning and went off to school.

5   Something had to have happened. You couldn't just do

6   nothing all day. What did you do at school?

7   ADAM: *(Thinks for a while.)* I had a test in history.

8   MOM: There, you see. Adam had a test in history today.

9   DAD: Yipee. Test in history. That's nice. Can I have the remote

10   back now?

11   MOM: *No!* You cannot have the remote back until we've spent

12   some quality family time together!

13   LEENA: These family nights suck.

14   MOM: Excuse me?

15   LEENA: I said family nights suck.

16   MOM: That is no way for a young lady to be speaking. Now, sit

17   down and shut up. We're going to talk about Adam's history

18   test! Adam, tell us about your history test!

19   DAD: Oh, please do. *(MOM hits DAD with magazine.)*

20   MOM: Adam?

21   ADAM: It was a history test.

22   MOM: And what was on the test?

23   ADAM: Questions about history.

24   DAD: Oooo. A history test with questions about history. Who

25   would have dreamed?

26   MOM: *(Glares at DAD for a moment, then resumes with ADAM.)* And

27   how do you think you did on the test?

28   ADAM: I did OK I guess.

29   MOM: Well that's nice. Isn't that nice, Dad?

30   DAD: Nice. *(Phone rings.)*

31   LEENA: That's probably Luke, I'll get it upstairs. *(LEENA tries to*

32   *exit. MOM catches her and puts her into a seat.)*

33   MOM: Oh, no you don't. *(Answers phone.)* I'm sorry nobody's

34   home. *(Hangs up phone.)*

35   LEENA: Mom! How could you?

1   MOM: You can call him back later. Right now you're sharing a
2   loving evening with your family! So sit back down and share!
3   *(Back to ADAM)* And that's it?
4   ADAM: Yeah.
5   MOM: Nothing else you'd like to share with us?
6   ADAM: I don't think so.
7   MOM: I see. *(Pause. ALL look at each other.)* That's nice dear. So
8   Leonard, how was your day?
9   DAD: It was just like every other day. I woke up, went to work for
10   a beanhead of a boss, got jack squat in pay for doing it, came
11   home to a nice meal and what I hoped was going to be a nice,
12   relaxing evening watching TV.
13   MOM: I see. *(Pause.)*
14   DAD: So, can I have the remote back now?
15   MOM: You'll get this remote back right up your butt if you don't
16   cooperate! I'm not asking for a lot. Just one evening where we
17   spend some time together. One measly night, where we can
18   exchange ideas, tell each other our dreams and hopes. Is that
19   too much to ask? Families are drifting apart more and more
20   these days. So much violence. Children bringing guns to
21   school. Young girls turning tricks in alleyways for God knows
22   what kind of men. Every time you turn around there's
23   something in the news that just amazes me. The world scares
24   me. Sometimes I wonder where we're all heading. It all boils
25   down to the family. Morals. Caring for each other. If we don't
26   have family, then there's nothing else worth having. Can't you
27   see? We're all we've got. It all starts right here. With the
28   family. *(Pause as ALL let speech sink in.)*
29   DAD: You're right dear. Why don't you tell us how your day was?
30   ADAM: Yeah.
31   LEENA: Yeah, Mom. How was your day?
32   MOM: Fine. *(Long pause. MOM hands remote back to DAD. LEENA*
33   *grabs phone and runs off. MOM begins reading.)*
34
35   *Curtain*

81

Feen Daning (Fine Dining)

Premise: A married couple finally saves up enough money to go on a honeymoon and has a unique experience ordering breakfast with the locals' native tongue.

Cast: Lyle — Husband on a honeymoon a few years into their marriage.

Ellenor — Wife on a honeymoon a few years into their marriage.

Robbay — Waiter in a foreign restaurant.

Props: Restaurant setting — menus, cups, plates, etc., brochure.

Scene: LYLE and ELLENOR are waiting Stage Left for a table in a restaurant. A table is set Center Stage.

Notes: ROBBAY's dialect should be extremely melodic with great inflections. It would be helpful to understand what ROBBAY is saying. The English translation is only given for reference.

1   LYLE: *(Reading from a brochure)* **The Golden Calf, four stars. Fine**
2   **cuisine, breakfast, lunch, and dinner.**
3   ELLENOR: **Oh, sweetie. This is the most wonderful idea you ever**
4   **had.**
5   LYLE: **I have always felt bad about not being able to afford the kind**
6   **of honeymoon you deserved. Now that I saved up some ...**
7   ELLENOR: **You know I was perfectly content with going to**
8   **Sheboygan.**
9   LYLE: **Yes, I know. But I wanted to take you somewhere nice.**
10   *(ROBBAY enters.)*
11 ROBBAY: **Morny. We coom to Da Gundun Coof. I Robbay u wait**
12   **are?** *[Morning. Welcome to the Golden Calf. I am Robbay, your*
13   *waiter.]*
14 LYLE: **Excuse me?**
15 ROBBAY: **Dawish taseet? Rye sway.** *(You wish to sit? Right this way.*
16   *Escorts LYLE and ELLENOR to seat.)* **You are minnow.** *[Here*
17   *are your menus.] (Hands them menus.)*
18 LYLE: **Just a minute.** *(Pages through brochure.)* **Min, mini,**
19   **minnow ... Menu.** *(Takes menu.)* **Thank you.**
20 ROBBAY: **Da Gundun Coof mining spee show eez flop jackets**
21   **weet so soje or a homanchie home lite. Robbay gaffew minnie.**
22   **Tuck your teem.** *[The Golden Calf morning special is flap jacks*
23   *with sausage or a ham and cheese omelet. Robbay will give you a*
24   *few minutes. Take your time.] (ROBBAY exits.)*
25 ELLENOR: **Oooo. The specials sound so exotic. I think I'll try the**
26   **hoo-manchie home lite. How about you?**
27 LYLE: **No. I think I'll just do some bacon and eggs. I'd hate to**
28   **have to pay for something I didn't enjoy.**
29 ELLENOR: **Oh, Lyle. Come on and take a chance. It's not every**
30   **year we take a second honeymoon.**
31 LYLE: **I don't think so.** *(ROBBAY returns.)*
32 ROBBAY: **Dawish to odor sunteen?** *[Do you wish to order*
33   *something?]*
34 LYLE: **Uh, yes. We'd like the homanshay home leet.**
35 ROBBAY: **Da hamanchie home lite?** *[The ham and cheese omelet?]*

1   LYLE: Yes. That. And I'd like some bacon and eggs.
2   ROBBAY: Ow july then? *[How would you like them?]*
3   LYLE: What?
4   ROBBAY: Aches. Ow july then? Pry, boy, pooch … ? *[Eggs? How*
5   *would you like them? Fried, boiled, poached?]*
6   LYLE: *(Looking through brochure)* Pry? Boy? Pooch?
7   ROBBAY: Your aches? *[Your eggs?]*
8   LYLE: Oh, the eggs! How do I like them? Sorry. Scrambled please.
9   ROBBAY: Ow july thee baycoom? Crease? *[How would you like*
10   *your bacon? Crisp?]*
11 LYLE: Baycoom?
12 ROBBAY: Baycoom, crease? *[Bacon, crisp?]*
13 LYLE: Uh, sure.
14 ROBBAY: OK. An santos? *[OK. And some toast?]*
15 LYLE: What?
16 ROBBAY: Santos. July santos? *[Some toast. Would you like some*
17   *toast?]*
18 LYLE: Ugh. I don't know. I don't think so.
19 ROBBAY: No. Judo one toes? *[No? You don't want toast?]*
20 LYLE: *(Paging through pamphlet)* Look, I feel really bad about this,
21   but I don't know what "judo one toes" means. I'm sorry.
22   *(ELLENOR takes brochure, begins looking through it.)*
23 ROBBAY: Toes! Toes! Why djew don juan toes? Ow bow cenglish
24   mopping we bother? *[Toast! Toast! Why don't you want toast?*
25   *How about English muffin with butter?]*
26 ELLENOR: English muffin! I've got it! You were saying toast!
27 LYLE: An English muffin will be fine.
28 ROBBAY: We bother? *[With butter?]* *(ELLEN shows LYLE the*
29   *brochure.)*
30 LYLE: No. Just put the bother on the side.
31 ROBBAY: Wad? *[What?]*
32 LYLE: I'm sorry. I meant butter. Butter on the side.
33 ROBBAY: Copy? *[Coffee?]*
34 LYLE: I feel terrible about this but …
35 ROBBAY: Copy. Copy, tea, mill? *[Coffee. Coffee, tea, milk?]*

1   **ELLENOR: Coffee! Yes, coffee please.**
2   **ROBBAY: Emu?** *[And you?]*
3   **LYLE: Yes. I'll have a coffee also. Black. And that's all.**
4   **ROBBAY: So, paddle bee, for loudy, the spee show hamanchie**
5   **home lite, for gen tea moon, strangle aches, crease baycome,**
6   **cenglish mopping we bother honey sigh, and copy. Rye?** *[So,*
7   *that will be, for the lady, the special ham and cheese omelet, for*
8   *the gentleman, scrambled eggs, crisp bacon, English muffin with*
9   *butter on the side, and black coffee, right?]*
10 **ELLENOR: That's right. Oh, can I please have a glass of orange**
11   **juice, too, please?**
12 **ROBBAY: Summer larj?** *[Small or large?]*
13 **ELLENOR: Small will be fine. Tendjewberrymud.**
14 **ROBBAY: Oooo. Tendjewberrymud.** *[Thank you very much]*
15   *(ROBBAY moves to counter.)*
16 **ELLENOR: Swee dis hiney moo one da foul. You da bees. Laffew.**
17   *[Sweetie, this honeymoon is wonderful. You are the best. I love*
18   *you.]*
19 **LYLE: I love you too? I guess this is kind of exotic. I'm glad you're**
20   **enjoying yourself.**
21 **ROBBAY:** *(At counter. No accent.)* **Benny, one ham and cheese**
22   **omelet with a small OJ and two yokes, bacon, with two**
23   **coffees.**
24
25   *Curtain*
26
27
28
29
30
31
32
33
34
35

The First Dictionary Salesman

Premise: The man who writes the world's first dictionary tries to peddle it door-to-door. Unfortunately, the majority of the population is illiterate and has no use for the book.

Cast: All should talk with English accents.

Salesman — The author of the world's first dictionary. He talks with an upper class English accent. He should be dressed a little better (maybe he has shoes).

Man — Husband and a father. He is illiterate but not dumb. He is poor and should be dressed so.

Mary — Mother and wife of Man, poor, also illiterate but not dumb.

Child — Should be played as a young child about seven years old. More literate than the parents, but not much.

Dirt-Guy — Another door-to-door salesman, but of the lower class. He is selling dirt, something the poor people can relate to.

Props: Table with a wobbly leg, three chairs, old-looking book that says "Words" on the cover.

Scene: Inside of a medieval home. There is a wobbly table with three chairs. Lights up on man sitting at the table. There is a knock on door. Man opens door to Salesman holding a book.

1   MAN: Can I help you?
2   SALESMAN: No, good sir, but I, perhaps, could be of grandiose
3   assistance to you.
4   MAN: Are you speaking a foreign language? We don't understand
5   foreigners here.
6   SALESMAN: No, I am offering you an opportunity for eloquence,
7   simply by listening to my diatribe, and partaking in a simple
8   remedy for a malady that has plagued mankind forever.
9   MAN: Oh my God! He's got the fever! *(MAN slams door shut. Knock*
10   *on door.)*
11   SALESMAN: *(Outside door)* **Open the door!**
12   MAN: No way! You're infected.
13   SALESMAN: I do not ...
14   MAN: Don't breathe on me!
15   SALESMAN: ... have the fever.
16   MAN: You don't?
17   SALESMAN: No, now may I please come in?
18   MAN: Are you sure you're clean?
19   SALESMAN: I'm clean. *(MAN opens door. SALESMAN enters.)*
20   MAN: Then why were you talking like that?
21   SALESMAN: I'm trying to sell you a book.
22   MAN: A book?
23   SALESMAN: Yes, my name is Dict Shunary, and I have a book
24   here of words.
25   MAN: Oh, a story ...
26   SALESMAN: No, no story.
27   MAN: *(Confused)* But there's words?
28   SALESMAN: Yes, it's words and their meanings.
29   MAN: What's the plot?
30   SALESMAN: There is no plot.
31   MAN: *(Calling Off-stage)* Mary, come here, someone's trying to sell
32   us a book. *(Enter MARY.)*
33   MARY: A book? Well, what's the story?
34   SALESMAN: There's no story.
35   MARY: *(Confused)* No story? Well, does it have words?

1   SALESMAN: Yes, it has all the words.

2   MARY: What's the plot?

3   SALESMAN: There is no plot.

4   MARY: A story with no plot?

5   SALESMAN: There is no story. *(Enter CHILD.)*

6   CHILD: Story? I love stories, read it to me.

7   SALESMAN: *(Beginning to get angry)* There is no story!

8   CHILD: *(Confused)* But, you've got a book.

9   SALESMAN: It's just got words and their meanings.

10 CHILD: A book with words but no story?

11 SALESMAN: Exactly!

12 MAN: What good is the book then?

13 SALESMAN: *(Finally getting a chance to explain)* Ah-ha! It's so you

14   can look up words that you don't know. *(Pause as FAMILY*

15   *seems to understand.)*

16 MAN: *(Confused again.)* Well, if I don't know them, how would I

17   look them up?

18 SALESMAN: Well, let's just say you heard someone use a word

19   that you didn't know, such as ... "assistance."

20 MAN: I don't know what that means.

21 MARY: Me neither.

22 SALESMAN: Exactly, then you could just look it up in this book.

23   *(Pause, as FAMILY seems to understand again.)*

24 MAN: *(Confused again.)* How?

25 SALESMAN: Well, all the words are in alphabetical order. *(Pause,*

26   *as FAMILY seems to understand again.)*

27 MAN: *(Confused again.)* What's an alphabet?

28 SALESMAN: An alphabet is a series of letters.

29 MARY: *(Confused.)* Letters?

30 SALESMAN: Yes, like A, S, Q, T, but they come in an order. A is

31   always first.

32 CHILD: I heard of that.

33 SALESMAN: See, and "assistance" starts with A. You simply go to

34   the section of the book with the A words and find "assistance."

35 CHILD: What's it mean?

1 SALESMAN: Help.

2 MAN: It's your book, how we suppose to help?

3 SALESMAN: No, *assistance* means *help*.

4 MARY: Then, why didn't you just say *help*?

5 MAN: Yeah, I understand *help*.

6 SALESMAN: Wait, OK, let's try this, you want to write a letter ...

7 MAN: But I don't know how to write.

8 SALESMAN: Oh, suppose you knew how to write and you wanted

9 to write a letter about your sick aunt ...

10 MAN: But ... none of my aunts are sick.

11 MARY: Maybe Aunt Tillie is sick.

12 CHILD: Aunt Tillie is sick, is she gonna be all right? *(FAMILY ad-*

13 *libs confusion.)*

14 SALESMAN: *(Beginning to get frustrated)* No wait, no one's sick!

15 Just suppose you had a sick aunt, and suppose you could

16 write, you'd want to send a letter to ...

17 MAN: But ... we ain't got no mail system.

18 SALESMAN: *(More frustrated) Suppose* there was a mail system,

19 and *suppose* your aunt was sick, and *suppose* you could write,

20 you'd want to send a letter to your relatives ...

21 MAN: But ... all my relatives live right here in this town.

22 MARY: We could walk to their huts in just a couple of minutes.

23 SALESMAN: *(Frustrated) Suppose* your relatives lived in Ireland,

24 *suppose* there was a mail system, and suppose your aunt was

25 sick, and *suppose* you could write, you'd want to send a letter

26 to your relatives so they could read about your aunt.

27 MAN: But none of my relatives can read.

28 SALESMAN: *Suppose they could!* They'd want to know about

29 your sick aunt!

30 CHILD: I thought you said Aunt Tillie wasn't sick.

31 SALESMAN: *She's not!*

32 MAN: *(Calmly)* Now let me get this straight, supposing my relatives

33 could read, which they can't, supposing my relatives lived in

34 Ireland, which they don't, supposing there was a mail system,

35 which there ain't, supposing my aunt was sick, which she

1   ain't, and supposing I could write, which I can't, then your
2   book would be useful.
3   SALESMAN: *(Exasperated)* Yes. *(Pause, SALESMAN is calm again.)*
4   Let's try this. Suppose you wanted to send a letter to the
5   Duke ... *(MAN begins to interrupt to say he can't write, but is cut*
6   *off by SALESMAN.) Suppose you could write ...* and you wanted
7   to send a letter to the Duke ...
8   MARY: Why would the Duke care if my aunt is sick?
9   SALESMAN: He wouldn't! Suppose ... suppose you weren't
10   happy with your taxes.
11   MAN: I'm not happy with my taxes!
12   SALESMAN: There you go! You could write a letter to the Duke
13   expressing your plight. *(FAMILY doesn't understand the word*
14   *plight)* ... your troubles.
15   MAN: This would help?
16   SALESMAN: Sure it would. *(Pause as the FAMILY thinks.)*
17   MAN: *(Standing up)* It's settled then, I'll send him a Q.
18   SALESMAN: Very well ... a what!?
19   MAN: A Q. I like that letter.
20   MARY: Me, too, can I send him a Q, too?
21   SALESMAN: *(Frustrated again)* No, you can't send him a Q.
22   MARY: That's discrimination, a man can send a Q but a woman
23   can't?
24   SALESMAN: No, no, no! Nobody can send him a Q. *(ALL pause.)*
25   MAN: Then T.
26   MARY: Oooo, T is good, but I do like Q.
27   SALESMAN: No, no T. *(ALL pause.)*
28   CHILD: How about S? *(MAN and WOMAN speak over each other*
29   *giving confusion to the scene.)*
30   MAN: Good one! The boy's got a good idea.
31   MARY: Yes, S, that is a good idea.
32   SALESMAN: *(Very frustrated now) You can't just send him a letter!*
33   MARY: But you just said to send him a letter.
34   SALESMAN: I meant a letter ... not just one letter, I meant a
35   whole ... If you just sent the Duke a Q he wouldn't know what

1   **you meant!** *(ALL pause.)*
2   **MAN: Maybe you could sell him a book.** *(Knock on door. MARY*
3   *answers. There stands DIRT-GUY, another salesman.)*
4   **MARY: Can I help you?**
5   **DIRT-GUY: Hi, I am selling a revolutionary new floor leveling**
6   **system.**
7   **MARY: What is it?**
8   **DIRT-GUY: It's a bag of dirt! You just spread it around to level out**
9   **the floor!**
10   **MAN: That sounds great!**
11   **MARY: We'll take one!**
12   **SALESMAN:** *You're buying dirt?!* **I'm trying to sell ... but ...**
13   **words and meanings ... this book could really help you!**
14   **MAN: Let's see!** *(MAN takes book, looks at it and shows table is*
15   *wobbly. Then uses the book to level out table.)* **He's right, we'll**
16   **take one.**
17   **SALESMAN:** *(Giving up)* **That'll be five pounds.**
18
19   *Curtain*
20
21
22
23
24
25
26
27
28
29
30
31
32
33
34
35

The Fish Tank

Premise: Life inside an aquarium. Fish are swimming around. Wayne, one of the fish, is missing. The police come looking. Nothing really happens. Hey they're fish, what did you expect?

Cast: Gil — Just a regular fish.
Sid — Just a regular fish.
Chip — A snail, he talks slow and moves even slower.
Goldie — Gil's wife.
Carp — Police fish.

Props: Large dead fish floating on the surface.

Scene: Inside a fish tank. Chip is Downstage Left moving very slowly across the stage.

Notes: Chip should be moving so slowly as to be barely noticeable, not even making it half way across the stage before the skit ends.

1   *(Enter GIL Stage Left and SID Stage Right, both swimming*
2   *towards the center.)*
3   GIL: *(To CHIP)* **Let's go, Chip. You're such a slow poke. Get**
4   **moving or get out of the way. Some of us have places to go.**
5   *(GIL and SID meet Center Stage.)*
6   SID: **Hey, Gil? How've you been?**
7   GIL: **Not bad. And you?**
8   SID: **Good.**
9   GIL: **What've you been up to lately?**
10   SID: **Well, you know. Just swimming around.**
11   GIL: **Yep, know what you mean.** *(Pause)* **Well, nice seeing you.**
12   **Catch you around.**
13   SID: **Take care.**
14   CHIP: *(Delayed reaction)* **Just go around.** *(FISH continue to swim to*
15   *the ends of the stage, then turn around and meet in the middle*
16   *again.)*
17   GIL: **Hey, Sid? How've you been?**
18   SID: **Not bad. And you?**
19   GIL: **Good.**
20   SID: **What've you been up to lately?**
21   GIL: **Well, you know. Just swimming around.**
22   SID: **Yep, know what you mean.** *(Pause)* **Well, nice seeing you.**
23   **Catch you around.**
24   SID: **Take care.**
25   CHIP: *(Delayed reaction)* **Just go around. Everyone's in such a**
26   **hurry.** *(SID and GIL give CHIP a puzzled glance.)*
27   GIL: **Chip's a little slow.**
28   SID: **Yep, know what you mean.** *(GIL and SID continue to swim to*
29   *the ends of the stage, then turn around and meet in the middle*
30   *again.)*
31   GIL: **Hey, Sid? How've you been?**
32   SID: **Not bad. And you?**
33   GIL: **Good.**
34   SID: **What've you been up to lately?**
35   GIL: **Well, you know. Just swimming around.** *(SID and GIL both*

1   *spot a cat outside the tank and scream.)*

2   **SID:** **What in the world is that?**

3   **GIL:** **Those big things that feed us every day call it a "cat."**

4   **SID:** **Something about the way he's looking at us freaks me out.**

5   *(GOLDIE enters.)* **Uh oh. Here comes the wife.**

6   **CHIP:** *(Looking to where cat was)* **It's a cat!**

7   **GOLDIE:** **Hi Sid.**

8   **SID:** **Hi Goldie.**

9   **GOLDIE:** **Hi Chip.** *(Pause)* **Gil, where in water have you been? I**

10   **had a heck of a time getting the kids off to school this morning.**

11   **I could have used your help.**

12   **GIL:** **Well, I woke up and swam a little. Then, Me, Wayne, and Sid**

13   **ate, then I swam a little.**

14   **SID:** **Speaking of Wayne, has anyfish seen him lately?**

15   **GOLDIE:** **Last time I saw him, he was swimming around.**

16   **SID:** **Oh, yeah. That's right.** *(Gesturing)* **I remember him swimming**

17   **over there.** *(Gesturing in a different direction)* **Then swimming**

18   **over there.** *(Gesturing in a different direction)* **Then over ...**

19   *(ALL the fish see a large dead fish, Wayne, floating. GOLDIE*

20   *screams and faints. GIL tries to revive her.)* **Holy Mackerel!**

21   **GIL:** **Hurry! Get me some air!**

22   **CHIP:** *(Delayed)* **Hiya, Goldie.** *(SID scoops some air from the surface*

23   *and gives it to GIL. GIL blows the air on GOLDIE's face to revive*

24   *her. ALL fish are swimming again.)*

25   **SID:** *(Looking at dead floating fish)* **That's freaky. Look.** *(Moves*

26   *around the tank.)* **No matter where you go, it's like his eyes just**

27   **follow you.**

28   **GOLDIE:** **What should we do?**

29   **GIL:** **Wait. Look. Here comes a** *carp.* *(Enter CARP.)*

30   **SID:** **Thank goodness you're here.**

31   **CARP:** **So what seems to be the problem?**

32   **CHIP:** **Anybody seen Wayne?**

33   **GOLDIE:** **It's Wayne!**

34   **CARP:** **Wayne?** *(ALL the fish gesture up.)* **Great mother of all things**

35   **that swim! All right everybody. Put your fins in the water**

1   where I can see them.

2   SID: But, it wasn't us.

3   GIL: We were just swimming here, minding our own business.

4   CARP: We'll see. All you fish, and Chip, I don't want any of you

5   leaving until I get to the bottom of this.

6   SID: Yeah, like one of us will skip tank and swim.

7   CARP: All I'm saying is that something smells a little human

8   around here. And by gum, I'm going to see to it that the

9   culprit responsible gets put away for a long, long time.

10   GOLDIE: *(Pointing outside the tank)* Hey, what's that?

11   SID: They're coming right at us. Everyfish, swim! *(ALL the fish take*

12   *cover. Floating dead fish gets removed.)*

13   CHIP: Thank goodness, it's the *carps*. *(ALL slowly come back out.)*

14   SID: Whew! That was close.

15   GIL: Last time I saw one of them do that is when I was separated

16   from my family and brought here.

17   GOLDIE: Yeah, but why did they take Wayne?

18   GIL: Good question. *(Toilet flush)*

19   CARP: Well then. I guess that about wraps it up. I should be

20   getting back to swimming my beat. *(CARP exits.)*

21   GOLDIE: And I have to go pick up the kids. *(To GIL)* See you later

22   at home. *(GOLDIE exits.)*

23   SID: I really should get back to swimming around.

24   GIL: Me too. Catch you later Sid.

25   SID: See you, Gil. *(SID and GIL swim to edge of stage and back to*

26   *center.)*

27   GIL: Hey, Sid? How've you been?

28   SID: Not bad. And you?

29   GIL: Good.

30   CHIP: Look out! It's a net!

31

32   *Curtain*

33

34

35

The Float Attendant

Premise: An airplane pilot and a flight attendant are put in charge of a lifeboat. They use their airline skills to keep control of the boat. One passenger is particularly upset.

Cast: Pilot — Crazy, takes over the raft.

Passenger — Gruff, mean, agrees with Flight Attendant and Pilot.

Sensible Person — Enough said. Becomes frustrated with others as skit goes along.

Flight Attendant — Upbeat, professional, but a bit ditzy (not a valley girl).

Props: Paper cup, Hershey's Milk Chocolate Bar, Hershey's Milk Chocolate Bar with Almonds, Life Savers Roll Candy, bottle of water, blow-up raft, cell phone.

Scene: Four people settling into a lifeboat.

1   PASSENGER: I can't believe the ship sank.

2   FLIGHT ATTENDANT: Believe it.

3   PASSENGER: I'd love to get my hands on that captain.

4   SENSIBLE PERSON: I'm sure he went down with the boat, that's

5   the rule.

6   PASSENGER: He's lucky, then.

7   FLIGHT ATTENDANT: At least we made it to the lifeboat.

8   PASSENGER: Great, from *The Love Boat* to the lifeboat.

9   FLIGHT ATTENDANT: *(Sings to the tune of* The Love Boat *theme*

10   *song.)* The lifeboat, exciting and new ...

11   PILOT: What are we going to do?

12   SENSIBLE PERSON: First things first, is anyone here a sailor?

13   *(ALL say no.)*

14   PILOT: I am an airplane pilot.

15   FLIGHT ATTENDANT: *(Forgetting the problem, and being*

16   *cheerful)* Really? I'm a flight attendant.

17   PILOT: *(Also forgetting)* Really, what airline?

18   FLIGHT ATTENDANT: TWA *(PILOT and FLIGHT ATTENDANT*

19   *ad lib job related stuff as:)*

20   SENSIBLE PERSON: *(Interrupting)* Excuse me? Back to the

21   matter at hand. Do you know anything about boats?

22   PILOT: Not really.

23   FLIGHT ATTENDANT: They float.

24   PASSENGER: I knew that.

25   PILOT: He didn't ask you. *(The THREE of them ad-lib arguing.)*

26   SENSIBLE PERSON: Excuse me! People. Listen! We're in a tough

27   situation here and we need some calm. *(ALL are calm.)* Now,

28   I've read the *Worst-Case Scenario Handbook* ...

29   FLIGHT ATTENDANT: Good, what's it say?

30   SENSIBLE PERSON: Well, in any emergency, someone needs to

31   be in charge. *(ALL agree.)*

32   FLIGHT ATTENDANT: How about you? *(Indicating SENSIBLE*

33   *PERSON)*

34   SENSIBLE PERSON: No ... I just ... *read* the *Worst-Case Scenario*

35   *Handbook*, I don't have any experience. *(To PILOT)* But you

1   do. Can you run a boat? *(Pause.)*

2   PILOT: Sure. How different can it be? We'll need a few things.

3   First, I'll need all the food to be inventoried.

4   SENSIBLE PERSON: Good idea. Here, I have a Hershey's Bar

5   with Almonds.

6   PILOT: I have a regular Hershey's Bar.

7   PASSENGER: I have a bottle of water

8   FLIGHT ATTENDANT: Oh, look! I have Life Savers.

9   PILOT: From now on everything will be communal. *(ALL agree.)* And

10   we'll need to establish directions ... let's see. *(Concentrating as he*

11   *looks for the sun, then inspired)* How about this? This will be the

12   front because I'm sitting here. I'm the pilot so I need to be in

13   front. Everyone face front. *(EVERYONE faces front. SENSIBLE*

14   *PERSON is confused as to why everyone needs to face front, but*

15   *follows.)* Next, I'll need a piece of paper, or a paper cup.

16   SENSIBLE PERSON: I have a Styrofoam cup.

17   PILOT: That's good. That'll work. *(Tears the bottom out.)* Let's get

18   started. *(ALL agree. PILOT speaks through cup.)* This is your

19   captain speaking, welcome aboard flight ... umm ... the

20   lifeboat.

21   FLIGHT ATTENDANT: *(Sings.)* The lifeboat ...

22   SENSIBLE PERSON: *(Getting frustrated)* What are you doing?

23   PILOT: *(Sets down cup.)* I'm addressing the passengers.

24   SENSIBLE PERSON: *(Still annoyed)* We're in a lifeboat!

25   FLIGHT ATTENDANT: *(Sings.)* The lifeboat ...

26   SENSIBLE PERSON: Shut up!

27   FLIGHT ATTENDANT: I'm just trying to lighten the mood.

28   PILOT: Listen, I know we're in a lifeboat ... but I'm not a lifeboat

29   captain, I'm an airline pilot ... this is how I run my plane.

30   PASSENGER: Would you just let him do his job? *(SENSIBLE*

31   *PERSON is annoyed through the next speech.)*

32   PILOT: Thank you ... *(Into cup)* We've gotten clearance to ... start

33   sailing ... and our flight ... boat ride will be approximately ...

34   a while. Once up to speed we'll be cruising at an altitude of ...

35   well, sea level. There are a few instructions, but I'll leave that

1   up to our capable flight ... *float* attendant.

2   SENSIBLE PERSON: This is ridiculous!

3   PASSENGER: Who else would give the rules?

4   FLIGHT ATTENDANT: Federal regulations require us to follow

5   certain procedures. Please remain in your seats for the entire

6   trip. In case of an emergency ...

7   SENSIBLE PERSON: What do you mean *in case of* an

8   emergency? We've been in a shipwreck; we're already in a

9   lifeboat!

10 FLIGHT ATTENDANT: Please, sir. In case of an emergency, your

11   seats are already a floatation device. In case of a drop in boat

12   pressure you will sink like this. *(Bends slowly at knees.)* Don't

13   panic: you can exit the boat from any side and proceed to

14   swim. Proper swimming techniques include this and this.

15   *(FLIGHT ATTENDANT demonstrates swimming techniques.)*

16 SENSIBLE PERSON: What are you doing?

17 FLIGHT ATTENDANT: The backstroke.

18 SENSIBLE PERSON: That's crazy ...

19 PASSENGER: No, I can swim and that's the proper technique.

20 SENSIBLE PERSON: *(More annoyed)* No! People, we've been in a

21   shipwreck. We need to focus. I've read the *Worst-Case*

22   *Scenario Handbook* ...

23 PILOT: *(Mad at SENSIBLE PERSON)* We've heard. Now let the

24   float attendant finish!

25 FLIGHT ATTENDANT: If you are unable to swim, please use a

26   fellow passenger as a floatation device. *(Demonstrates the*

27   *following on SENSIBLE PERSON.)* Proper techniques for holding

28   on are this, and this. Never hold on like this ... or this ... or this.

29 SENSIBLE PERSON: Let me go!

30 FLIGHT ATTENDANT: I'll be serving rations momentarily. *(To*

31   *PASSENGER)* Would you like a Hershey with Almond, Plain

32   Hershey, or a Life Saver?

33 PASSENGER: Life Saver.

34 FLIGHT ATTENDANT: *(To SENSIBLE PERSON)* Would you like

35   Plain Hershey's, or a Life Saver?

1   SENSIBLE PERSON: Hershey's with Almond.

2   FLIGHT ATTENDANT: I'm sorry. We only serve Hershey's with

3   Almonds to the first class passengers.

4   SENSIBLE PERSON: First class? I'm sitting right beside him.

5   FLIGHT ATTENDANT: No, you're sitting right behind him,

6   weren't you paying attention? *(Demonstrates.)* Pilot, first class,

7   coach.

8   SENSIBLE PERSON: *(Frustrated)* But it was my candy to start

9   with.

10   FLIGHT ATTENDANT: But now it's communal property and I'm

11   in charge of serving meals, and first class passengers always

12   get better meals. You should have gone first class.

13   SENSIBLE PERSON: I was in first class on the cruise ship.

14   FLIGHT ATTENDANT: We're not on the cruise ship anymore.

15   PASSENGER: Yeah, what are you some kind of troublemaker?

16   SENSIBLE PERSON: No, I'm just trying to be realistic.

17   PASSENGER: Well, realistically, first class passengers do get

18   better meals!

19   PILOT: *(Through cup)* Your attention please. If you look to your

20   left, you can see the Pacific Ocean, to your right, is more of the

21   Pacific Ocean.

22   FLIGHT ATTENDANT: *(To PASSENGER)* Drink?

23   PASSENGER: Thanks.

24   FLIGHT ATTENDANT: *(To SENSIBLE PERSON)* Drink?

25   SENSIBLE PERSON: He just drank straight from the bottle ...

26   don't we have a cup or something? *(FLIGHT ATTENDANT*

27   *gives cup to SENSIBLE PERSON. He pours drink into it and all*

28   *over self.)*

29   PASSENGER: He's wasting water!

30   FLIGHT ATTENDANT: Great!

31   SENSIBLE PERSON: This cup has no bottom!

32   PASSENGER: I say we throw him out. You've been nothing but

33   trouble since this trip began.

34   SENSIBLE PERSON: What trip? We're in a lifeboat.

35   FLIGHT ATTENDANT: *(Sings.)* The lifeboat!

1   **PILOT:** *(Taking back cup and speaking through)* **And you've done**
2   **nothing but complain.**
3   **PASSENGER: And spill water!**
4   **SENSIBLE PERSON: I read the *Worst-Case Scenario Handbook***
5   **and ...**
6   **PASSENGER: What's your worst-case scenario say about a**
7   **broken nose?**
8   **PILOT: People can you hold it down ... I have something to say.**
9   **We're about to crash into the land. Please assume crash**
10 **positions.**
11 **SENSIBLE PERSON: Land? That's what we've been waiting for!**
12 **FLIGHT ATTENDANT: Sir, please sit down.**
13 **PILOT: I'll try to make the landing as gentle as possible.**
14 **FLIGHT ATTENDANT: Once the craft has come to a complete**
15 **stop, please exit on the emergency exit slide.** *(Takes out blow-*
16 *up raft and begins blowing it up. After second breath, ALL*
17 *pantomime hitting shore.)*
18 **SENSIBLE PERSON: We're saved!** *(He stands up.)*
19 **FLIGHT ATTENDANT: Please sir, sit down.**
20 **PASSENGER: Yeah, sit down!**
21 **PILOT:** *(Through cup)* **Sit down.**
22 **SENSIBLE PERSON: Screw you! This is land. I can step out of the**
23 **boat.** *(He does.)* **This isn't an airplane. You people didn't read**
24 **the *Worst-Case Scenario Handbook* ... I did! You're all nuts.**
25 **You're crazy! You'll be sitting in this boat for thirty minutes**
26 **while he blows up that raft!** *(SENSIBLE PERSON steps out of*
27 *boat and exits.)*
28 **FLIGHT ATTENDANT: Troublemaker.**
29 **PASSENGER: Someday, he's gonna get hurt.** *(Cell phone rings.)*
30 **PILOT:** *(Answering phone)* **Hello? Yes, can I call you back honey,**
31 **can't talk during work time!** *(Hangs up.)* **He'll never survive.**
32
33 *Curtain*
34
35

Halloween Candy

Premise: This scene takes place on the inside of a trick-or-treat bag on Halloween. The pieces of candy interact with each other, each with their own personality befitting their name.

Cast: Voices — Off-stage, children's voices.
Chunky — Slightly overweight, whiny person. "Why me?" attitude.
Snickers — Constantly laughing, everything is funny to this candy.
Tootsie Roll — Gum chewing, truck stop waitress.
Mr. Goodbar — Sophisticated, suave, ladies' man.
Watchamacallit — Big oaf-like person. Not very bright.
Juicy Fruit — Effeminate man.

Costumes: All should be dressed as the candy bars that they are named after.

Scene: The inside of a trick-or-treat bag. The top of the bag is on one side of the stage.

Notes: All candy will enter from the same side moving quickly to center stage and stopping abruptly. The "pile" of candy should become larger and more tangled as the scene goes on.

1   *(Doorbell rings.)*

2   **VOICES:** *(Off-stage)* **Trick-or-treat!** *(Enter CHUNKY.)*

3   **CHUNKY:** Aw, geez, I'm on the bottom. Why'd I have to be on the

4   bottom? This kid'll probably get a ton of candy, and I'll end

5   up squished and rotten here on the bottom of the pile. Why's

6   the fat guy always have to be on the bottom? *(Doorbell rings.)*

7   **VOICES:** *(Off-stage)* **Trick-or-treat!** *(Enter SNICKERS.)*

8   **SNICKERS:** Hi. *(Snicker, snicker)* **How's it going?** *(Snicker, snicker)*

9   **CHUNKY:** What's so funny?

10   **SNICKERS:** Nothing. *(Snicker, snicker)*

11   **CHUNKY:** You're laughing at me. Why do people always laugh at

12   the Chunkies? Am I that amusing to you that you have to

13   laugh right in front of me?

14   **SNICKERS:** No, it's not you. *(Snicker, snicker)* **It's just that ...**

15   *(Snicker, snicker)*

16   **CHUNKY:** What? What's so funny?

17   **SNICKERS:** It's just that I'm not on the bottom this year. *(Snicker,*

18   *snicker. Doorbell rings.)*

19   **VOICES:** *(Off-stage)* **Trick-or-treat!** *(Enter TOOTSIE ROLL.)*

20   **TOOTSIE ROLL:** Hiya, big fellah! How's tricks?

21   **SNICKERS:** Hi.

22   **CHUNKY:** Hi, toots.

23   **SNICKERS:** Toots! *(Snicker, snicker)*

24   **CHUNKY:** What's so funny now?

25   **SNICKERS:** You called her ... toots.

26   **TOOTSIE ROLL:** What's so funny about that, sweetheart?

27   **SNICKERS:** He's not a *Sweet-Tart*. He's a Chunky bar. *(Doorbell*

28   *rings.)*

29   **VOICES:** *(Off-stage)* **Trick-or-treat!** *(Enter MR. GOODBAR.)*

30   **MR. GOODBAR:** Whoa, what a ride!

31   **TOOTSIE ROLL:** Hi, there! I've been looking for you.

32   **MR. GOODBAR:** Yeah, well, get in line. *(SNICKERS snickers.)*

33   What's so funny?

34   **SNICKERS:** She's looking for Mr. Goodbar!

35   **CHUNKY:** No one's ever looking for the Chunky guy, that's for

1   sure.
2   MR. GOODBAR: Chin-up, Chunky! Maybe we'll get a Mounds
3   bar in here.
4   CHUNKY: Yeah, with my luck, though, she'll be an Almond Joy.
5   *(Doorbell rings.)*
6   VOICES: *(Off-stage)* Trick-or-treat! *(Enter WHATCHAMACALLIT.)*
7   WHATCHAMACALLIT: Duh, where am I?
8   TOOTSIE ROLL: You're in a Halloween bag, kid.
9   WHATCHAMACALLIT: Duh, what's that?
10   SNICKERS: You don't know what Halloween is?
11   WHATCHAMACALLIT: Duh … no.
12   TOOTSIE ROLL: Halloween is the holiday where all the boys and
13   girls dress up and go house to house begging for candy.
14   WHATCHAMACALLIT: I never heard of that.
15   CHUNKY: What a dork!
16   WHATCHAMACALLIT: At least I'm not on the bottom.
17   CHUNKY: What? … Even the dork makes fun of the fat guy. I
18   can't win. When it comes to the socializing totem pole, fat guys
19   are always on the bottom.
20   SNICKERS: Kind of ironic, huh? *(Snicker, snicker)*
21   CHUNKY: That's not funny!
22   MR. GOODBAR: Where's all the girls?
23   WHATCHAMACALLIT: Maybe they're here but just dressed
24   differently.
25   MR. GOODBAR: I don't think so. It's just that I don't like the
26   odds here.
27   WHATCHAMACALLIT: You calling me odd?
28   MR. GOODBAR: No, son, I'm talking about guys and girls, the
29   ratio is way too high.
30   TOOTSIE ROLL: You got me, handsome.
31   MR. GOODBAR: *(Sarcastically)* Oh, great! I hope someone new
32   comes in. *(Doorbell rings.)*
33   VOICES: *(Off-stage)* Trick-or-treat! *(Enter JUICY FRUIT.)*
34   JUICY FRUIT: Well, I'll be spit out, it's crowded in here.
35   WHATCHAMACALLIT: Hey, mister. Your odds just got better.

1   *(SNICKERS snickers.)*
2   **MR. GOODBAR: Not what I had in mind, kid.**
3   **CHUNKY: Hey, Goodbar, I think the fruit likes you.**
4   **JUICY FRUIT: Who said that?**
5   **CHUNKY: I did, sister.**
6   **SNICKERS: Sister.** *(Snicker, snicker)* **That's funny.**
7   **JUICY FRUIT: Well, chubby, you know the difference between**
8   **you and me?**
9   **CHUNKY: What's that?**
10   **JUICY FRUIT: I'd never be caught dead on the bottom.**
11   **TOOTSIEROLL: He got ya there, sweetheart.**
12   **CHUNKY: Great! Even the Juicy Fruit makes fun of the fat guy, I**
13   **can't win.**
14
15   *Curtain*
16
17
18
19
20
21
22
23
24
25
26
27
28
29
30
31
32
33
34
35

Husbands Hypnotized

Premise: A wife can't get her husband to listen to her and in a desperate measure orders the Husband Hypnosis Video. It works but she never knows.

Cast: Lydia — Frustrated wife of Fred.
Fred — Husband of Lydia.
Ben — Friend of Fred.
Tony — Friend of Fred.
Delivery Person
Announcer — Commercial announcer voice, Off-stage.

Props: Television, VCR, video tape, dinner settings, newspaper, football game sounds.

Scene: Lydia and Fred have just finished dinner, Fred is reading a newspaper while Lydia talks.

1   LYDIA: ... And it would only be two nights a week, and I can get
2   a ride with Rita. I'll pay for them myself with the tips that I've
3   been saving. What do you think? Freddy?
4   FRED: *(Looking up from newspaper)* Uh ... I'm sorry. What?
5   LYDIA: Night classes. I was thinking of taking some night classes
6   at the community college. Then I can help out with the ...
7   FRED: Yeah, yeah. We'll talk about it later.
8   LYDIA: But the registration deadline is Tuesday. It's not like we
9   can't ...
10   FRED: *(Getting up to leave)* Later, Liddy. Hey, listen. Ben and Tony
11   are heading over to check out the new John Deere. Just send
12   them to the garage when they get here, OK? *(FRED exits.)*
13   LYDIA: *(Begins cleaning table.)* "Later, Liddy." "We'll talk about it
14   later." That's all I ever hear. *(Knock on door. Lydia answers.*
15   *Enter TONY and BEN. TONY and BEN "ignore" LYDIA.)*
16   BEN: Hiya, Linda. How ya doin'? Fred in the garage?
17   LYDIA: Yeah. And it's *Lydia*.
18   TONY: Rita says hi. Ooh, French fries!
19   LYDIA: Yeah. You know your wife and I were going to take ...
20   *(TONY and BEN exit.)* some night ... classes. Don't mind me,
21   I'm just another *human being!* I think I could talk until I'm
22   blue in the face and they still wouldn't notice me. *(Turns on*
23   *TV.)*
24   ANNOUNCER: *(Off-stage)* Do you talk until your blue in the face
25   and still can't get your husband to notice you? Does it seem
26   like no one listens to what you have to say? Would you like the
27   final word just once? Well now you can get it with the new
28   Husband Hypnosis Video. This video will provide you with all
29   the material you'll need to grab your better half's attention so
30   that you'll not only be able to get a word in edgewise, but
31   actually get him to respond to it as well. Call 1-800-IM-
32   TALKING for the Husband Hypnosis Video. Call today and
33   be heard tomorrow. Individual results may vary. No purchase
34   necessary. Void where prohibited. Under eighteen need not
35   apply. Consult a physician before engaging in any hypnotic

1   regimen. **All rights reserved. Any reproduction of the**
2   **Husband Hypnosis Video is strictly prohibited. Employees of**
3   **any husband that has been hypnotized not eligible. All rights**
4   **reserved. Sorry, Tennessee.** *(As disclaimer is being said, LYDIA*
5   *is writing the number down. She reaches for phone and dials.)*
6   **LYDIA: Hello? Yes. I would like to purchase the Husband Hypno ...**
7   **Yes, I'll hold.** *(Singing to Muzak)* **Up, up and away in my**
8   **beautiful, my beauti ...** *(Spoken)* **Yes. I was saying that I would**
9   **like to purch ... Yes I'll hold.** *(Singing)* **I bless the rains down**
10   **in Africa, I bless the ...** *(Spoken)* **Yes. I want the Husband**
11   **Hypnosis Video ... Yes ... It's Three, Two, One Norwan Place,**
12   **Rochester, Pennsylvania. Thank you. Buh-bye.** *(Hangs up.*
13   *Knock on door. LYDIA answers. Enter DELIVERY PERSON.)*
14   **DELIVERY PERSON: Mrs. Nix?**
15   **LYDIA: Yes?**
16   **DELIVERY PERSON: Sign here please.** *(LYDIA signs.)* **Bye now.**
17   **LYDIA: Bye.** *(Opens tape and puts it in VCR. We hear the sounds of a*
18   *football game.)* **This is it? A lousy football game? How am I**
19   **going to get him to notice me when a football game is on?**
20   *(Enter FRED who gets absorbed into the game and goes into*
21   *trance-like state. Phone rings and LYDIA pauses tape. FRED*
22   *snaps out of it and gets a drink as LYDIA answers phone.)* **Hello?**
23   **Oh. Hi, Rita.** *(Enter BEN.)* **Oh, nothing. I'm just watching a**
24   **video.** *(LYDIA starts tape again and now both FRED and BEN*
25   *are hypnotized.)* **Yes, I told him about it. "We'll talk about it**
26   **later." Fred gets me so mad sometimes I feel like he needs to**
27   **get slapped in the head.** *(BEN slaps FRED.)* **Ben too, huh?**
28   *(FRED slaps BEN.)* **I know but they drive me crazy.** *(FRED and*
29   *BEN make crazy gestures and faces.)* **They act like they're deaf**
30   **sometimes.** *(FRED and BEN act deaf, either signing or cupping*
31   *hands to ears.)* **Well, I tried but he's as stubborn as a mule.**
32   *(FRED and BEN act like mules as TONY enters and gets*
33   *hypnotized.)* **Just once I'd like him to be me and see how it**
34   **feels.** *(ALL men start acting feminine and chatty.)* **So anyway.**
35   **What else is new? Ooh. She's sick again?** *(FRED, BEN, and*

1	*TONY start showing signs of nausea.)* **She threw up?** *(MEN start*
2	*gagging and puking.)* **We took Sparky to the vet to have him**
3	**neutered.** *(MEN all start grabbing crotch and sniffing each*
4	*other.)* **Oh, well. I'll talk to you later. Bye, Rita.** *(Hangs up and*
5	*ejects tape. MEN snap back to normal not realizing what has*
6	*happened and exit.)* **Husband hypnosis. What a scam!**
7	
8	*Curtain*
9	
10	
11	
12	
13	
14	
15	
16	
17	
18	
19	
20	
21	
22	
23	
24	
25	
26	
27	
28	
29	
30	
31	
32	
33	
34	
35	

I Done Got Happy

Premise: Blind Boy is a blues singer, but he regained his sight, which has made him happy. He arrives at the recording studio but is too cheerful to sing the blues. The producer and his agent try to make him "blue" again.

Cast: Blind Boy Larry — Extremely happy blues musician. Not blind anymore.

Executive — Record company executive worried about record sales. Wants to hear the blues.

Manager — Blind Boy's manager. Promises to deliver the blues.

Studio Musician — Plays guitar with Blind Boy.

Props: Two guitars, plate with burgers.

Costumes: Blue shirt for Manager.

Scene: The inside of a recording studio, Executive and Manager are waiting for Blind Boy. A Studio Musician is waiting off to the side.

1   EXECUTIVE: OK, I'm getting worried. The session started at
2   nine and it's now nine-forty. Where's your boy?
3   MANAGER: He'll be here, he'll be here. You know how those
4   musicians are, a little flighty, living in their own world.
5   EXECUTIVE: What if something bad happened to him?
6   MANAGER: I'm sure he's just running late, but if something did
7   happen, hey, it might make a great song. You know how those
8   blues musicians are.
9   EXECUTIVE: We signed Blind Boy to this deal because you
10   promised us he'd have some great songs, but if he doesn't
11   show up to record them, what good are they?
12   MANAGER: He'll be here, he'll be here.
13   EXECUTIVE: He better be here, and quick. This is costing me a
14   lot of money with studio rental, musicians, techies ...
15   MANAGER: Trust me, he's coming. *(Enter BLIND BOY, wearing*
16   *dark glasses.)*
17   BLIND BOY: Hey, guys!
18   MANAGER: See, I told you!
19   EXECUTIVE: It's about time, where were you?
20   BLIND BOY: You'll never believe what happened to me!
21   EXECUTIVE: I'm sure it's bad, but let's hear it in a song, huh?
22   Time is money.
23   BLIND BOY: No, no, no, it's not bad.
24   MANAGER: You look a little different Blind Boy, did you change
25   your hair?
26   BLIND BOY: No, but I really like your *blue* shirt.
27   EXECUTIVE: Speaking of blue, can we record some here?
28   MANAGER: Blind Boy, you're not blind anymore!
29   BLIND BOY: *(Removing sunglasses)* No! It was the most amazing
30   thing, I woke up and I could see!
31   EXECUTIVE: Great! There goes a ton of money to have CD
32   covers reprinted.
33   MANAGER: That's great Blind Boy or ... umm. What should I
34   call you?
35   EXECUTIVE: How about the artist formerly known as Blind Boy?

1   **BLIND BOY:** Hey, that's really funny!

2   **EXECUTIVE:** Yeah, can we start? I'm really glad you can see, so

3   I'm sure you can see how many people I'm paying to record

4   the blues.

5   **BLIND BOY:** Why do they call sad music the blues? I mean, I saw

6   the sky, it's blue and it looks really happy!

7   **MANAGER:** I don't know. Let's just get started, huh?

8   **BLIND BOY:** Alrighty, then!

9   **EXECUTIVE:** OK, we'll do the first one. *(Pointing to studio*

10   *musician)* Do you want to tell him what you want, what to play?

11   **BLIND BOY:** Sure! *(BLIND BOY goes to MUSICIAN.)*

12   **EXECUTIVE:** *(To MANAGER)* Is this going to affect his singing?

13   **MANAGER:** No, no, he's a professional.

14   **EXECUTIVE:** I just mean, his blues were so heartfelt, you know,

15   how sad, low-down dirty, and it's because he felt sorry for

16   himself, being blind and all.

17   **MANAGER:** No, he'll give you the blues, because that's what

18   Blind ... umm ... that's what he does.

19   **EXECUTIVE:** Are you ready people? Let's take one.

20   **BLIND BOY:** One, two, three, four ... *(STUDIO MUSICIAN begins*

21   *playing an upbeat tune — not the blues — as BLIND BOY sings*

22   *the following words.)*

23   **BLIND BOY:** *The clouds in the sky are fluffy/My dog his name is*

24   *Scruffy/And I love him —*

25   **EXECUTIVE:** *Cut!* What was that?

26   **BLIND BOY:** Hey, I write and sing what I feel, and now that I can

27   see, that's what I feel.

28   **EXECUTIVE:** *(Turns to MANAGER.)* This is not the blues.

29   **MANAGER:** It sounded good.

30   **EXECUTIVE:** It's not the blues! This just isn't going to work out.

31   I need the blues!

32   **MANAGER:** Are you sure? Because I bet you could sell that song.

33   **EXECUTIVE:** On the Muddy Creek label?

34   **MANAGER:** I guess not.

35   **EXECUTIVE:** I'm going to get fired.

1   MANAGER: *(Thinks.)* I know! Let's tell him some sad things, you
2   know, and give him the blues.
3   EXECUTIVE: I'll try anything. Hey look, it's raining outside.
4   BLIND BOY: Great, I won't have to water the grass!
5   MANAGER: *(With burgers)* Blind Boy, want a bite to eat? Oh, no,
6   you're a vegetarian and we only have burgers.
7   BLIND BOY: *(Taking a burger)* No, I saw a cow on the way in and
8   decided they're really ugly, so I can eat them now!
9   EXECUTIVE: Don't you owe Big Bad Willy a lot of money?
10 BLIND BOY: Nope, paid him off.
11 MANAGER: How's that gambling problem?
12 BLIND BOY: Great, how do you think I paid Willy off?
13 EXECUTIVE: *(Puts arm around BLIND BOY.)* I want you to
14   remember. Think back to your childhood, remember growing
15   up on the street, living in the alleys, your family struggling just
16   to survive, wearing bread bags that you got from the dumpster
17   as shoes because you couldn't afford real ones, do you got it?
18 BLIND BOY: *(Starting to cry)* I'm there.
19 EXECUTIVE: Okay, let's start. *(Play "Those Were the Days.")*
20 EXECUTIVE: *Cut!*
21 MANAGER: How's the alcohol problem?
22 BLIND BOY: On the wagon.
23 EXECUTIVE: IRS problem?
24 BLIND BOY: They owe me a refund.
25 MANAGER: How's the rash?
26 BLIND BOY: Cleared up.
27 EXECUTIVE: Ring, ring ... hello ... oh no, Blind Boy, it's your
28   wife, she's leaving you!
29 BLIND BOY: Great! Now I can marry my girlfriend! And you're
30   all invited.
31 EXECUTIVE: That's it. You're fired!
32 MANAGER: No, wait ... *(EXECUTIVE exits, MANAGER chases.)*
33 BLIND BOY: Fired? But I really love music.
34 GUITARIST: Feeling a little blue?
35 BLIND BOY: I sure am. *(BOTH play blues as curtain closes.)*

The Interview Come-On

Premise: A seemingly self-assured professional interviews a loser for a job, and they end up switching roles.

Cast: Boss — Very dynamic woman who seems extremely happy.
Ms. Newbom — Nervous and self-conscious interviewee.
Mr. Dink — Interviewee (one line).

Props: Resumé (piece of paper), desk, two chairs, goodie tray, coffee pitcher, cups.

Scene: An office with one desk, an interview chair, and a small table with pitcher and cups. BOSS sits behind desk.

1   *(MS. NEWBOM enters.)*

2   **BOSS: Hello. Ms. Newbom I presume?**

3   **MS. NEWBOM: Uh, yes.** *(BOSS moves to MS. NEWBOM and gives*

4   *her the company greeting. MS. NEWBOM is caught off guard,*

5   *and doesn't know how to participate. The hug/shake should be as*

6   *goofy as possible, with high fives, slaps, and whole body shakes.)*

7   **BOSS: Come on in, have a seat.**

8   **MS. NEWBOM: Uh … thanks.** *(MS. NEWBOM and BOSS sit.)*

9   **BOSS:** *(Looking at the resumé)* **Can I just call you Edna?**

10   **MS. NEWBOM: My name is Fran.**

11   **BOSS: Well, how about Fran then?**

12   **MS. NEWBOM: Sure.** *(BOSS gets tray and offers it.)*

13   **BOSS: Something to eat?**

14   **MS. NEWBOM: No, thank you. I'm not hungry.**

15   **BOSS: Come on, have a treat.**

16   **MS. NEWBOM: No, thank you.**

17   **BOSS:** *(Moves to coffee table.)* **Drink?**

18   **MS. NEWBOM: No. Thanks.**

19   **BOSS: Back massage?** *(BOSS begins massaging MS. NEWBOM, who*

20   *is startled and pulls away.)*

21   **MS. NEWBOM: No! Really, I'm fine. If we could just get on with**

22   **the interview.**

23   **BOSS:** *(Moving back to seat)* **Yes. Of course, Fran. I was just**

24   **looking over your resumé. Quite impressive.**

25   **MS. NEWBOM:** *(In disbelief)* **Really?**

26   **BOSS: Says here you worked for the Burger Hut.**

27   **MS. NEWBOM: Yes. I flipped burgers for about three weeks.**

28   **BOSS: A Grill Coordinator? Well, Fran. I've never met a Culinary**

29   **Technician before. OK. I see here you also dabbled in the**

30   **communications services.**

31   **MS. NEWBOM: I did?**

32   **BOSS: Come on. So modest. The newspaper job?**

33   **MS. NEWBOM: I just subbed for my nephew's paper route one**

34   **weekend.**

35   **BOSS: Yes. A Journalism Representative. Fran, come give me a**

1   hug. *(Moves to the front of the desk.)*
2   MS. NEWBOM: Pardon me?
3   BOSS: Come on. We're all one big happy family here. Give me a
4   hug. *(Pulls MS. NEWBOM out of her chair.)* You know our
5   motto around here?
6   MS. NEWBOM: No. I'm afraid I don't. *(BOSS repeats the earlier*
7   *company greeting as she recites the company motto.)*
8   BOSS: Shake me up, like a soda pop. And I'll fizz with happiness
9   and never stop. *(MS. NEWBOM is startled. BOSS revels in the*
10   *moment then returns to her seat.)* Any other hidden talents or
11   qualifications, Fran, you'd like to share?
12   MS. NEWBOM: No.
13   BOSS: Nothing?
14   MS. NEWBOM: No.
15   BOSS: Somebody as talented as you must have loads of experiences
16   you can share. Come on, you can admit it.
17   MS. NEWBOM: No, not really. I spend most of my time sitting on
18   the couch, eating Cheezy Curlers and watching reruns of
19   *Charlie's Angels.*
20   BOSS: Whoa!
21   MS. NEWBOM: Yeah. I know. I'm not proud of the way I am, but
22   I …
23   BOSS: A Consumer Broadcasting Specialist.
24   MS. NEWBOM: A what?
25   BOSS: And you invest your free time wisely in Popular Pop
26   Culture Dramatic Studies. Well, Fran, your credentials seem
27   impeccable. By the way, that's a beautiful top, Fran.
28   MS. NEWBOM: Thanks. Can you tell me how long this is going to
29   take?
30   BOSS: Wow! And a forward-thinker as well. Not many of you left,
31   I'm afraid. The last person I interviewed for the job had no
32   sense of success. Not the slightest idea of ambition. But I know
33   talent when I see it, and believe me when I say it looks as though
34   the gods of promising employees smiled down on us when you
35   walked through our door. I knew instantly that the …

1   MS. NEWBOM: Excuse me, but I really don't think that I belong
2   here.
3   BOSS: Nonsense. You belong Fran! You're perfect.
4   MS. NEWBOM: Look, I don't even know what this job is. My
5   mother saw the ad in the paper and insisted that I apply.
6   BOSS: And we are so fortunate that she did. Thanks Fran's mom.
7   I'm sure she's as wonderful as you.
8   MS. NEWBOM: Look, don't patronize me. I know I'm totally
9   unqualified for whatever it is you're looking for. Go ahead,
10   you can tell me the truth. It's not as though I haven't heard it
11   before. You won't hurt my feelings. Say it. I'm pathetic. I
12   couldn't get a job as a failure. I'd even fail at that. Say it. I'm
13   a loser. At least give me the decency of admitting it. *Come on*,
14   say it! *I am a failure! (Pause. BOSS changes from gung-ho to*
15   *depressed.)*
16   BOSS: You're right, Fran.
17   MS. NEWBOM: I knew it.
18   BOSS: *I am a failure!*
19   MS. NEWBOM: What?
20   BOSS: It feels so good to finally admit it. It's uncanny. You hit the
21   nail right on the head. You have me down to a *T*. I'm a failure.
22   Fran, your instincts are impeccable and your way of reading
23   people seems almost unreal. You got the job.
24   MS. NEWBOM: I got the job?
25   BOSS: Sure do. You're practically over-qualified. As a matter of
26   fact, you make me feel inadequate.
27   MS. NEWBOM: Really? I have the job?
28   BOSS: Welcome aboard Fran. *(BOSS does the hug/shake*
29   *halfheartedly as MS. NEWBOM does it with more enthusiasm.)*
30   Sign here please. The passion you have is so refreshing ... and
31   here. If I could only experience an ounce of that drive you
32   have, and here, and motivation. But I don't. That's the
33   difference between the movers and the shakers like you, and
34   the go-nowhere dead-end types like me. You definitely have a
35   future here, Fran. Make no mistake about that. But as for me,

1   well …

2   MS. NEWBOM: I don't know what to say.

3   BOSS: Just say you'll take the job.

4   MS. NEWBOM: Sure. When do I start?

5   BOSS: How's now sound?

6   MS. NEWBOM: Well, I'm really not prepared. I …

7   BOSS: Come on, Fran. You were born prepared. As for me, I think

8   it's time for me to admit that I'm a useless piece of barnacle

9   on the ship of life. I think it's time for me to move on. Good

10   luck, Fran. *(BOSS exits.)*

11   MS. NEWBOM: Uh … Thank you. *(MR. DINK enters.)*

12   MR. DINK: *(Cautiously)* Hello, I'm here for the job interview.

13   MS. NEWBOM: Yes, Mr. Dink, I take it. Come on in. *(MS.*

14   *NEWBOM gives the company greeting very enthusiastically as*

15   *MR. DINK is dumbfounded.)* Have a seat. Something to eat?

16

17   *Curtain*

18

19

20

21

22

23

24

25

26

27

28

29

30

31

32

33

34

35

Keeping Up with the Joneses

Premise: Two construction workers try to outdo each other in their conversation, which then carries over into their work, until they begin purposefully hurting themselves.

Cast: Jones One — Construction worker.
Jones Two — Also a construction worker.
Violinist (or other musician) — No lines.
Woman — Just to walk past.

Props: (Any prop designated "large" would work best if it's as big as possible in your theater) three cigars, pictures, videotape, suspenders, bibbed overalls, work boots, large rubber boots, earplugs, earphones, safety glasses, safety goggles, small gloves, large gloves, hardhat with "Jones" written on front which also can light up, hardhat with "Jones" written on front in bigger letters, nail apron, bigger nail apron, small saw, large saw, small piece of wood, large piece of wood, work bench, ladder, regular hammer, sledgehammer, nails, spike, small lunch pail, large cooler, little bottle with drink, large thermos, small cup, large cup (see text for special directions), napkin, table cloth, lunch pie, regular size pie, small bag of chips, large bag of chips, large boom box, violin (or appropriate instrument), large hoagie, extra large hoagie, knife, electric cord, edible nails (such as small pretzel sticks), stick of dynamite, lighter.

Scene: Work area, props are on stage but the "funny" props should not be visible to the audience. Jones One and Jones Two enter from opposite sides.

1   **ONE: How was your weekend?**

2   **TWO: Good. How was yours?**

3   **ONE: Great.** *(This should be said as the first "one-ups-manship"*

4   *statement.)* **I went to the air show.**

5   **TWO: Oh, yeah? I went skydiving. And guess what, Mary was in**

6   **labor Saturday for seven hours.**

7   **ONE: Really? Suzie was in labor for seventeen hours. She had a**

8   **baby boy, seven pounds six ounces.** *(JONES ONE hands JONES*

9   *TWO a cigar.)*

10   **TWO: Really. Mary had twins, both nine pounds three ounces.**

11   *(JONES TWO hands JONES ONE two cigars.)* **Here's some**

12   **pictures.**

13   **ONE: Here's the video.** *(Pause)* **We almost didn't make it to the**

14   **hospital because the car didn't start, I had to call a taxi.**

15   **TWO: Ours wouldn't start either, so we took the bus.**

16   **ONE: Oh, well, the taxi didn't come, so I actually had to ride her**

17   **on my bicycle.**

18   **TWO: Well, the bus broke down, so I had to carry her the rest of**

19   **the way. Five blocks.**

20   **ONE: That's why there was so much traffic backed up and I**

21   **couldn't get across the bridge. I actually had to hollow out a**

22   **tree for a canoe and paddle across then carry her to the**

23   **hospital.** *(A whistle blows. Note: The following is done without*

24   *speaking and with music in the background. As each outdoes the*

25   *other, he should feel good about himself, and then when he's*

26   *outdone, he should feel deflated.*

27   *ONE removes his jacket and is wearing suspenders. TWO*

28   *removes his jacket and has on bibbed overalls. TWO removes*

29   *sneakers, puts on work boots. ONE puts on large rubber boots.*

30   *ONE puts in earplugs. TWO puts on earphones. TWO puts on safety*

31   *glasses. ONE puts on goggles. ONE puts on gloves. TWO puts on*

32   *bigger gloves. TWO puts on hardhat with "Jones" written across*

33   *the front. ONE puts on hardhat with "Jones" written bigger and*

34   *bolder. TWO reaches to helmet, flips a switch and his name lights*

35   *up. ONE puts on nail apron. TWO puts on bigger apron.*

1   *TWO picks up saw. ONE picks up bigger saw. ONE grabs a*
2   *small piece of wood. TWO grabs a big piece of wood. TWO pulls*
3   *out bench to set wood against. ONE brings out a ladder. ONE*
4   *pulls out a regular hammer. TWO pulls out a sledgehammer. TWO*
5   *pulls out a regular nail. ONE pulls out a spike.*

6   *As the two get set to hammer, whistle blows. TWO removes*
7   *earphones. Louder whistle blows, ONE removes earplugs. ONE*
8   *gets small lunch pail. TWO gets large cooler. TWO pulls out little*
9   *bottle. ONE pulls out large Thermos. ONE pulls out little cup and*
10   *fills. TWO pulls out large cup and fills. Note: The cup should look*
11   *like it holds more than the little bottle, but the little bottle should*
12   *fill it. When this skit was first done, a large cup with a smaller cup*
13   *turned over inside it was used. Also, a small piece of plastic the*
14   *same color as the drink was positioned to unfold and look like the*
15   *pouring drink.*

16   *TWO pulls out napkin. ONE pulls out tablecloth. ONE pulls*
17   *out lunch-size pie. TWO pulls out a real size pie. TWO pulls out*
18   *lunch-size bag of chips. ONE pulls out large bag of chips. ONE*
19   *gets out a large boom box and turns it on. TWO claps his hands*
20   *and a VIOLINIST enters. TWO pulls out large hoagie [This*
21   *sandwich should be bigger than JONES ONE's whole lunch pail.]*
22   *ONE pulls out a giant hoagie. Note: The sandwich could be made*
23   *from pliable Styrofoam and squeezed into the lunch pail.*

24   *WOMAN enters and walks past the two, pauses as they whistle*
25   *and then exits. ONE whistles at girl. TWO whistles louder and*
26   *more fancy.*

27   *Whistle blows again, and both stand to work. Except for the*
28   *splinter, the following should all be done on purpose. ONE, as he*
29   *picks up his piece of wood, gets a splinter. TWO tries getting*
30   *splinter, but can't so picks up knife and cuts his own finger. ONE*
31   *bashes thumb with hammer. TWO cuts finger off. ONE drops*
32   *regular hammer on foot. TWO drops sledgehammer on foot.*
33   *BOTH are woozy, and each hops on one foot.*

34   *ONE smacks head on ladder and falls to ground. TWO eats*
35   *nails from apron, begins choking, and also falls. ONE puts*

1   *electric cord to tongue and shocks himself. TWO pulls out a stick*
2   *of dynamite, puts it in his mouth, and begins lighting with lighter.*
3   *Lights out. Large explosion is heard.)*
4
5   *Curtain*
6
7
8
9
10
11
12
13
14
15
16
17
18
19
20
21
22
23
24
25
26
27
28
29
30
31
32
33
34
35

Kid to Work Day

Premise: An emergency room surgeon decides to participate in "bring-your-child-to-work" day. He shows little Timmy the operating room and lets him participate in actual surgery. The nurses are not amused.

Cast: Doctor — Likes the idea of spending time with Timmy. Tries to make the experience as fun as possible. Likes to try "fatherly" practical jokes.

Timmy — Son who gets to come to work with Dad. He likes all the new stuff and isn't afraid to do things he knows are wrong, as long as Dad isn't looking.

Ritter — Operating room nurse. Very professional, but tries to appease the surgeon.

Green — Anesthesiologist. Also professional, trying to do a good job.

EMT 1 — Small role.

EMT 2 — Nonspeaking role.

Patient — Nonspeaking role.

Props: Operating table, monitors (computer screens will do), tray with scalpel and other surgery tools, x-ray viewer, gas mask and tank, paddles and machine for shocking patients.

Scene: Operating room. A surgery table is Down Center Stage. There is a set of monitors at the head of the table along with anesthesiologist's equipment. Ritter and Green are in the room, dressed for surgery.

Note: If you have the means, monitors that look like real heart machine monitors with the heartbeat line could be facing the audience. If not, old computer monitors or other boxes could be facing away from the audience.

1   **RITTER: I hate these "bring-your-kid-to-work" days.**

2   **GREEN: I know. It's like for one day we suddenly become a**

3   **daycare.** *(DOCTOR and TIMMY enter.)*

4   **DOCTOR: Everybody, this is my son, Timmy.**

5   **RITTER:** *(Away from DOCTOR and Timmy)* **Great.**

6   **DOCTOR: This is where it all happens, Timmy. The O.R.** *(Pause)*

7   **This is Nurse Ritter.**

8   **RITTER: Hiya, Timmy.**

9   **TIMMY: Hi.**

10   **DOCTOR: Nurse Ritter is responsible for assisting me in the**

11   **surgery and this is Doctor Green.**

12   **GREEN: Hi, Tim.**

13   **TIMMY: Hi.**

14   **DOCTOR: Doctor Green is the anesthesiologist. He puts the**

15   **patient to sleep and then watches these monitors to make sure**

16   **everything is OK.**

17   **TIMMY:** *(Seeing the monitors with lights and displays)* **Cool! Video**

18   **games.**

19   **DOCTOR: Oh, no Timmy. These aren't games. That's an EKG. We**

20   **connect that to the patient's heart and can tell how the patient**

21   **is by watching the graph. You see Timmy, we use sophisticated**

22   **equipment to assist us in surgery. All of these machines ...**

23   *(EMT 1 and EMT 2 enter.)*

24   **EMT 1: We have an automobile accident victim, contusions to the**

25   **lower abdomen. Patient is dilated. BP at one-twenty over**

26   **eighty with possible subdural hematoma.** *(EMTS place*

27   *PATIENT on operating table, turn over control to RITTER and*

28   *GREEN, then exit. GREEN puts gas mask on PATIENT, and hooks*

29   *PATIENT to the heart monitor which should begin beeping*

30   *rhythmically.)*

31   **DOCTOR:** *(Excited)* **Oooo, Timmy, you're in luck. This is a great**

32   **example of the types of decisions doctors are faced with every**

33   **day ...**

34   **RITTER: Doctor?**

35   **DOCTOR: One wrong decision can mean the difference between**

1   life and death.
2   RITTER: Doctor!?
3   DOCTOR: Each second that passes can be the point of no return.
4   No time to second guess yourself ...
5   RITTER: Doctor, we're ready!
6   DOCTOR: Oh, yes. Of course. Ready, Timmy?
7   TIMMY: Sure.
8   DOCTOR: First, we prep the patient.
9   RITTER: He's already prepped, doctor.
10   DOCTOR: Oh, I see that he is.
11   TIMMY: Daddy, what's this?
12   DOCTOR: That? That's an occipital retractor. We use that to hold
13   back the skin while we operate.
14   TIMMY: Oooo. Can I try it?
15   RITTER: Doctor, I really don't think that would be wise.
16   DOCTOR: *(Serious)* I'm afraid I agree with the nurse, Timmy.
17   *(Excited)* We don't use that until later. How'd you like to jump
18   up here and help cut him open?
19   TIMMY: Sure.
20   DOCTOR: OK. We're going in. Scalpel.
21   RITTER: Scalpel. *(DOCTOR begins incision.)*
22   DOCTOR: We're going to begin the incision starting at — ow! My
23   finger! Just kidding. Ha, ha, ha.
24   TIMMY: Aw, Dad.
25   DOCTOR: Gotcha.
26   RITTER: Doctor, please!
27   DOCTOR: Nag, nag, nag. *(To TIMMY)* Worse than your mother!
28   OK. Before we dig in, let's give the old x-rays a gander.
29   *(DOCTOR, RITTER, and GREEN move to x-ray viewer and are*
30   *no longer watching TIMMY. TIMMY begins playing with*
31   *PATIENT, pushing on his chest. Everytime he pushes, the heart*
32   *monitor beeps out of turn. Note: Have fun with this idea. As*
33   *DOCTOR recites the following lines, TIMMY should push on the*
34   *chest, apprehensively at first, then more playfully. If the timing is*
35   *right, TIMMY could play a "song" with the beeps and dance*

1	*around. DOCTOR speaks as TIMMY plays with patient.)* **You see**
2	**Timmy, subdural hematoma is a collection of blood clots in the**
3	**subdural space between the brain and the duramater. If a**
4	**hematoma is on the left side, speech will be slurred. CAT and**
5	**MRI scans show abnormal blood clots and indentation of the**
6	**skull. And here in the abdominal region, we see an**
7	**abnormality that we'll need to check out.** *(DOCTOR continues*
8	*explaining until the heart machine flatlines.)*
9	**GREEN: Doctor, we've lost the patient!**
10	**TIMMY: You didn't lose him. He's right here, Dad.**
11	**DOCTOR: Good one, son.** *(DOCTOR and TIMMY high-five.)*
12	**GREEN: Doctor?**
13	**DOCTOR: Get the paddles.** *(To TIMMY)* **We're going to try to**
14	**revive the patient by shooting electricity through his body.**
15	*(GREEN hands paddles to DOCTOR.)* **Clear.** *(GREEN removes*
16	*gas mask from PATIENT, EVERYONE backs up and DOCTOR*
17	*shocks PATIENT.)*
18	**RITTER: Nothing.**
19	**DOCTOR: Clear.** *(DOCTOR shocks PATIENT. Rhythmic beeping*
20	*begins again. DOCTOR sets paddles down.)*
21	**GREEN: We have a pulse.**
22	**DOCTOR: How about that son?**
23	**TIMMY: Cool!**
24	**DOCTOR: There's something you don't see every day. All right**
25	**nurse, administer the lythane.** *(RITTER prepares syringe.)* **You**
26	**see Timmy, we have to administer a powerful nerve**
27	**suppressant to inhibit the possibility of adverse reactions.**
28	*(DOCTOR ad-libs turning away from the others so as not to see*
29	*the following exchange. TIMMY picks up paddles to examine them*
30	*more closely. He decides to zap RITTER who accidentally injects*
31	*GREEN with the muscle suppressant. RITTER turns and takes*
32	*paddles from TIMMY while GREEN falls to the floor. GREEN's*
33	*whole side is limp. RITTER tends to GREEN. TIMMY then pulls*
34	*off the PATIENT's mask, sniffs and falls to floor. PATIENT starts*
35	*to wake. RITTER puts mask back on PATIENT. TIMMY wakes.*

1   *ALL back to normal.)* **And although we have the patient**
2   **sedated, we take secondary precautions. Now, we begin the**
3   **incision, beginning at the Vylar region.**
4   **GREEN: BP holding, lipids down to twenty-three.**
5   **DOCTOR: All right, Timmy. Now if you look in here you see the**
6   **appendix and ... oooo, here we go Timmy. Feel this.**
7   **RITTER: Doctor! I don't think that's wise.**
8   **DOCTOR: Once again, you're correct, nurse. Be sure to put on**
9   **your gloves first.** *(TIMMY puts on gloves then sticks hand in*
10   *PATIENT.)*
11 **TIMMY: Cool!**
12 **DOCTOR: Just keep your finger pressing on this artery right here.**
13   **I have to check the x-ray real quick.**
14 **TIMMY: Cool!**
15 **RITTER: But, Doctor?!**
16 **DOCTOR: Oh, relax. He's a very bright boy.** *(DOCTOR, RITTER*
17   *and GREEN again turn away from PATIENT and TIMMY.*
18   *DOCTOR points at x-ray.)* **Tell me what you think of this,**
19   **nurse.** *(RITTER and GREEN begin to confer with DOCTOR;*
20   *TIMMY begins searching through the insides of the PATIENT. He*
21   *pulls out innards, returns innards, DOCTOR returns.)* **All right**
22   **then. Looks like it wasn't a subdural after all. With a little**
23   **medication I'm sure that swelling will go down. And as for the**
24   **abdominal protrusion ...** *(DOCTOR snips something inside*
25   *patient.)* **There we go. Nurse, would you be so kind as to close**
26   **for me? I'm going to take my son golfing. So there you go**
27   **Timmy. The exciting life of a surgeon and all the ...** *(DOCTOR*
28   *and TIMMY exit.)*
29 **RITTER: I hate these "bring-your-kid-to-work" days.**
30
31   *Curtain*
32
33
34
35

Little Thoughts

Premise: Time has a way of affecting a couple's point of view on fond memories, but some things never change.

Cast: Kim — A nostalgic wife, with a great memory.
Joe — Forgetful husband.
Kimmy — A young Kim.
Joey — A young Joe.
Jones — An angry old man (voice only).

Props: Tree trunk, pocket knife, books.

Costumes: T-shirt, ball cap, and shorts for Joe and Joey.

Notes: The scene should be conducted as a split screen, with the attention and the stage lights switching when marked.

1   KIM: Oh, honey. This brings back so many memories.

2   JOE: The old neighborhood hasn't changed much. Seems a lot

3   smaller.

4   KIM: We were just a lot smaller.

5   JOE: Those were the days.

6   KIM: Look, there's the tree. This is where it all started.

7   JOE: Yep. Where it all started. *(Pause)* What all started?

8   KIM: Us. Where we started. You mean to tell me you don't

9   remember the first time we met?

10 JOE: Oh, yeah, right. I knew that. I thought you were talking

11   about something else.

12 KIM: Sure you did. All right then, Mr. Sentimental, what was I

13   wearing?

14 JOE: What were you wearing? Kim, that was fifteen years ago.

15 KIM: Seventeen. Told you you didn't remember. You probably

16   don't even remember what we had for breakfast this morning.

17 JOE: Waffles. See.

18 KIM: Whooo, somebody mark this one on a calendar. He

19   remembered something.

20 JOE: All right, smarty pants, what was I wearing?

21 KIM: A T-shirt, ball cap, and short pants. You had the cutest bony

22   little legs. Still do.

23 JOE: Well, that was a tough one. That's all I ever wore.

24 KIM: I'll never forget the way you winked at me to catch my

25   attention.

26 JOE: Huh?

27 KIM: You were so cute. *(Lights switch to younger couple scene.*

28   *JOEY is digging in the dirt with a stick and gets something in his*

29   *eye. He is blinking furiously when KIMMY walks in. JOEY notices*

30   *and straightens up.)*

31 JOEY: Uh, hi.

32 KIMMY: Hi. *(JOEY goes back to digging. Lights switch to older*

33   *couple scene.)*

34 KIM: It was magical.

35 JOE: It was? *(Notices KIM daydreaming, smiling.)* Uh … yeah, it

1   was.
2   KIM: And then the next day in school, when you met me at my
3   locker. *(Lights switch to younger couple scene. JOEY rushes in*
4   *carrying books, bumps into KIMMY and drops books. JOEY*
5   *stoops to pick them up.)*
6   KIMMY: Hello.
7   JOEY: Hi. *(Lights switch to older couple scene.)*
8   KIM: You had such a way with words.
9   JOE: I did?
10   KIM: You were a sweet talker. *(Lights switch to younger couple*
11   *scene.)*
12   JOEY: T'sup?
13   KIMMY: Not much.
14   JOEY: Cool. *(Lights switch to older couple scene.)*
15   KIM: You gave me goose bumps when you asked me to the
16   homecoming game.
17   JOE: I did?
18   KIM: I remember it like it was yesterday. *(Lights switch to younger*
19   *couple scene.)*
20   JOEY: You going to homecoming tonight?
21   KIMMY: Yes.
22   JOEY: Maybe I'll see you there then. Later. *(JOEY exits. Lights*
23   *switch to older couple scene.)*
24   KIM: I remember on our first real date, you were such a
25   gentleman. We just sat there and talked all night.
26   JOE: I was? We did?
27   KIM: You don't remember? We talked about everything.
28   Philosophy, food, movies, religion. It was so enlightening.
29   *(Lights switch to younger couple scene.)*
30   KIMMY: … and I told her, you wouldn't know good taste if it
31   walked up and bit you. Then she said she was going to the
32   movies and didn't care what we did. Who would you believe?
33   I just said the heck with both of them and went to the mall.
34   Can you imagine her face when she realized she didn't have a
35   ride? I would have paid to see that. Who does she think she is

1   **anyway? And then there was the whole shoe disaster ...** *(JOEY*
2   *just nods. Lights switch to older couple scene.)*
3   **JOE: Are you sure?**
4   **KIM: Yes, I'm sure. I could've listened to you all night. I wish you**
5   **remembered things like I do. Look, honey. It's our initials.**
6   **You were so romantic. And remember ol' Mr. Jones?**
7   **JOE: Now, him I remember. How old was he, a hundred and three?**
8   **Mean old coot.**
9   **KIM: He wasn't that bad.** *(Lights switch to younger couple scene.)*
10   **KIMMY: Hey, Joey, what ya doin'?**
11   **JOEY: Nothing. Just carving.**
12   **KIMMY: What are you carving?**
13   **JOEY: My name.**
14   **KIMMY: Where's mine?**
15   **JOEY: I don't know.**
16   **KIMMY: Well, put mine on, too.**
17   **JONES:** *(Off-stage)* **Hey, what are you kids doin' to my tree?**
18   **JOEY: Nothin'.**
19   **JONES:** *(Off-stage)* **Nothin' my patoot. Get outta here 'fore I call**
20   **the cops.**
21   **KIMMY: We better go Joey.**
22   **JOEY: I'm not afraid of him.**
23   **KIMMY: I know. Let's go.** *(Lights switch to older couple scene.)*
24   **JOE: That was a long time ago.**
25   **KIM: Do you regret any of it?**
26   **JOE: Na. Not any that I can remember.**
27
28   *Curtain*
29
30
31
32
33
34
35

The Mirror Marriage

Premise: The same couple eating morning breakfast, except it's thirty years later. See how the more things change, the more things stay the same.

Cast: Young Husband — Very enamored with his new wife.
Young Wife — In love and trying very hard to please her husband.
Old Husband — In a routine, takes his wife for granted.
Old Wife — In a routine, takes her husband for granted.

Props: Two each of the following: toaster, toast, music box. One briefcase. Bouquet of flowers.

Scene: The stage is set with two tables, each with two chairs, and two storage areas with the appropriate props on each. The pieces should look like a mirror image of each other. Young Wife is sitting at table Stage Right. Old Wife is sitting at table Stage Left. A newspaper sits on both tables. Young Husband enters Stage Right. Old Husband enters Stage Left.

Notes: The two sets, husbands and wives, should take every opportunity to make the same or similar movements. For example, when the husbands first come on stage, they should both stretch and yawn at the same time, and maybe scratch themselves. This should go on for the rest of the skit.

132

1   YOUNG WIFE: Good morning, my little sleepyhead.

2   OLD WIFE: Hey, look who decided to finally crawl out of bed.

3   OLD HUSBAND *(Mad)* and YOUNG HUSBAND *(Lovingly)*: I'm a
4   hard working man.

5   OLD WIFE *(Sarcastically)* and YOUNG WIFE *(Lovingly)*: Yeah.

6   OLD WIFE: You kept me up half the night. You were snoring like
7   a horse.

8   YOUNG WIFE: You kept me up half the night. How did you sleep,
9   my sweetheart?

10 YOUNG HUSBAND: Like a baby.

11 OLD HUSBAND: Quit your whining. *(YOUNG HUSBAND starts to*
12   *get up for coffee, but YOUNG WIFE gets it for him. OLD WIFE*
13   *gets herself coffee. OLD HUSBAND goes to fridge and gets beer.)*

14 YOUNG WIFE: I made you some breakfast. Some homemade
15   bran muffins, fresh orange juice. I know how concerned you
16   are about your health, so I made an eggbeater vegetable
17   omelet for you. *(As YOUNG WIFE speaks, OLD HUSBAND*
18   *grabs cereal, donuts, bowl, milk, spoon and sits back again. As*
19   *the following goes on, the OLD HUSBAND pours the cereal, puts*
20   *donuts in the bowl, realizes the milk is sour, and decides to pour*
21   *beer on the cereal. He then begins eating.)*

22 YOUNG HUSBAND: You're a sweety. *(YOUNG WIFE gives*
23   *YOUNG HUSBAND the newspaper. OLD HUSBAND reaches for*
24   *the newspaper. OLD WIFE grabs paper before he gets it and hits*
25   *a fly. OLD HUSBAND picks up paper and flicks bug, begins*
26   *reading. YOUNG WIFE brings breakfast to YOUNG HUSBAND.)*

27 YOUNG WIFE: Would you like some toast?

28 YOUNG HUSBAND: Sure. *(YOUNG WIFE turns, gets out bread,*
29   *pushes down toast. OLD WIFE also makes toast. YOUNG*
30   *HUSBAND sneaks out and brings in flowers. YOUNG WIFE*
31   *turns around.)* Happy anniversary!

32 YOUNG WIFE: Anniversary?

33 YOUNG HUSBAND: It was exactly one year, three months and
34   two days ago since our first date.

35 YOUNG WIFE: You are such a darling. *(YOUNG WIFE and*

1   *YOUNG HUSBAND embrace.)* **But it was four months.**

2 **YOUNG HUSBAND: Four months?**

3 **YOUNG WIFE: One year, four months and two days.**

4 **YOUNG HUSBAND: Are you sure?**

5 **YOUNG WIFE: Positive. It was in January. I still have the ticket**

6   **stubs. I keep them in the music box you gave me for my**

7   **birthday.** *(She stands and picks up the music box lovingly.)*

8 **YOUNG HUSBAND: I feel like such a heel.**

9 **YOUNG WIFE: It's the thought that counts.**

10 **YOUNG HUSBAND: You know, I do think the world of you?**

11 **YOUNG WIFE: I know.** *(YOUNG WIFE and YOUNG HUSBAND*

12   *embrace. YOUNG WIFE moves to toaster and has problems with*

13   *toaster, YOUNG HUSBAND comes to rescue. OLD WIFE moves*

14   *to toaster, both YOUNG HUSBAND and OLD WIFE*

15   *simultaneously bang on toaster, retrieve toast. ALL sit at tables.*

16   *YOUNG WIFE starts to brush back hair.)*

17 **YOUNG HUSBAND: Hold it.**

18 **YOUNG WIFE: What?**

19 **YOUNG HUSBAND: That. The way you do that to your hair. It's**

20   **so beautiful. Like locks of silk.** *(OLD WIFE begins to brush*

21   *hair.)*

22 **OLD HUSBAND: For criminy sakes, Gladys, do you gotta rake**

23   **that mop at the table? I'm tryin' to eat here.** *(YOUNG WIFE*

24   *and YOUNG HUSBAND gaze into each others eyes.)*

25 **YOUNG HUSBAND: You have such beautiful eyes.**

26 **YOUNG WIFE:** *(Gives YOUNG HUSBAND affectionate slap on the*

27   *arm acting bashful but eating it up.)* **Awww. Stop it.**

28 **OLD HUSBAND: By the way, you got some eyesnot in your eye.**

29 **OLD WIFE:** *(Slaps HUSBAND, then cleans her eye.)* **Stop it!** *(OLD*

30   *HUSBAND picks up paper and buries his nose in it. YOUNG*

31   *HUSBAND is listening to YOUNG WIFE attentively.)*

32 **YOUNG HUSBAND: I love your voice. It's like an angel singing. I**

33   **could listen to you all day long.**

34 **YOUNG WIFE: Really?**

35 **OLD WIFE and YOUNG WIFE: Did I tell you my mother is**

1   coming over tonight for dinner?

2   **YOUNG HUSBAND** *(Excited)* **and OLD HUSBAND** *(Annoyed)*:

3   She is? Great.

4   **OLD HUSBAND:** There goes my appetite.

5   **YOUNG HUSBAND:** She's such a treat.

6   **OLD WIFE and YOUNG WIFE:** My, look at the time, you better

7   get going.

8   **YOUNG WIFE:** The newest head chef at the Royal Crown Hotel

9   shouldn't be late for his first big day at work.

10   **OLD WIFE:** And just because free Whoppers are a benefit doesn't

11   mean you have to eat them everyday. Take a banana. And

12   don't forget your drive-through head-set. *(OLD HUSBAND*

13   *and YOUNG HUSBAND exit. After a pause OLD HUSBAND*

14   *enters.)*

15   **OLD HUSBAND:** Oh, yeah. Happy anniversary.

16   **OLD WIFE:** Anniversary? Our Anniversary isn't until next week

17   you old coot.

18   **OLD HUSBAND:** Mmmm. I knew that.

19   **OLD WIFE:** It's the thought that counts. *(As the conversation goes*

20   *on, YOUNG HUSBAND enters, picks up his briefcase, looks at*

21   *WIFE and sets it down.)*

22   **OLD HUSBAND:** You know, I do think the world of you?

23   **OLD WIFE:** I know. *(OLD HUSBAND and YOUNG HUSBAND open*

24   *music box on counter, and both couples begin to dance.)*

25

26   *Curtain*

27

28

29

30

31

32

33

34

35

Mixed-Up Father and Son

Premise: A father and son switch roles. The son becomes the adult while the father acts like a child.

Cast: Dad — An ex-hippie, although he looks like a normal dad. Son.

Scene: Dad is sitting in a living room. He lights a cigarette.

1   SON: *(Off-stage)* I'm home. *(DAD panics, tries waving smoke away.)*
2   Where are you?
3   DAD: In here. *(DAD hides his cigarette as SON enters.)*
4   SON: Hi, Dad.
5   DAD: Hi Son! You're home earlier than usual.
6   SON: Don't start with me again ... I have homework!
7   DAD: Homework, huh? I heard through the grapevine that today
8   was senior skip day, where were you?
9   SON: In school.
10 DAD: That's so like you. Why can't you be more like Marty's kids?
11   You know what they did? They slept in 'til eleven and then
12   went to the park.
13 SON: I don't do things just because other kids are doing them!
14 DAD: Right, I know ... I suppose if other kids went bungee
15   jumping off a bridge, you wouldn't go.
16 SON: Not if I was only getting a B in Spanish.
17 DAD: Look, Son, I don't expect you to be perfect!
18 SON: Well, congratulations, I'm not ... I got a detention today.
19 DAD: *(Excited)* Really?! For what?
20 SON: Praying in class.
21 DAD: *(Disappointed)* That's my boy ... are you at least going to
22   fight it?
23 SON: No. That's how the system works. Plus, I am grounding
24   myself for a week.
25 DAD: A week?
26 SON: I think that's fair punishment.
27 DAD: But we were supposed to go to the school picnic this
28   Saturday.
29 SON: There will be other picnics.
30 DAD: Not like this one.
31 SON: I am grounded for a week and that's final.
32 DAD: But, I really ...
33 SON: Do you want me to make it two?
34 DAD: No. *(Pause)* We'll miss taco night, too.
35 SON: *(In a lecturing voice)* Look, what I did was wrong, and I have

1	to take responsibility for that. I know a week seems like a long
2	time. But it will give me time to think about what I did wrong.
3	That's what growing up is all about. Learning to take
4	responsibility for your actions. *(SON finds hidden cigarette.)*
5	What's this?
6	DAD: Cigarette. You want one?
7	SON: You know I don't smoke.
8	DAD: Right ... *(Making quotations with fingers in the air)* "It's bad
9	for you," gives you "cancer."
10	SON: And yet you continue to smoke.
11	DAD: I am old enough to make my own decisions.
12	SON: Not when I'm living under your roof! *(Pause)* I can leave ...
13	do you want that?
14	DAD: No.
15	SON: How would you survive without me? Who else would rent
16	that room for two hundred dollars a month?
17	DAD: *(In a loud mumble)* One of your "friends"?
18	SON: What's that supposed to mean?
19	DAD: I'm saying, your friends would do something like that if they
20	knew I needed it. I'm saying maybe you could use some new
21	friends.
22	SON: Those kids I hang out with are good influences; they have
23	short hair and clean clothes. And every night we're home by
24	ten.
25	DAD: Like those kids I keep seeing on the news with their "clean
26	up the neighborhood" attitudes, with their "humor the anti-
27	drug" ... what's wrong with good old-fashioned dope?
28	SON: That's just not who we are, Dad. Sometimes I wish ... I
29	wish ... I didn't have this image. I wish I could stay up late for
30	no reason ...
31	DAD: People can change ... you could be bad just once ... maybe
32	stay out 'til midnight?
33	SON: I don't know ...
34	DAD: Sure ... maybe you could even go to the prom. You could stay
35	out all night, then go to that after-prom in the morning, you'd

1   be gone for ...
2 SON: Dad! One step at a time.
3 DAD: Right.
4 SON: Funny, Mary Beth keeps asking me to the prom.
5 DAD: See, you should go!
6 SON: She is attractive, but ... she gets Cs in Algebra.
7 DAD: Son, you don't have to date girls who are just smart and
8   have great personalities. Sometimes it's OK to date a girl
9   purely on the way she looks. You can ask her at the picnic.
10 SON: But I'm grounded, remember the detention?
11 DAD: I could take care of that detention for you, and then you
12   wouldn't have to ground yourself.
13 SON: You'd do that for me?
14 DAD: Son, that's what fathers are for ... and hey, I am the
15   principal.
16
17   *Curtain*
18
19
20
21
22
23
24
25
26
27
28
29
30
31
32
33
34
35

My Fellow Cavemen

Premise: The leader of the caveman tribe was eaten, and now the clan must elect a new leader. Meet the candidates as they answer questions from the media about how they will lead into the first millennium.

Cast: Mediator — Host of the press conference. Tries to keep the peace.

Kegor — Caveman reporter.

Talsee — Caveman reporter. Very annoying to everyone else.

Bantee — Caveman reporter.

Tonga — Caveman candidate. His platform is education.

Korg — Caveman candidate. Strongest man in clan. Violence is his answer.

Sally — Cavewoman candidate. Wife of former leader. She is most intelligent caveperson.

Props: Three stone tablets with hammer and spikes for writing, clubs, three sticks, rocks to sit on.

Scene: Kegor, Talsee, and Bantee sit on rocks as Mediator addresses them.

1   MEDIATOR: Cavemen and cavewomen. It with great pain that I

2   make following announcement. Slock, our clan leader for last

3   two years found dead outside of cave near tar pits last night.

4   *(REPORTERS raise hands. He points to KEGOR.)* Yeah ... you.

5   KEGOR: Kegor, from the Chicago Mammoth. What cause of death?

6   MEDIATOR: We think tyrannosaur ate him.

7   KEGOR: Why you think that?

8   MEDIATOR: Well ... teeth marks on half of him that found

9   looked big. We have team trailing one we think did it ...

10   studying poop.

11   KEGOR: Wait, wait, wait. *(All REPORTERS begin chiseling*

12   *quickly.)* OK. *(REPORTERS raise hands again.)*

13   MEDIATOR: *(Pointing to TALSEE)* You, go.

14   TALSEE: Talsee from Boston Big Ball of Light in Sky, what we do

15   now?

16   MEDIATOR: Now we hold election to see who new clan leader.

17   TALSEE: What about vice-clan leader?

18   MEDIATOR: We no have vice-clan leader.

19   TALSEE: Don't you think that be wise?

20   MEDIATOR: Give us break; we still evolving.

21   TALSEE: Wait ... you thought to study dinosaur poop, but you no

22   plan ahead to elect vice-clan leader?

23   MEDIATOR: *(Tempted to club her.)* OK now, if no more questions,

24   we bring out candidates. First, Tonga *(Enter TONGA)* ...

25   richest caveman in our clan. He invent wheel, fire, and, most

26   notably, little stick to pick teeth with. Next, we have Korg

27   *(Enter KORG)* ... his biggest achievement was barehandedly

28   killing giant sloth that was getting into old lady Nantor's trash

29   cans. And finally, the widow of our deceased leader, Sally.

30   *(Enter SALLY.)* We now take questions. *(REPORTERS raise*

31   *hands. He points to BANTEE.)* Yes.

32   BANTEE: Bantee, from the Little Rock Fossil. My question for

33   Tonga. Tonga, you think being linked to biggest sex scandal in

34   history going to hurt your chances?

35   TONGA: No. First of all, history only go back few million years. So

1   to say biggest sex scandal in history, not saying a lot.
2   TALSEE: Still, you seen clubbing cavewoman other than wife over
3   the head.
4   TONGA: Exactly my point. Clubbing someone on head not
5   constitute actual sex. Believe me, I have feeling scandals and
6   politics going to get worse before better.
7   TALSEE: Still, you degraded woman and should have to answer to
8   someone.
9   TONGA: I swung, but I did not hit.
10 MEDIATOR: Next question please. *(Points to KEGOR.)* Yes.
11 KEGOR: For Korg. If elected, what your plan?
12 KORG: Make more weapons. Bigger clubs, more axes to attack
13   and kill tyrannosaur.
14 KEGOR: Sally, how you feel about what Korg say?
15 SALLY: It wild-boar-wash. We no need more weapons. We need to
16   concentrate on more hunting and gathering.
17 KEGOR: So you saying no new weapons.
18 SALLY: Read my lips: "No new axes."
19 BANTEE: What if tyrannosaur comes back to eat rest of us?
20 SALLY: We nothing to fear but fear itself.
21 KORG: Tell that to Slock!
22 TALSEE: How you propose protect us?
23 SALLY: We have enough clubs for protection, and tyrannosaur
24   only come when there noise, so we talk softly and carry big
25   club.
26 TALSEE: That your national defense plan? Be quiet? You think
27   that work?
28 SALLY: *(Tempted to club TALSEE.)* I show you how well it works!
29   *(MEDIATOR stops her.)*
30 TONGA: Violence is not the answer, you kook! We protect
31   ourselves by becoming smarter.
32 MEDIATOR: Next question.
33 KEGOR: Sally, if elected how you help me?
34 SALLY: Ask not what clan can do for you, ask what you can do for
35   clan.

1   KEGOR: *(Pause)* **OK, how I help clan?**

2   SALLY: **Well ... umm ... Don't know.**

3   TALSEE: **You just said to ask and you have no answer?**

4   SALLY: **It rhetorical.** *(SALLY goes to club TALSEE, but is stopped by*

5   *MEDIATOR.)*

6   KEGOR: **Korg, what you do for me?**

7   KORG: **I kill!**

8   TALSEE: **Kill what?**

9   KORG: **Anything I have to!**

10   TALSEE: **Could you be little more specific?**

11   KORG: **I kill sloths in garbage.**

12   TALSEE: **What if there no sloths in garbage?**

13   KORG: **I kill other nuisances!** *(KORG goes toward TALSEE with*

14   *club. MEDIATOR stops him.)*

15   TONGA: **If elected, I make sure everyone has clean teeth by**

16   **building factory to make little sticks to pick teeth with.**

17   *(TONGA hands sticks — not small — to each REPORTER.)*

18   TALSEE: **Isn't this something you invented?**

19   TONGA: **Yes, but I not making money from it.**

20   KORG: **I make sure everyone has big stick to stab tyrannosaur**

21   **with, so he not have to clean you from his teeth.**

22   TALSEE: **You think arming all citizens good idea? Violent crime**

23   **rate already higher than ever.**

24   KORG: **I kill anyone who use stick wrong way!**

25   TALSEE: **You support death penalty?**

26   KORG: **Fully!** *(KORG starts toward TALSEE. MEDIATOR stops him.)*

27   BANTEE: **What you think biggest problem facing clan as clan on**

28   **verge of first millennium?**

29   TONGA: **Big business. We need bring in wheel-making factory,**

30   **create new jobs.**

31   TALSEE: **And you would own this factory, right?**

32   TONGA: **Well, wheel my invention. I have patent pending.**

33   TALSEE: **You think that make it OK? Then you exploit working**

34   **class and don't pay enough to even afford wheel?**

35   SALLY: **I say biggest problem is gap between upper and lower**

1   class, we need new deal, I say, wheel in every cave and dodo in

2   every pot!

3   **KORG: Korg say all problems easily solved — just kill.**

4   **BANTEE: That typical caveman response, does it always have to**

5   **be violence?**

6   **KORG: Give us break, we just barely evolved from animals.**

7   **TONGA: But we have evolved, and if elected I promise to lead clan**

8   **into first millennium. If elected I promise to help evolve. I**

9   **have dream, that we all stand up straighter, smell better and**

10   **be less hairy.**

11   **TALSEE: If we less hairy, wouldn't we all freeze at night? How you**

12   **propose we keep warm?**

13   **TONGA: Fire.**

14   **TALSEE: Another of your inventions? The rich get richer? So**

15   **what we have to choose from is maniac, money grubber, or**

16   **kook.**

17   **SALLY:** *(Imitating Richard Nixon)* **I am not a kook.**

18   **MEDIATOR: OK, now time for election, ready? Vote!** *(All three*

19   *CANDIDATES club each other until only one is left.)* **Medicine**

20   **man swear you in tomorrow.**

21

22   *Curtain*

23

24

25

26

27

28

29

30

31

32

33

34

35

Needs Instruction

Premise: A new worker arrives at a job where the "old hand" shares his notes for getting the job done. Soon the new worker "passes" the experienced.

Cast: Chris — A little nervous about his first day at work.
Jamie — An old-hand at work, but still using notes to get things right.
Boss — A typical boss.

Props: Empty boxes, note books, paper or other packing material, tape, lunch bags, lunch.

Scene: A mail room, with three tables. One is filled with boxes.

1   CHRIS: Hello, I'm Chris. This is my first day on the job.

2   JAMIE: Good to meet you. I'm Jamie.

3   CHRIS: Good to meet you Jamie. I'm a little nervous. Never did

4   anything like this before. *(CHRIS sits. JAMIE pulls out*

5   *notebook. CHRIS looks curious.)*

6   JAMIE: Notes. They help me keep things straight.

7   CHRIS: You new here, too?

8   JAMIE: No. Been here three years.

9   CHRIS: And you still need notes?

10 JAMIE: Makes things easier.

11 CHRIS: I see. So where do we start?

12 JAMIE: *(Checking notes)* Let's see. First we check incoming

13 packages. *(Both move to boxes. JAMIE checks notes.)* Check for

14 any damage and look at the labels for the package's

15 destination. In-office packages go here. *(Points at table.)* And

16 the other packages go over there.

17 CHRIS: OK. *(CHRIS picks up box and moves toward appropriate*

18 *table when:)*

19 JAMIE: *(Checking notes)* Step one. *(CHRIS stops and returns to listen*

20 *to JAMIE.)* Lift box, inspect box for damage. Rotate box to

21 completely ensure that there are no signs of mishandling.

22 *(CHRIS looks at JAMIE, puzzled, as JAMIE does this deliberately.*

23 *CHRIS inspects as he moves towrd table until JAMIE says:)* Step

24 two. *(CHRIS stops short again and returns to listen to Jamie.)*

25 After examining the package and concluding that the package

26 is in satisfactory condition, check all sides of box for label to

27 determine the destination of the item.

28 CHRIS: Got it. In-office over there, and other packages over here.

29 Thanks. *(A third time CHRIS moves to place package but JAMIE*

30 *speaks, stopping him.)*

31 JAMIE: Let me check. *(Checking notes, surprised)* That's right! And

32 this is your first day?

33 CHRIS: Uh, yes.

34 JAMIE: And you say you never did anything like this before?

35 CHRIS: No.

1   JAMIE: **Wow. OK, where was I?** *(Phone rings. JAMIE begins to*
2   *panic, looking through notes.)* **Oh, umm, umm, phone ... phone.**
3   CHRIS: **You want me to answer it?**
4   JAMIE: **No thanks rookie, this is important. The boss wouldn't**
5   **like it if you messed it up.**
6   CHRIS: **All right.**
7   JAMIE: *(Finds phone in notebook.)* **Phone ... here it is.** *(Reading)*
8   **Pick up handle from cradle, hold ear piece to ear, hold mouth**
9   **piece near mouth.** *(Is holding the phone upside down)* **See**
10   **illustration next page — oh!** *(Turns it over.)* **Say hello. "Hello."**
11   *(Checking notes constantly during conversation)* **Yes, Mr.**
12   **Murphy ... a package for you ... umm. Can you hold?** *(Reads,*
13   *pushes button, then becomes confused about what to do with the*
14   *phone after pushing hold button.)* **This isn't very clear.**
15   CHRIS: **Just set it down.**
16   JAMIE: *(Still confused. Looks around, checks notes again, then says:)*
17   **I'll read the instructions and you do them, OK?**
18   CHRIS: **I guess.**
19   JAMIE: **Good.** *(Reading)* **Step one: check each package label for**
20   **name of inquirer.**
21   CHRIS: **Mr. Murphy's package is right here.**
22   JAMIE: **OK, good job.** *(Checks notes. Pushes button.)* **Hello ... Mr.**
23   **Murphy? Your package is here ... you're welcome ... good-**
24   **bye.** *(Checks notes again. Hangs up receiver.)* **OK, where was I?**
25   CHRIS: **Checking the label.**
26   JAMIE: **Right. OK. Observe the label.** *(Reading label)* **Mr. Klink in**
27   **Accounting. That would be in-office, so it would go here.**
28   **Alrighty then. One down. We're cookin' with gas now.**
29   CHRIS: *(Sarcastically, starts to question JAMIE's experience.)* **Yeah,**
30   **cookin'.**
31   JAMIE: **Next.** *(Reading)* **Repeat steps one and two until all**
32   **packages are distributed.** *(Checking notes)* **Step one. Lift box,**
33   **inspect box for damage. Rotate box to completely ensure that**
34   **there are no signs of mishandling.** *(CHRIS finishes other boxes*
35   *while JAMIE messes with his second.)* **Step two. After**

1	examining the package and concluding that the package is in
2	satisfactory condition, check all sides of box for label to
3	determine the destination of the item. *(JAMIE checks box but*
4	*does not find label. Begins to panic.)* **Oh, my heavens! Oh, great**
5	**gravy from above! Sheeshcabob!**
6	CHRIS: **What's the matter?**
7	JAMIE: **There's no label on this one! What do I do? What do I**
8	**do?!?!**
9	CHRIS: **Settle down. Let me see.** *(CHRIS takes box and examines it.*
10	*Finds label on the bottom.)* **It's right here. This one goes to**
11	**purchasing.**
12	JAMIE: *(Frustrated)* **On the bottom? No wonder I didn't see it.**
13	**Who in their right mind would think of looking on the**
14	**bottom?**
15	CHRIS: **Are you serious?**
16	JAMIE: *(Referring to his notes)* **It clearly says here to check all the**
17	**sides, nothing about the bottom.**
18	CHRIS: **The bottom is a side.**
19	JAMIE: **I'll make a note of that.** *(JAMIE writes in notebook.)*
20	CHRIS: **Forget it. What's next?**
21	JAMIE: **Let me check my notes.**
22	CHRIS: **Oh, brother.**
23	JAMIE: *(Checks notes. Reads.)* **After sorting incoming packages,**
24	**prepare outgoing items for shipping. Step one, open empty**
25	**box.** *(Follows instruction.)* **Step two, place item to be shipped in**
26	**box.** *(Follows instruction.)* **Step three, secure item with packing**
27	**material.** *(Follows instruction.)* **Step four, close box and adhere**
28	**packaging tape to lid flaps to prevent the box opening during**
29	**shipping.** *(JAMIE grabs tape while CHRIS continues packing.)*
30	**Step one, locate the end of tape on the exterior of tape roll.**
31	*(Follows instruction.)* **Step two, with thumb and forefinger,**
32	**grasp the end and pull away from roll until desired length is**
33	**established.** *(Follows instruction.)* **Step three, tear tape along**
34	**base of extended strip to remove tape portion from roll.**
35	*(CHRIS loses patience, grabs tape from JAMIE, rips a piece and*

1   *sticks it to JAMIE's box. JAMIE examines the job, checking it to*
2   *his notes, feels a tad threatened when he realizes it's done right.)*
3   **Show off.**
4   **CHRIS: What? It's just tape on a box. I learned that when I was a**
5   **kid.**
6   **JAMIE: I thought you said you didn't have any experience at ... Oh,**
7   **hold on.** *(JAMIE checks notes.)* **Excuse me, I have to go to the**
8   **bathroom.** *(JAMIE sets down his notebook, then picks up a*
9   *different one, and exits. CHRIS looks through JAMIE's notebook,*
10   *erases something and laughs. JAMIE returns, and whistle sounds.)*
11   **CHRIS: What's that?**
12   **JAMIE:** *(Checks notes.)* **That's the lunch whistle, we can stop and**
13   **eat.**
14   **CHRIS: Great I'm starving.** *(Both grab lunch bags.)*
15   **JAMIE: Step one, unroll top of bag.** *(Follows instruction.)* **Step two,**
16   **remove food items and place them on flat surface.** *(Follows*
17   *instruction.)* **Step three, unfold napkin and spread out on flat**
18   **surface.** *(CHRIS finally totally frustrated, grabs the notebook and*
19   *tears it up.)*
20   **CHRIS: Just eat your lunch!**
21   **JAMIE: But my notes!**
22   **CHRIS: Eat!** *(JAMIE tries to put back together the pieces of the notes,*
23   *but can't. He starts to mope.)* **Just eat!** *(JAMIE attempts to eat*
24   *without his notes but to no avail, smashing his sandwich in his*
25   *face, spilling his drink, etc. He gets frustrated. Enter BOSS.)*
26   **BOSS: What's going on here?**
27   **JAMIE: He tore up my notebook!**
28   **BOSS: Is this true?**
29   **CHRIS: It's ridiculous. He needed notes for everything.**
30   **BOSS:** *(Pulls out notebook and checks it. Turns to CHRIS.)* **You're**
31   **fired.** *(CHRIS, astounded, exits. BOSS sees JAMIE is distraught,*
32   *checks his notes.)* **Don't worry, we'll find a good one some day.**
33   *(Checks notebook again and pats JAMIE on back three times.)*
34
35   *Curtain*

New Neighbors

Premise: New neighbors are coming over to visit, but can't stay. Sounds simple, until the skit is run a second time except faster, and then a third time even faster. Just watch the chaos develop.

Cast: Director — Director of the production.

Gwen — Wants to be friendly to the new couple who just moved in.

Rodney — Gwen's husband, would rather not spend time with the new people.

George — New neighbor and taxidermist. A bit eccentric.

Vita — New neighbor and wife of George. Also a bit eccentric.

Props: Remote control, deck of cards, card table, four cups, tray with cheese and crackers, two coats, phone.

Scene: Director addresses audience before curtain is pulled.

1   DIRECTOR: Excuse me ladies and gentlemen. We have such a
2   wonderful audience tonight, and it seems we have been
3   making really good time on our show, so I was wondering if I
4   could ask you for a favor. You see we were working on this
5   sketch that we thought was good, but we're not sure. We were
6   hoping to test it in front of a live audience to get their reaction.
7   Since we have some extra time I thought it might be OK to try
8   this sketch. So if you would be so kind as to bear with us, we'll
9   be getting back to our show in just a minute right after *The*
10   *New Neighbors. (Curtain opens to a living room. RODNEY is*
11   *watching television Stage Right. Four chairs and a card table not*
12   *yet set up are Stage Left. Enter GWEN Stage Left with a shirt in*
13   *her hand approaching RODNEY.)*
14 GWEN: Honey? Aren't you ready yet? George and Vita will be
15   here any minute now.
16 RODNEY: Next commercial.
17 GWEN: HBO has no commercials, sweetie. *(GWEN takes remote*
18   *from RODNEY and shuts off TV.)* And besides, you've been
19   saying that for the last half hour. *(Hands RODNEY a shirt.)*
20   Now. Please, get ready. *(Notices table.)* You haven't even set up
21   the table yet. You remember what it was like when we first
22   moved here? Not knowing a soul?
23 RODNEY: *(Begins to set up card table.)* Sometimes I think we were
24   better off.
25 GWEN: I'd just like to show the Wallaces that this is a great place
26   to live.
27 RODNEY: What did you say he does?
28 GWEN: He's a taxidermist.
29 RODNEY: He stuffs animals for a living?
30 GWEN: That's what Vita said. *(Doorbell rings.)* There they are. Now,
31   please, don't embarrass me. *(GWEN moves to answer door.)*
32 RODNEY: *(Hikes his pants up and picks nose.)* Wouldn't think of it.
33   *(GEORGE and VITA enter, GEORGE with hiked-up pants and*
34   *picking nose like RODNEY.)*
35 GWEN: Hello. Come in.

1   **VITA: Hello, Gwen. This is my husband George.**

2   **GWEN:** *(Taking coats)* **So glad to finally meet you George. This is**

3   **my husband ...** *(Turns and sees RODNEY picking nose.)* **Rod!**

4   *(VITA simultaneously turns, sees GEORGE, and smacks him.*

5   *Both HUSBANDS straighten up.)* **This is my husband Rodney.**

6   **VITA: Glad to meet you.** *(HUSBANDS go to shake hands.)*

7   **RODNEY: So, you mount dead animals for a living, huh?**

8   **GWEN:** *(Slaps RODNEY.)* **Rod, behave.**

9   **GEORGE: Yes, I'm a taxidermist. It's actually a very rewarding**

10   **career.**

11   **GWEN: We'll be playing cards over here. Can I get anybody**

12   **something to drink?**

13   **RODNEY: I'll take a brew.**

14   **GWEN:** *(Glares at RODNEY.)* **I meant our guests, honey.** *(To*

15   *GEORGE and VITA)* **Anything?**

16   **VITA: Oh, I'll have something diet.**

17   **GEORGE: Do you have any kiwi nectar?**

18   **GWEN: Uh, no.**

19   **GEORGE: Anything carbonated would be great.**

20   **GWEN: All right. Honey, would you help me with the drinks and**

21   **the cheese plate please?**

22   **RODNEY: Sure.** *(RODNEY and GWEN exit. GEORGE and VITA start*

23   *scavenging through the room. RODNEY and GWEN enter.*

24   *GEORGE and VITA quickly sit.)*

25   **GWEN: Here we are, one something diet and one carbonated**

26   **anything.** *(All sit, begin to play cards.)*

27   **RODNEY: George, would you like to deal first?**

28   **GEORGE: Sure.** *(GEORGE does some dramatic, exaggerated deal*

29   *movements. GWEN offers cheese plate.)*

30   **GWEN: Cheese and crackers?**

31   **GEORGE: Do you have any raspberry sherbet?**

32   **GWEN: Uh, no.**

33   **GEORGE: Oh well, cheese would be fine.** *(GEORGE takes a piece.)*

34   **GWEN: Vita?**

35   **VITA: I'll have just a taste.** *(Puts some in her mouth, then a few in her*

1   *purse and pockets. Phone rings. GWEN moves over to answer the*
2   *phone.)*
3   **GWEN: Hello? Yes, just a minute. George it's for you.**
4   **GEORGE:** *(Moves to phone.)* **Hello ... You don't say ... Down by**
5   **McGafferty's? Yes, I know where that is ... OK. Thanks.**
6   *(Hangs up.)* **Sorry folks. Gotta run. Just got a call on a fresh**
7   **hit down on the four lane. Let's go Vita.**
8   **GWEN: We'll, I'm sorry you couldn't stay.** *(To RODNEY)* **Honey,**
9   **would you get their coats please?** *(RODNEY leaves to get*
10   *coats.)* **Maybe we can try again next week?**
11   **VITA: That would be great.** *(RODNEY returns with coats.)*
12   **GEORGE: We'll have you over to our place next time. Nice to meet**
13   **you Rodney. So long folks.**
14   **GWEN: Bye, bye.**
15   **VITA: Bye.** *(GEORGE and VITA exit.)*
16   **GWEN: They seem like nice people.** *(RODNEY looks at watch, grabs*
17   TV Guide *and remote. Plunks down in front of TV.)* **Nice people.**
18   *(GWEN begins to straighten up. DIRECTOR enters. Note: As the*
19   *DIRECTOR gives the following speech, he can be helping reset*
20   *the scene to the beginning [unfolding the table, gathering cards,*
21   *etc.]. The ACTORS can also help, but must play along like*
22   *repeating the scene isn't planned. Even asking, "You want us to*
23   *do it faster?")*
24   **DIRECTOR:** *(To audience)* **I'm sorry. I thought this was better**
25   **than that and I think it is, I think we can do it better. It just**
26   **needs more energy, a quicker pace. Please, bear with us, we're**
27   **going to try this again only faster this time.** *(To CAST)* **Pick up**
28   **the pace.** *(To audience)* **They're really good at this.** *(The scene*
29   *now repeats itself, with the exact dialog but with the ACTORS*
30   *doing everything faster. For example, GWEN begins by coming in*
31   *faster [although not running yet, save that for the third time],*
32   *throwing the shirt at RODNEY sooner, etc. GEORGE and VITA*
33   *enter taking coats off, and check out the house a little faster. When*
34   *scene finishes, DIRECTOR again asks the cast to repeat the scene*
35   *only faster.)*

1   **GWEN: Honey? Aren't you ready yet? George and Vita will be**
2   **here any minute now.**
3   **RODNEY: Next commercial.**
4   **GWEN: HBO has no commercials, sweetie.** *(GWEN takes remote*
5   *from RODNEY and shuts off TV.)* **And besides, you've been**
6   **saying that for the last half hour.** *(Hands RODNEY a shirt.)*
7   **Now. Please, get ready.** *(Notices table.)* **You haven't even set up**
8   **the table yet. You remember what it was like when we first**
9   **moved here? Not knowing a soul?**
10   **RODNEY:** *(Begins to set up card table.)* **Sometimes I think we were**
11   **better off.**
12   **GWEN: I'd just like to show the Wallaces that this is a great place**
13   **to live.**
14   **RODNEY: What did you say he does?**
15   **GWEN: He's a taxidermist.**
16   **RODNEY: He stuffs animals for a living?**
17   **GWEN: That's what Vita said.** *(Doorbell rings.)* **There they are. Now,**
18   **please, don't embarrass me.** *(GWEN moves to answer door.)*
19   **RODNEY:** *(Hikes his pants up and picks nose.)* **Wouldn't think of it.**
20   *(GEORGE and VITA enter, GEORGE with hiked-up pants and*
21   *picking nose like RODNEY.)*
22   **GWEN: Hello. Come in.**
23   **VITA: Hello, Gwen. This is my husband George.**
24   **GWEN:** *(Taking coats)* **So glad to finally meet you George. This is**
25   **my husband ...** *(Turns and sees RODNEY picking nose.)* **Rod!**
26   *(VITA simultaneously turns, sees GEORGE, and smacks him.*
27   *Both HUSBANDS straighten up.)* **This is my husband Rodney.**
28   **VITA: Glad to meet you.** *(HUSBANDS go to shake hands.)*
29   **RODNEY: So, you mount dead animals for a living, huh?**
30   **GWEN:** *(Slaps RODNEY.)* **Rod, behave.**
31   **GEORGE: Yes, I'm a taxidermist. It's actually a very rewarding**
32   **career.**
33   **GWEN: We'll be playing cards over here. Can I get anybody**
34   **something to drink?**
35   **RODNEY: I'll take a brew.**

1   GWEN: *(Glares at RODNEY.)* **I meant our guests, honey.** *(To*
2   *GEORGE and VITA)* **Anything?**
3   VITA: **Oh, I'll have something diet.**
4   GEORGE: **Do you have any kiwi nectar?**
5   GWEN: **Uh, no.**
6   GEORGE: **Anything carbonated would be great.**
7   GWEN: **All right. Honey, would you help me with the drinks and**
8   **the cheese plate please?**
9   RODNEY: **Sure.** *(RODNEY and GWEN exit. GEORGE and VITA*
10   *start scavenging through the room. RODNEY and GWEN enter.*
11   *GEORGE and VITA quickly sit.)*
12   GWEN: **Here we are, one something diet and one carbonated**
13   **anything.** *(All sit, begin to play cards.)*
14   RODNEY: **George, would you like to deal first?**
15   GEORGE: **Sure.** *(GEORGE does some dramatic, exaggerated deal*
16   *movements. GWEN offers cheese plate.)*
17   GWEN: **Cheese and crackers?**
18   GEORGE: **Do you have any raspberry sherbet?**
19   GWEN: **Uh, no.**
20   GEORGE: **Oh well, cheese would be fine.** *(GEORGE takes a piece.)*
21   GWEN: **Vita?**
22   VITA: **I'll have just a taste.** *(Puts some in her mouth, then a few in*
23   *her purse and pockets. Phone rings. GWEN moves over to answer*
24   *the phone.)*
25   GWEN: **Hello? Yes, just a minute. George it's for you.**
26   GEORGE: *(Moves to phone.)* **Hello ... You don't say ... Down by**
27   **McGafferty's? Yes, I know where that is ... OK. Thanks.**
28   *(Hangs up.)* **Sorry folks. Gotta run. Just got a call on a fresh**
29   **hit down on the four lane. Let's go Vita.**
30   GWEN: **We'll, I'm sorry you couldn't stay.** *(To RODNEY)* **Honey,**
31   **would you get their coats please?** *(RODNEY leaves to get*
32   *coats.)* **Maybe we can try again next week?**
33   VITA: **That would be great.** *(RODNEY returns with coats.)*
34   GEORGE: **We'll have you over to our place next time. Nice to meet**
35   **you Rodney. So long folks.**

1 **GWEN: Bye, bye.**
2 **VITA: Bye.** *(GEORGE and VITA exit.)*
3 **GWEN: They seem like nice people.** *(RODNEY looks at watch, grabs*
4 TV Guide *and remote. Plunks down in front of TV.)* **Nice people.**
5 *(GWEN begins to straighten up. DIRECTOR enters again. Note:*
6 *As the DIRECTOR gives the following speech, he again can be*
7 *helping reset the scene to the beginning [unfolding the table,*
8 *gathering cards, etc.]. The ACTORS can also help, but must play*
9 *along like repeating the scene isn't planned. Even asking, "You*
10 *want us to do it faster?")*
11 **DIRECTOR:** *(To audience)* **I'm sorry. I still thought this was better**
12 **than that. I think we can do it better. It just needs more**
13 **energy, a quicker pace. Please, bear with us, we're going to try**
14 **this once again only faster this time.** *(To CAST)* **Pick up the**
15 **pace.** *(To audience)* **They're really good at this.** *(The scene now*
16 *repeats itself again, but with the ACTORS doing everything faster.*
17 *For example, GWEN begins by running in, throwing the shirt at*
18 *RODNEY sooner, etc. GEORGE and VITA enter taking coats off,*
19 *and check out the house even faster. Note: The following is done*
20 *with as much chaos as possible. Characters should be almost*
21 *yelling to add to the confusion and frantic pace.)*
22 **GWEN:** *(Enters running.)* **Honey? Get ready!** *(Throws shirt at*
23 *RODNEY.)*
24 **RODNEY: Commercial.**
25 **GWEN: HBO!** *(GWEN takes remote from RODNEY and shuts off TV.)*
26 **Set up the table!**
27 **RODNEY:** *(Begins to set up card table.)* **He stuffs animals?**
28 **GWEN: That's what Vita said.** *(Doorbell rings.)* **Don't embarrass**
29 **me.** *(GWEN begins toward door as VITA and GEORGE enter.)*
30 **RODNEY and GEORGE:** *(Picking noses)* **Duh!** *(VITA and GEORGE*
31 *throw coats at RODNEY. WIVES hit their HUSBANDS.)*
32 **GWEN: Drink?**
33 **RODNEY: Brew!**
34 **GWEN: Guests!**
35 **VITA: Something diet.**

1   **GEORGE: Got kiwi nectar?**
2   **GWEN: No.** *(GWEN and RODNEY exits. GEORGE and VITA start*
3   *scavenging through the room. RODNEY and GWEN enter again*
4   *almost immediately. GEORGE and VITA sit.)* **Here.** *(Gives drinks*
5   *to GEORGE and VITA. ALL sit.)*
6   **RODNEY:** *(To GEORGE)* **You deal.**
7   **GEORGE: Sure.** *(GEORGE throws cards around. GWEN offers*
8   *cheese plate.)*
9   **GWEN: Cheese and crackers?** *(GWEN throws plate toward VITA.*
10   *VITA grabs crackers stuffs them in her mouth, in her purse and*
11   *dumps plate down shirt. Phone rings. GWEN picks up phone.)*
12   **George.** *(Throws phone at GEORGE.)*
13   **GEORGE: Thanks.** *(Hangs up.)* **Gotta run.**
14   **GWEN:** *(To RODNEY)* **Honey, coats?** *(RODNEY grabs coats Off-*
15   *stage and throws across to GEORGE and VITA.)*
16   **GEORGE: Our place.**
17   **VITA: Bye.** *(GEORGE and VITA exit.)*
18   **GWEN: Nice people.**
19   **RODNEY:** *(Jumps in seat.)* **Nice people.** *(DIRECTOR enters.)*
20   **DIRECTOR: Perfect.**
21
22   *Curtain*
23
24
25
26
27
28
29
30
31
32
33
34
35

PBS Plus

Premise: Public television is having trouble paying its bills. Cutbacks are being made even as the telethon is being aired. Shows are combined and the telethon hosts are becoming more distraught at the lack of support.

Cast: Molly — Telethon host.
Brink — Telethon host.
Cook — Host of the Cajun Cook public television show.
George — Host of a public television show.
Galaxy Man — Host of a public television show.
Mr. Rogers — Host of a public television show.
Cookie Monster — Host of a public television show.
Antique Collector — Host of a public television show.

Props: WBEG mug, plate with shrimp, sander, gun, phone.

Scene: Brink and Molly are in front of the curtain running a public television telethon.

1   BRINK: ... and for those of you that donate ten dollars or more,
2   we are offering one of these fine WBEG mugs. So, please, give
3   us a call!
4   MOLLY: That's right folks. Without your pledges we will not be
5   able to continue to bring you fine quality entertainment like
6   the show we're watching today.
7   BRINK: We need these phones ringing. Public television depends
8   on you, the public, to keep us alive, and well, unfortunately,
9   we here at WBEG already had to make some cut backs.
10 MOLLY: That's right, Brink. We like to call them programming
11   enhancements. Because of the high cost of producing so many
12   high quality programs, we here at WBEG found it necessary
13   to combine a few of the shows.
14 BRINK: Please, give us a call. *(Pause, wait for phone to ring)* I guess
15   we'll be returning you now to our program.
16 MOLLY: So please sit back and enjoy *This Old Cajun Cook.*
17   *(Curtain opens to COOK and GEORGE in a kitchen.)*
18 COOK: Thank you for joining us today for *This Old Cajun Cook.*
19   Today we will be preparing our famous shrimp stuffed with
20   crab ...
21 GEORGE: ... and installing the new Econoline Electromaster 520
22   Range and Indoor Grill.
23 COOK: So to begin, we have to bring four cups of water to a boil.
24 GEORGE: That's right Remi, and the Electromaster 520 is perfect
25   for the job. It's the most efficient stove on the market and will
26   help cut costs in the final production. That always looks good
27   on the final invoice.
28 COOK: Thanks, George. While we're waiting for you to install the
29   Electromaster 520 so we can boil our water, we will carefully
30   peel the shrimp.
31 GEORGE: Here, let me get that. *(GEORGE picks up a sander.)* The
32   new Sandmaster 200 strips and peels paints and varnishes
33   faster and more efficiently than any of the competitors, but be
34   sure to wear your safety goggles.
35 COOK: You are always thinking of safety, George.

1   GEORGE: Well you have to. OSHA has been bearing down.

2   *(GEORGE hits the shrimp with the sander and they spray across*

3   *the room.)*

4   COOK: I see. Well, since it seems I'm a little short on shrimp,

5   we're going to have to improvise. Let's see what I have in the

6   refrigerator. *(Opens refrigerator.)* Whew! What is that smell?

7   Hey! Everything is spoiled. There's no power here.

8   GEORGE: That's right, Remi. Safety first. Be sure to shut off all

9   breakers while the preliminary wiring is done.

10   COOK: Great! Now what?

11   GEORGE: Now we drill a one-and-a-half inch bore hole for the

12   electrical lead. *(Begins drilling, Lights fade On-stage and come*

13   *up on telethon.)*

14   MOLLY: Unfortunately, we are still not getting any calls. We here

15   at WBEG rely on your pledges to keep us going.

16   BRINK: That's right, Molly. Please, people! For crying out loud.

17   Give us a call. Fifty dollars, ten dollars, or even a nickel! Is

18   that too much to ask? I'll tell you what. Anyone with a fifty-

19   dollar or more pledge, I will personally wash your car.

20   MOLLY: *(Shocked)* Well … you heard him, folks. A car wash for a

21   pledge of fifty dollars or more.

22   BRINK: So get off your fat, lazy butts and give us a call.

23   MOLLY: *(To BRINK)* Brink! *(To audience)* We now return you to

24   our program, *This Old Cajun Neighborhood and Galaxy Show.*

25   *(Lights go down on telethon and up On-stage.)*

26   GEORGE: Now, we can turn the power back on.

27   COOK: *(COOK gets shocked.)* Yeeeooooww! *(COOK falls to ground.)*

28   GEORGE: Remi? Are you OK?

29   COOK: I see stars. *(GALAXY MAN enters.)*

30   GALAXY MAN: That would be Orion's Belt. And if you look up

31   into the eastern night sky, Jupiter shines bright as the lunar

32   phase begins. *(MR. ROGERS enters.)*

33   MR. ROGERS: Hello, neighbors.

34   GALAXY MAN and GEORGE: Hello, Fred!

35   MR. ROGERS: It is so wonderful to join you today. I understood

1   that you were going to be preparing Cajun today, so I took the
2   trolley to Chef Brocket's, and he made a special secret crab
3   meat stuffing for you.
4 GALAXY MAN: And Cancer, the crab, twinkles in the southwest,
5   near Delphi's Nebula.
6 MR. ROGERS: That's a fun word. Can you say that boys and
7   girls? *(Slowly)* Nebula. Very good. *(To GEORGE)* Do you know
8   what that means?
9 GEORGE: It means any of many immense bodies of highly
10   rarefied gas or dust in interstellar space.
11 MR. ROGERS: That's right. You were always very bright. *(To*
12   *audience)* You are special, too. *(Exits. Lights down On-stage, up*
13   *on telethon.)*
14 MOLLY: We did get a pledge over the last segment.
15 BRINK: Really?
16 MOLLY: That's right. Let's go to the Pledge Meter. The new
17   pledge brings our grand total to ... one dollar and sixteen
18   cents.
19 BRINK: *(Getting irate.)* One dollar and sixteen cents? One dollar
20   and sixteen cents!? You're telling me that you people out there
21   can't spare more than one dollar and sixteen cents?
22 MOLLY: Brink!
23 BRINK: A lousy dollar and sixteen cents. You people are the worst
24   excuse for a public that I have ever seen. Un-freaken-believable!
25 MOLLY: *Brink?*
26 BRINK: An entire bunch of low-lifes, probably watching reruns of
27   *Friends*, who don't care if we're on the air or not!
28 MOLLY: Brink. Please! I'm sure our watchers realize that we need
29   their support.
30 BRINK: Bunch of cheapskates!
31 MOLLY: Our goal is to continue to air the fine programs that
32   you're accustomed to seeing here on WBEG.
33 BRINK: So just sit back and enjoy the free show. Jerks.
34 MOLLY: We now return you to *This Old Cajun Antique and Galaxy*
35   *Report. (Lights down on telethon, up On-stage.)*

1   **GALAXY MAN:** *(Handing telescope to ANTIQUE)* **It used to be my**
2   **grandfather's.**
3   **ANTIQUE COLLECTOR: Mint condition, one to three thousand**
4   **power lens, Heinzfeld, Inc. Could be worth one hundred and**
5   **twenty thousand dollars.**
6   **GALAXY MAN: Really?**
7   **ANTIQUE COLLECTOR: Could be. If it didn't say made in Japan**
8   **here on the stem.**
9   **COOK: Could everyone please, just clear out so I can finish my**
10   **orange custard cookies?** *(COOKIE MONSTER enters.)*
11   **COOKIE MONSTER: Cookie!**
12   **COOK: That's it. I'm out of here.**
13   **GALAXY MAN: Remember, keep looking up.** *(Lights down On-*
14   *stage, up on telethon)*
15   **BRINK:** *(BRINK is now holding MOLLY hostage.)* **We need pledges!**
16   **If we don't get them, then she gets it! I'm serious here, if this**
17   **phone doesn't ring soon …** *(Phone rings.)* **Hello?**
18   **VOICE: Hello. Brink?**
19   **BRINK: Yeah.**
20   **VOICE: You guys are cool.**
21   **BRINK: Huh?**
22   **VOICE: This is better than cable. Action. Gunplay. I'll donate fifty**
23   **dollars.**
24   **BRINK: Thanks.** *(Takes the actors On-stage hostage.)* **More pledges**
25   **or they all get it!** *(Phone rings.)* **Hello?**
26   **VOICE: You guys are great. I'll pledge a hundred dollars.**
27
28   *Curtain*
29
30
31
32
33
34
35

Penny for Your Thoughts

Premise: A man on his lunch break meets a strange man who won't leave him alone until he gets some things off his chest.

Cast: Ted — Strange man, wants to talk.
Brent — Business man on his lunch break, just wants to be left alone.
Chris — Ted's second victim.

Props: Newspaper, two pennies, book.

Scene: Ted is sitting on a park bench. Brent enters with a newspaper and sits.

1 TED: Hello.

2 BRENT: Hi.

3 TED: Beautiful day, isn't it?

4 BRENT: Yep. *(BRENT begins to read paper. Pause)*

5 TED: Penny for your thoughts.

6 BRENT: Pardon me?

7 TED: I said, penny for your thoughts. You look down. Just curious
8   what's bothering you.

9 BRENT: Nothing's bothering me. Thanks.

10 TED: You sure?

11 BRENT: I'm sure. *(BRENT goes back to reading.)*

12 TED: You know what they say?

13 BRENT: Excuse me?

14 TED: What they say. You know. Sometimes it's easier to talk to a
15   complete stranger.

16 BRENT: Look buddy. No offense, but there's nothing wrong, and
17   even if there was, I wouldn't want to talk about it.

18 TED: So, there is something bothering you?

19 BRENT: No. Nothing's bothering me. Now, please if you don't
20   mind, I'd like to get back to my paper.

21 TED: I'm sorry, go right ahead. *(Pause)* You'd feel a lot better
22   though, *(BRENT gives TED a dirty look)* ... if you got it off your
23   chest. You know, purge yourself.

24 BRENT: I've got nothing to purge. Look, I'm just on my lunch
25   break and figured I'd get out and catch a breath of fresh air.

26 TED: Co-workers getting to you, huh?

27 BRENT: No.

28 TED: That's OK. I mean, nobody gets along with everybody.

29 BRENT: I get along with my co-workers just fine. I'm just enjoying
30   the beautiful day. Now, please ...

31 TED: Sure. I'm sorry. *(Pause)* Then it's your family?

32 BRENT: What?

33 TED: Been pretty busy lately, haven't gotten around to calling your
34   mom. Finally get around to it and she lets you hear all about
35   it. Hey, I have a mom too, you know.

1   BRENT: You don't say. Sorry to disappoint you but my mother
2   and I are doing great. Not that it's any business of yours. My
3   dad is fine, my sister, her husband, their kids. Everybody is
4   doing just great. Now please, can I get back to my paper?
5   TED: Sure. Be my guest. *(Pause)* Women ... can't live with 'em,
6   can't shoot 'em.
7   BRENT: Would you please!
8   TED: They confuse the living daylights out of me, too. Right when
9   you think you got them figured out, bang-zowee, back to
10   square one.
11   BRENT: I don't have women problems either! I'm not even dating
12   anyone right now.
13   TED: Oh, don't worry, you'll find someone.
14   BRENT: I don't want to find someone. I'm happy with the way
15   things are. I would just really appreciate it if you'd let me
16   finish my paper before my lunch hour is up. Could you do that
17   for me? Huh?
18   TED: You betcha. You go ahead and read your paper. *(Pause)* But
19   hiding from the world won't solve your problems.
20   BRENT: I have no problems! None! I'm as content as anyone can be.
21   TED: Under your circumstances.
22   BRENT: Under any circumstances. I'm a very happy person with
23   a life I'm very satisfied with.
24   TED: Really?
25   BRENT: Really!
26   TED: And nothing's bothering you?
27   BRENT: Nothing. *(Pause)*
28   TED: You're sure?
29   BRENT: I'm sure. *(BRENT looks for acknowledgment and a signal to*
30   *get back to reading the paper. TED nods. After a moment TED*
31   *pulls out a penny and tosses it on the ground.)*
32   TED: Whoops. How clumsy of me. I dropped a penny. *(BRENT*
33   *notices the penny, slowly moves to pick it up, snatches penny.)*
34   BRENT: *(Suddenly)* You were right, OK? My boss is a real moron
35   and I should have got that promotion instead of Gibson, but

1   no. Gibson had his nose stuck so far up the boss's butt. Then,
2   I get home yesterday to four messages on the machine from
3   *dear old Mom* telling me how it's been a whole whopping three
4   days since I called her last. What? I don't have a life of my
5   own? And get off my back already about settling down and
6   grandchildren. It's not easy finding the right person. It's not
7   like I don't want to. And besides, I can't even afford to treat
8   myself to a night out every once in a while, let alone someone
9   else. My car needs brakes, I lost my wallet, I've had a
10   migraine all morning, I have a root canal appointment
11   tomorrow at three. My dog pooped on the rug this morning
12   and I found out by stepping in it and tracking it all through
13   the house. Then, I figure I'd take a little break from this lousy
14   life I'm leading to go to the park for a breath of fresh air and
15   some joker insists on playing my shrink. *(Pause)* Well there
16   you go, doc, I hope you're happy and my life is all you thought
17   it wasn't. Now, if you don't mind, I have five minutes to finish
18   my paper. *(BRENT goes back to reading but keeps glancing at*
19   *TED, finally giving in.)*
20 **BRENT:** What?
21 **TED:** Nothing.
22 **BRENT:** *What?!* *(TED holds out his hand, BRENT deposits penny.*
23   *TED continues to hold out his hand. Frustrated, BRENT digs for*
24   *another penny.)*
25 **TED:** I was just thinking how much better you must feel getting all
26   that off your chest.
27 **BRENT:** *(Sarcastically)* Yeah, so much better. *(BRENT storms off.*
28   *CHRIS enters and sits, begins to read book.)*
29 **TED:** Penny for your thoughts.
30 **CHRIS:** Pardon me?
31
32   *Curtain*
33
34
35

Pirate Training

Premise: A new baseball player has just come over from the Pirates. Not from Pittsburgh, but from the Caribbean.

Cast: Owner — Worried about the team's finances.
Coach — A grizzled baseball veteran.
Brown Beard — A pirate, not from Pittsburgh, complete with eye patch and hook.
Trainer — Has to train Brown Beard to play ball.

Props: Two gloves, bag with bats, ball, trophy, hot dog vending box, and hot dogs.

Costumes: Baseball uniform, pirate's outfit.

Scene: Coach and Owner are standing in locker room.

1	OWNER: I just can't do it. We aren't selling tickets like we used to
2	and we certainly can't afford any more bad press.
3	COACH: That flagpole thing?
4	OWNER: The flagpole thing. What was he doing up there anyway?
5	COACH: He said it's some kind of tradition where he comes from.
6	OWNER: That's just great. Not only can't he play ball, he has a
7	background for climbing flagpoles?
8	COACH: I think he was trying to get the flag.
9	OWNER: What's he want that for?
10	COACH: Tradition.
11	OWNER: I've been thinking about this and as much as I like
12	Brown Beard, I'm just going to have to let him go. He's
13	costing us way too much for what he's producing.
14	COACH: But the kid's got so much potential.
15	OWNER: Well potential isn't making this franchise any stronger
16	or richer. I realize you're the one that discovered him, but my
17	hands are tied. What can I do? The fans want a winning team.
18	I figure we'll take the contract option and trade him for two
19	minors. I hear there's a player down in Phoenix who's pretty
20	hot now. Maybe we can ...
21	COACH: Give me one more chance. I got a new trainer coming in
22	to work with the kid this afternoon.
23	OWNER: All right. But this is it. If he doesn't shine like MVP
24	material in Friday's game, we might even have to reconsider
25	our coaching staff. Last chance. You're up at bat. Don't whiff.
26	*(OWNER exits.)*
27	COACH: Great! Now what? Three days? Turn the kid around in
28	three days. *(TRAINER enters.)*
29	TRAINER: I'm looking for coach Bartlet?
30	COACH: That's me.
31	TRAINER: I'm Dorin Gil, the trainer you sent for.
32	COACH: Oh, great! It's good to see you. I sure hope you can help us.
33	TRAINER: Trust me. I worked with all the greats. I could train a
34	kindergarten class to win the pennant.
35	COACH: This might be a little tougher. *(To Off-stage)* Brown Beard,

1   **get in here!** *(To TRAINER)* **This guy just came from the pirates'**
2   **organization.**
3 **TRAINER: Pittsburgh?**
4 **COACH: No, Caribbean.** *(BROWN BEARD enters.)*
5 **BROWN BEARD: Yo, coach?**
6 **COACH: Listen Brown Beard, you know I think you've got great**
7   **potential, but lately …**
8 **BROWN BEARD: Yeah. Been sailin' in circles at half-mast lately.**
9   **But the north wind, she's about to catch. There be land on the**
10   **horizon. Me voyage won't last much longer, eh?**
11 **COACH: Can't last any longer. They're looking to trade ya.**
12 **BROWN BEARD: Trade me?**
13 **COACH: Seems there's a clause in your contract that let's them**
14   **trade you before you play ten games.**
15 **BROWN BEARD: Trade me?**
16 **COACH: And since Friday is game nine, they want to exercise that**
17   **option unless we show 'em your stuff, and show it fast.**
18 **BROWN BEARD: Trade me? Those scurvy dogs. I should cut**
19   **their tongues out and use 'em for bait.**
20 **COACH: Brown Beard listen, no more ruckus. That flagpole**
21   **incident is what started this …**
22 **BROWN BEARD: But I had to get that flag …**
23 **COACH: I know, I know, tradition. But look, we got one more**
24   **chance. Either you shape up or they're going to ship you out.**
25 **BROWN BEARD: Aye, let 'em try. I'll gut 'em like filet.**
26 **COACH: You're not going to gut anyone. Listen up, this is Dorin**
27   **Gil. He's going to work with you. You got that?**
28 **BROWN BEARD: Aye, who we playing Friday?**
29 **COACH: The Marlins.**
30 **BROWN BEARD: Aargh? I'll be guttin' them!**
31 **COACH:** *No!* **Listen, I want you to do exactly what Gil tells you to**
32   **do. I'll see you both on the field at six.** *(COACH exits.)*
33 **BROWN BEARD: Gil, eh?**
34 **TRAINER: That's right. Now, let's see what we got to work with.**
35 **BROWN BEARD: I'm all yours, laddie.**

1   TRAINER: Let's start by catching some flies.

2   BROWN BEARD: What for?

3   TRAINER: For the game Friday.

4   BROWN BEARD: Aaargh, if we're goin' fishin' for marlins we'll
5   need something bigger than flies to use for bait.

6   TRAINER: No, not bait, I mean fly balls. Put the glove on, let's see
7   you catch. *(TRAINER throws ball, BROWN BEARD catches.)*
8   Good job! Throw it back. *(BROWN BEARD puts hook in glove,*
9   *ball gets stuck on hook as he tries to throw. They both fumble with*
10   *it, finally pull it off.)* Let's try some hitting.

11   BROWN BEARD: Aye, now you're talkin'.

12   TRAINER: We'll start with some grounders.

13   BROWN BEARD: Aye, grounders you say, what that be?

14   TRAINER: Grounders, you know, they go across the ground. We'll
15   hit some grounders.

16   BROWN BEARD: Aye, landlubbers! I'd love to hit 'em, scurvy
17   dogs.

18   TRAINER: No, not landlubbers, grounders. I mean baseballs.

19   BROWN BEARD: Baseballs, eh? Not landlubbers?

20   TRAINER: Yes, baseballs. Here take one of these. *(Offers BROWN*
21   *BEARD the bats.)*

22   BROWN BEARD: That's quite a collection of prosthetic limbs you
23   got there, you expectin' to be attacked by sharks?

24   TRAINER: Those are bats.

25   BROWN BEARD: Aye, they must be petrified. What happened to
26   their wings?

27   TRAINER: No, baseball bats, to swing.

28   BROWN BEARD: Oh, like a club?

29   TRAINER: Sort of, but you hit the balls. Let's see your stance.
30   *(BROWN BEARD poses as if attacking someone.)* Here, try it
31   like this.

32   BROWN BEARD: *(Picks bat up and swings it like a club.)* Like that?

33   TRAINER: Well, not exactly, but now I'm going to throw the ball
34   and I want you to hit it.

35   BROWN BEARD: I'm with ya, matey. *(TRAINER throws ball,*

1   *BROWN BEARD doesn't move.)*
2   **TRAINER: Let's try it again.** *(TRAINER throws ball, BROWN*
3   *BEARD doesn't move.)* **You've got to swing.**
4   **BROWN BEARD: At what?**
5   **TRAINER: The baseba ... Wait a minute.** *(TRAINER moves*
6   *BROWN BEARD's eye patch to the other eye.)* **Now let's try it.**
7   *(TRAINER throws ball. BROWN BEARD jumps out of the way.)*
8   **BROWN BEARD:** *Aargh!* **He shot one across our bow? We're**
9   **under attack! Hoist the main sails! Hard to starboard,**
10   **prepare for boarding!** *(BROWN BEARD swings at TRAINER*
11   *and misses knocking over a trophy.)*
12   **TRAINER: What the ... What are you doing?**
13   **BROWN BEARD: Ye'll pay for that ye scurvy dog!**
14   **TRAINER: I'm not paying for that! You broke it!** *(BROWN BEARD*
15   *continues to attack TRAINER, who keeps running.)*
16   **BROWN BEARD: Fight like a man, ye yellow coward.** *(Swings and*
17   *misses again.)*
18   **TRAINER: Would you stop that? Cut it out!**
19   **BROWN BEARD: Aye. Cutting it out is exactly what I 'spect ta do.**
20   **Cuttin' out yer heart!**
21   **TRAINER:** *(To Off-stage)* **Help! Hey, could someone get in here?**
22   *(Enter OWNER and COACH.)*
23   **COACH: What's going on in here? Brown Beard! Stop trying to kill**
24   **the trainer!**
25   **BROWN BEARD: Well, he started it. Hurled a cannon ball right**
26   **square at me, he did.**
27   **OWNER: That's it! You know Brown Beard, I brought you on**
28   **because I thought you would bring the team some color. I**
29   **figured it would be worth it. But it's just not working out. I'm**
30   **afraid I'm going to have to let you go.**
31   **BROWN BEARD:** *(Beaten)* **Really? I understand. I'll be gatherin'**
32   **me lot from me Davy Jones' Locker.** *(Starts shuffling off.)*
33   **TRAINER: Brown Beard wait.** *(To OWNER)* **If you let me train him**
34   **for one more day, I'll bet you'll find a place for him in this**
35   **organization.**

1   OWNER: *(Hesitant)* You have one day.

2   TRAINER: Great. Brown Beard. Let's get to work! *(BROWN*

3   *BEARD and TRAINER exit.)*

4   COACH: Do you really think that he can be taught anything?

5   OWNER: Oh. I think I can find something for him to do. *(COACH*

6   *and OWNER exit as BROWN BEARD enters from opposite side*

7   *with a vendor's tray as TRAINER follows with pointers.)*

8   BROWN BEARD: Arr! Get yer scurvy dogs here! Who wants a

9   scurvy dog? *(Throws some hot dogs around.)*

10

11   *Curtain*

12

13

14

15

16

17

18

19

20

21

22

23

24

25

26

27

28

29

30

31

32

33

34

35

The Pizza Audition

Premise: A has-been actor looks for her last big break and, inadvertently, lands a pizza delivery job.

Cast: Mona Toadstoy — Extreme method actress.
Shawny Klumpnickle — Laid-back pizza delivery guy.
Mr. Malonovich — Hollywood casting director.
Receptionist — Typical receptionist.

Props: Table or desk with chair.

Scene: Receptionist sits at desk working, and Mona enters.

1   RECEPTIONIST: Yes, may I help you?

2   MONA: Mona, Mona Toadstoy. I'd like to see Mr. Malonovich.

3   RECEPTIONIST: Do you have an appointment?

4   MONA: No, I do not have an appointment, but ...

5   RECEPTIONIST: Can I tell him to what this regards?

6   MONA: Please, just tell him it's Mona Toadstoy, and I just need a

7   moment of his time.

8   RECEPTIONIST: Mona ...

9   MONA: Toadstoy. *Beyond Recollection? (Looks for recognition.)*

10   *Another Twice As Nice? (Looks for recognition.) Darker Than*

11   *Night? (No response from RECEPTIONIST.)*

12   RECEPTIONIST: Right. Toadstoy. Please, just have a seat. I will

13   let Mr. Malonovich know you're here. *(MONA has a seat and*

14   *SHAWNY enters.)*

15   SHAWNY: Shawny Klumpnickle. I'm here to see Mr. Malonovich.

16   RECEPTIONIST: *(Checks appointment book.)* Right, Shawny. I will

17   let Mr. Malonovich know you're here. Please have a seat.

18   *(RECEPTIONIST exits, SHAWNY sits.)*

19   SHAWNY: *(To MONA)* Hi. You here for the job? *(MONA continues*

20   *to review part.)* I'm Shawny. *(Extends hand. MONA continues to*

21   *review part.)* Funniest thing happened to me. I was delivering

22   a pizza to advertising upstairs yesterday and stopped to get a

23   drink at a fountain.

24   MONA: Whoa, now that's funny.

25   SHAWNY: Well, I took a drink and the guy behind me said I

26   looked like somebody Mr. Malonovich could use.

27   MONA: How interesting.

28   SHAWNY: It seems that this guy cleans rugs. His brother-in-law

29   got him a job doin' the rugs on the third floor.

30   MONA: His brother-in-law?

31   SHAWNY: Morris.

32   MONA: Morris?

33   SHAWNY: Yeah, Morris. He sells doughnuts in the cafeteria.

34   MONA: Doughnuts. And this interests me because?

35   SHAWNY: It seems that Morris and Gabriel have sort of a thing

1   going.
2   MONA: A thing going?
3   SHAWNY: Yeah, a thing. Well, anyway, Gabriel used to clean the
4   offices on the fifth floor.
5   MONA: Look, I find this all very amusing, but I'm busy. *(MONA*
6   *continues to go over part, time elapses.)*
7   SHAWNY: You here to see Mr. M?
8   MONA: I'm Mona Toadstoy. *(Blank look from SHAWNY. MONA*
9   *preps for scene, performs monolog.)* Doth not, in any instance,
10   find it undeniable? The love for which I have endured such
11   agony. The love for which I have bequeathed unto you. My
12   heart grows heavier with each tear that crawls down my
13   cheek. Draining my soul. Thus, the emptiness which envelopes
14   my life. My being. Doth not one find sympathy for my plight?
15   Doth not one care?
16   SHAWNY: I care. That's why I'm asking. Are you here to see Mr.
17   Malonovich?
18   MONA: I'm Mona Toadstoy! *My Heart is Broken. Never Again.*
19   *Melancholy Mistress. The Duchess of Toledo.*
20   SHAWNY: Well. We all have to start somewhere.
21   MONA: Listen here you little delivery twerp, I was in this business
22   before you were crawling. I've trained with DeBon in France
23   and am known worldwide, and if you think you even have a
24   remote chance in winning this job over me, then you have
25   another think coming.
26   SHAWNY: That's cool. Good luck. *(Brief silence)*
27   MONA: Gabriel?
28   SHAWNY: Excuse me?
29   MONA: Morris and Gabriel. You said that Gabriel used to clean
30   the offices on the fifth floor, and … ?
31   SHAWNY: Oh, yes. Gabriel used to clean offices on the fifth floor
32   before she moved to the cafeteria. Her and Beatrice …
33   MONA: *(Very interested)* Beatrice?
34   SHAWNY: Mr. Malonovich's assistant. You see, Beatrice and
35   Gabriel both took the E-14 train to and from work.

1   MONA: Of course. The assistant. Why didn't I think of that? Easy
2   to get to. No appointment needed. That's a great idea.
3   SHAWNY: *(Confused)* Yeah, right, whatever. Anyway, somewhere
4   in conversation, Beatrice mentioned that Mr. Malonovich was
5   looking for someone new.
6   MONA: Someone new?
7   SHAWNY: Seems he was tired of the same ol', same ol'.
8   MONA: The same ol'?
9   SHAWNY: Then when Gabriel got hired at the cafeteria and met
10   Morris, she mentioned it and he told Harvey at his nephew's
11   birthday party.
12   MONA: Harvey, the gentleman at the fountain?
13   SHAWNY: Yes. And here I am.
14   MONA: That's it?
15   SHAWNY: That's it.
16   MONA: I've been doing this longer than I care to remember,
17   dedicating the majority of my life to establishing myself and
18   my career. You stop for a drink at a fountain and the next
19   thing you know you're sitting here with an appointment to see
20   Mr. Malonovich. And you say he's looking for someone new?
21   SHAWNY: That's what Beatrice tells Gabriel who told Morris who
22   mentioned it to Harvey.
23   MONA: The man at the fountain. This is just great! *(Performing*
24   *again)* I'm washed up. My career is over. I strive for
25   perfection, and what does it get me? Poor little ol' me. If I
26   don't get this job I don't know what I'll do. How will I
27   survive? I don't think I can afford another rejection. I'm at
28   the end of my rope.
29   SHAWNY: Look, I'm sure Mr. Malonovich isn't the only game in
30   town. There's got to be plenty of other people out there that
31   could use you.
32   MONA: Oh no you don't. You're so sure of yourself. You're still
33   wet behind the ears for pity's sake. I didn't get where I'm at
34   by chance. I earned the right to be here waiting for someone
35   else to tell me I'm not good enough, I don't need some

1 sniveling wannabe to tell me. Or ... you know what I mean.
2 *(MR. MALONOVICH enters.)*
3 MR. MALONOVICH: All right then. *(Sees SHAWNY.)* Oh,
4 Shawny. Beatrice told me you'd be stopping.
5 MONA: Wait just a minute. I was here first. Oh, sure, I may have
6 been around a while, but I have experience. I have talent.
7 *(Performing again)* My years account for the riches that I can
8 offer. My life is the pallet on which I create. Dare not destroy
9 this masterpiece. *(SHAWNY and MR. MALONOVICH turn to*
10 *each other confused.)* How dare you take him before me just
11 because your ex-cleaning lady knows the doughnut guy. I was
12 here first and demand that you give me a chance.
13 MR. MALONOVICH: But ...
14 MONA: But nothing. I demand you try me first.
15 MR. MALONOVICH: Shawny, that OK with you?
16 SHAWNY: Sure. Sounds like she needs the work a lot worse than
17 me.
18 MR. MALONOVICH: *(Handing MONA an order)* OK. Here you go.
19 Two with pepperoni and one with hot peppers.
20
21 *Curtain*
22
23
24
25
26
27
28
29
30
31
32
33
34
35

Real Job Morale

Premise: An enthusiastic employee gets disillusioned when she finds out the real motivation behind her company's policies.

Cast: Barbara — Enthusiastic employee believing the customer comes first.

Linda — Negative employee, just wants to get back to work.

Henrietta — Energetic motivational speaker.

Props: Two chairs.

Scene: Linda is sitting in a chair waiting for a meeting. Barbara enters.

1   BARBARA: Hi, how ya doing? I'm Barbara Haversham from
2   accounting.
3   LINDA: Linda Dingle from shipping.
4   BARBARA: Good to meet you Linda. So, do you know what's up?
5   LINDA: Nope. Got to my locker today and there was this note
6   taped to the door. *(Pulls out note and begins reading.)* **Dear**
7   **valued employee, we here at Microshaft, in a continuing effort**
8   **to keep up with the times, are implementing workshops ...**
9   LINDA and BARBARA: ... to help increase efficiency and
10   employee morale.
11   BARBARA: Mine was left on my desk.
12   LINDA: Keeping up with the times? Please! It's just some suit
13   somewhere deciding what we should do or how we should act.
14   I don't like it.
15   BARBARA: Maybe it won't be that bad.
16   LINDA: What makes them think they know what will boost my
17   morale? They're just treating us like mindless cattle. Every
18   company in the chain doing the same as the other. It's just
19   easier for them to control us that way.
20   BARBARA: I really don't think that's it. The last company I was
21   at had us gather every morning for a pep cheer.
22   LINDA: Are you serious?
23   BARBARA: Yes siree, Linda. It got all the juices flowing.
24   LINDA: I don't need anyone flowing my juices.
25   BARBARA: No, really. We all gathered in the main lobby before
26   opening and joined hands. *(BARBARA holds out hand for*
27   *LINDA, LINDA gives scowl.)* **Well, anyway, we all gave our**
28   **little cheer,**
29   *Smile with teeth all pearly white,*
30   *The customer is always right,*
31   *We work together all as one,*
32   *And make the job lots of fun.*
33   *Yeah, Walmarket!*
34   LINDA: Get a grip.
35   BARBARA: It made us all feel as we were one big team.

1 LINDA: Team of morons. You fell for that junk?
2 BARBARA: It's not junk, Linda. This type of motivational
3   interaction has been proven to enhance productivity in
4   Japanese industries for years.
5 LINDA: Yeah, well sometimes all it takes is some good hard work
6   and knowing you're going to get canned if you don't do your
7   job. Problem with things today is everyone's trying to find the
8   quick fix answers. Time-outs, positive reinforcements, over-
9   analyzing, motivational gobbledygook. It's all a big scam. Just
10   do your job and let me do mine.
11 BARBARA: Times change, Linda. Gotta keep up with the times, or
12   the times are going to leave you behind.
13 LINDA: My behind is just fine the way it is.
14 BARBARA: I'm telling you, this is the wave of the future.
15   Management is looking for the cooperators, not the
16   deadwood. Nora Nutwhistle, a friend of mine, used to work
17   for Balgaro's, they implemented one of these motivational
18   campaigns and she wanted nothing to do with it.
19 LINDA: Good for Nutwhistle.
20 BARBARA: Sure was, Linda, if the unemployment line is good.
21   The company wanted nothing to do with her. She had fourteen
22   years with the company, then woosh.
23 LINDA: Whoosh?
24 BARBARA: Whoosh. She wasn't a cooperator.
25 LINDA: She was probably just a goof off.
26 BARBARA: Nora was employee of the month fourteen times.
27 LINDA: And they canned her?
28 BARBARA: Deadwood Linda. She wasn't a cooperator. Wasn't
29   willing to grow and keep up with the times.
30 LINDA: Sheesh. You gotta be kidding me.
31 BARBARA: I wouldn't kid you. We're co-workers. We see each
32   other more than we see our own families. Linda, Linda, Linda.
33   *(BARBARA goes to embrace LINDA, LINDA pushes BARBARA*
34   *back.)* Now, now, Linda. I'm only trying to help.
35 LINDA: I just can't believe they're making us do this. Free country

1   my foot. Government, boss, co-workers, always someone
2   telling me what to do or how to act.
3   BARBARA: It's really not that bad, Linda. You just have to try a
4   little harder to be a cooperator.
5   LINDA: A cooperator.
6   BARBARA: Right. *(HENRIETTA enters.)*
7   LINDA: More like a butt kisser. *(LINDA spots HENRIETTA.)*
8   HENRIETTA: Hello, I'm Henrietta Yodle. I've been hired by
9   Microshaft Inc. to work with you in advancing this company
10   into a mindset for the twenty-first century.
11   LINDA: *(Sarcastically)* Yippee.
12   BARBARA: *(To LINDA)* Cooperator.
13   HENRIETTA: By the time we're through today, hopefully I will
14   have you looking at work a whole new way.
15   BARBARA: Yippee!
16   LINDA: *(To BARBARA)* Butt kisser.
17   HENRIETTA: There are four principles to a successful business.
18   Number one. Does anyone know the most important element
19   to keeping a business on top? *(BARBARA raises hand.*
20   *HENRIETTA points at BARBARA.)* Yes?
21   BARBARA: The customers?
22   HENRIETTA: That's right, the customers. *(BARBARA turns to*
23   *LINDA and gloats.)* We must realize how important they really
24   are to the success of this company.
25   BARBARA: *(To LINDA)* See?
26   HENRIETTA: They're all a bunch of mindless lemmings.
27   BARBARA: What?
28   HENRIETTA: Clumps of clay that wouldn't know the difference
29   between antiques or garbage rejects unless they read our
30   circular in the newspaper.
31   BARBARA: *(Raising hand)* Excuse me, Mrs. Yodle?
32   HENRIETTA: Yes?
33   BARBARA: Shouldn't we value each customer like a star?
34   HENRIETTA: Are you serious?
35   LINDA: She's serious.

1   **HENRIETTA:** Where have you been hiding? They'll buy what we
2   want them to buy.
3   **BARBARA:** But what if they don't?
4   **HENRIETTA:** They have to. *(BARBARA looks confused.)* We got the
5   market cornered. Even if they buy from another company,
6   where do you think that company got it from? One way or
7   another we're getting their money and that's all that really
8   matters. As a matter of fact, that's even better. Then we don't
9   have to deal with the sniveling and whining every time
10   something breaks or they have to update. This way the other
11   poor sap's got to deal with them.
12   **BARBARA:** But …
13   **HENRIETTA:** Number two, selectively inform the public. In other
14   words, what they don't know won't hurt them until their
15   money is in our pockets with a no refund policy and it's too
16   late. One way or another we're getting their money and that's
17   all that really matters.
18   **BARBARA:** But that's just not honest.
19   **HENRIETTA:** Number three, I'm going to show you how to
20   substitute materials to be more cost effective. I mean why use
21   metal when plastic will do, right?
22   **BARBARA:** But what about value, respect, quality? Doing what's
23   right by your loyal customers?
24   **HENRIETTA:** Number four, I'm going to show you all how to be
25   cooperators. Something apparently some of us know nothing
26   about.
27   **LINDA:** Here, here!
28   **HENRIETTA:** That's the spirit.
29   **BARBARA:** *(To LINDA angrily)* **Cooperator!** *(BARBARA exits.)*
30
31   *Curtain*
32
33
34
35

The Real Scoop

Premise: Two neighbors host a show and gossip about the local news of their town, which ends up being news about the other neighbors' private lives.

Cast: Deloris — Sassy gossiping woman.
Abigale — Housewife and gossiper.

Props: Newspaper, kitchen stuff.

Scene: Abigale and Deloris are seated at a kitchen table with coffee and a newspaper.

1   *(Music)*

2   ABIGALE: Hello, I'm Abigale.

3   DELORIS: And I'm Deloris.

4   ABIGALE: Welcome to *The Real Scoop.* *(DELORIS opens*

5   *newspaper and hands half to ABIGALE.)*

6   DELORIS: Let's see what we got going on in the headlines today.

7   *(Both scan the paper.)*

8   ABIGALE: In the local news, says here two men were arrested for

9   the convenience store robbery in Aliquippa last week.

10   DELORIS: That store deserved to get robbed. They've been

11   robbing customers for years with the prices they charge.

12   ABIGALE: Says here it was a Milton Biner and — well, doesn't this

13   just figure — Bryan Dobey. That boy was trouble from day one.

14   DELORIS: You're telling me. That whole family can use a good

15   slap upside the head.

16   ABIGALE: I heard that his mother had a thing going on with with

17   Ed Middleton down at the dairy.

18   DELORIS: Old man Middleton?

19   ABIGALE: The one and only.

20   ABIGALE and DELORIS: Ewwww.

21   DELORIS: *(Back to paper scanning)* Let's see what else we have.

22   Middle East unrest escalates ...

23   ABIGALE: ... impeachment imminent ...

24   DELORIS: ... meltdown evacuation ... bridge collapses ...

25   ABIGALE: Ooo, listen to this. At a press conference this morning, it

26   was announced that a new drug is being approved by the Food

27   and Drug Administration that helps you to stop smoking.

28   DELORIS: Those things don't never work.

29   ABIGALE: It could be worth a try.

30   DELORIS: Trust me. You name it, I tried it. I'm even up to a three-

31   patch-a-day habit. *(Lifts sleeve and reveals patches, starts hacking.)*

32   ABIGALE: *(Back to paper scanning)* OK. So what else do we have?

33   DELORIS: Want some more coffee?

34   ABIGALE: Sure.

35   DELORIS: *(To the audience)* We'll be right back after this

1	**commercial break.** *(Music. DELORIS gets up to get coffee.)*
2	**ABIGALE: What kind of coffee is this? It's pretty good.**
3	**DELORIS: It's Maxamus, with a blend of the finest Colombian**
4	**coffee beans hand picked by Julio Vandeel.** *(BOTH take a sip.)*
5	**DELORIS and ABIGALE: Ahhhh.** *(Music)*
6	**ABIGALE: So where were we?**
7	**DELORIS: Page ... three.**
8	**ABIGALE: Right. In education news it says here that the Monaca**
9	**School Board will be meeting ... I guess we'll never know why**
10	**the Monaca School Board will be meeting.** *(ABIGALE glares at*
11	*DELORIS.)*
12	**DELORIS: What?** *(ABIGALE holds up paper with coupon holes.)*
13	**Rump roast for a dollar thirty-three a pound. How was I**
14	**supposed to pass that up?**
15	**ABIGALE: You could at least wait until after the show. Now what**
16	**are we supposed to do?** *(Pause)*
17	**DELORIS: Gladys?**
18	**ABIGALE: Gladys?**
19	**DELORIS: Gladys Finkle.**
20	**ABIGALE: Isn't she the one with the ...** *Red!!!!*
21	**DELORIS: Yeah.** *Red!!* **The most unnatural color I've ever seen.**
22	**ABIGALE: And what was it last week?**
23	**ABIGALE and DELORIS:** *Yellow!!!*
24	**DELORIS: She changes her color more often than Dennis Rodman.**
25	**ABIGALE: And now the roots are starting to show.**
26	**DELORIS: Her head looks like a giant candy corn.**
27	**ABIGALE: So what about her?**
28	**DELORIS: She's on Monaca's PTA. She would know what's going on.**
29	**ABIGALE: Right. Like a correspondent.**
30	**DELORIS: A candy corn correspondent.** *(DELORIS picks up phone*
31	*and starts dialing.)*
32	**ABIGALE: Good thing it's not Halloween.**
33	**DELORIS: Trick or freak. Wait, it's ringing. Hello, Gladys, this is**
34	**Del. Yeah, a long time. No, not much. He is? Really. Uh-huh.**
35	**Ouch. OK. Keep in touch. No really. We'll get together and do**

1   lunch. Bye-bye.

2   ABIGALE: What'd she say?

3   DELORIS: You know Kevin Glick?

4   ABIGALE: Tight buns at the supermarket?

5   DELORIS: Right. Well apparently Gladys says that Sylvia's
6   daughter went out with him Saturday.

7   ABIGALE: Betty or Linda?

8   DELORIS: Linda. They went to the movies.

9   ABIGALE: What did they see?

10   DELORIS: *Days Gone By.*

11   ABIGALE: I loved the end of that movie.

12   DELORIS: Then they both left together. *(BOTH get teary.)* And
13   then Darla.

14   ABIGALE: Myrtle's youngest?

15   DELORIS: Right. Darla spotted them in the back ... *(Wiggles eyebrows.)*

16   ABIGALE: No.

17   DELORIS: Yep. So what's the first thing that Darla does?

18   ABIGALE and DELORIS: Run home to tell Mommy.

19   DELORIS: And what's the first thing she does?

20   ABIGALE: Calls Gladys?

21   DELORIS: And what do you think happened when Gladys found
22   out that her daughter's prom date went to the theater *(Wiggles*
23   *eyebrows)* with her sister's kid?

24   ABIGALE: What?

25   DELORIS: She nearly popped her stitches.

26   ABIGALE: That's all we need.

27   DELORIS: Her face dropping back down.

28   ABIGALE: All that skin ...

29   DELORIS: ... flapping all over. *(DELORIS and ABIGALE shudder.)*
30   Everybody run! Candy corn avalanche.

31   ABIGALE: You are so bad, but so right. So what about the school
32   board meeting? *(DELORIS looks dumbfounded.)*

33   DELORIS: Well, that wraps up our news for the day.

34   ABIGALE: Be sure to join us next time on *The Real Scoop. (Music)*

35   *Curtain*

The Royal Pet Store

Premise: Because of technical difficulties, two skits need to be put on at one time. Unfortunately, one actor is in both skits. See how he handles running from a medieval English castle to a modern-day pet store.

Cast: King — King of a medieval country.
Queen — Wife of the king.
Clerk/Servant — Actor playing pet store clerk and King's servant.
Customer 1 (Benny) — Younger boy.
Customer 2
Customer 3
Director — The director of the show. Could be the real one or just someone acting as a director.
Guard — King's guard.
Mime, minstrel, juggler, lawyer — Keep trying to "entertain" the King and Queen.

Props: Club for Guard, bell for King, bell for pet store counter, small bag of pet food, spoon, "iguana" or something that looks like one, large dragon (a person with a face mask).

Costumes: The medieval side should have appropriate costumes, as should the pet store. The Clerk/Servant should have to change clothes as he switches sides.

Scene: Stage Right is a King's throne room. Stage Left is a pet store. The King and Queen are sitting on their thrones. The Guard is standing behind them.

1   **KING:** *(Out of character)* **Director!** *(DIRECTOR enters.)*

2   **DIRECTOR:** We have a show going on here.

3   **KING:** Why's the pet store skit set up with our medieval skit?

4   **DIRECTOR:** We had them both scheduled, and we're running out

5   of time, so I decided to run them both at the same time.

6   **KING:** At the same time? Is that going to work?

7   **DIRECTOR:** Yes, let's get on with it. *(CLERK/SERVANT enters.)*

8   **CLERK/SERVANT:** Excuse me, but I'm in both of these skits.

9   **DIRECTOR:** That's all right, you can handle it. Ready? Action.

10   *(DIRECTOR and CLERK/SERVANT exit. KING rings bell.*

11   *CLERK/SERVANT enters Stage Right.)*

12   **CLERK/SERVANT:** Yes, Sire? You called?

13   **KING:** We are getting hungry. Have the cook send up a snack.

14   *(MIME enters Stage Right, begins entertaining. CUSTOMER 1*

15   *enters Stage Left and pretends to look around, eventually picking*

16   *up small bag of pet food.)*

17   **QUEEN:** In the name of all that irritates us, *(To KING)* you know

18   that we deplore mimes.

19   **KING:** We think that they are quite amusing.

20   **QUEEN:** Nonsense. *(QUEEN claps and GUARD steps up, whacks the*

21   *MIME and removes him from the stage. To SERVANT.)* **And this**

22   **time, someone will be sure to pay if the morsel is as**

23   **indigestible as the last. That is all.** *(CUSTOMER 1 rings bell on*

24   *counter in pet store. CLERK/SERVANT exits Stage Right.*

25   *CUSTOMER 1 rings the bell again. CLERK/SERVANT enters*

26   *Stage Left.)*

27   **CUSTOMER 1:** I'll just take this, today.

28   **CLERK/SERVANT:** OK. So how's that tarantula doing, Benny?

29   **CUSTOMER 1:** Real good. My sister hates it.

30   **CLERK/SERVANT:** Great. Let's see. Meal worms, crickets. Ooo.

31   **Someone's going to eat good tonight. This is it, then?**

32   **CUSTOMER 1:** That's it. *(KING rings bell.)*

33   **CLERK/SERVANT:** Ummm. I'll be back in just a sec, Benny.

34   *(CLERK/SERVANT exits Stage Left with package of food, then*

35   *enters Stage Right.)* **Yes, your majesty? You called?**

1   QUEEN: What is the delay with our food? Oh, splendid. Bring it
2   here. Smells delicious. *(MINSTREL enters. CLERK/SERVANT*
3   *gives pet food to QUEEN.)*
4   KING: In the name of all that irritates us, *(To QUEEN)* Mother, you
5   know that we deplore wandering minstrels.
6   QUEEN: We think that they are quite cute.
7   KING: Nonsense. *(KING claps and GUARD whacks the wandering*
8   *MINSTREL, removing him Stage Right. QUEEN picks up spoon,*
9   *takes a bite from pet food leaving spoon in pet food. CLERK/*
10   *SERVANT shields head from GUARD's club.)*
11   KING: Servant? *(CLERK/SERVANT flinches.)*
12   QUEEN: Scrumptious.
13   KING: I have a telegram to be delivered to King Ali Quippa.
14   CLERK/SERVANT: Yes, Your Majesty. *(CLERK/SERVANT grabs*
15   *scroll and searches for pen as KING talks.)*
16   KING: It is imperative that we should speak. The turmoil and
17   devastation which is ravaging our lands must cease. We
18   suggest to combine our efforts in approaching a peaceful
19   resolution. We hope to meet with you to discuss such matters
20   at the Perennial Gardens two nights forthwith. Signed, Lord
21   Cuvington III. That is all. *(JUGGLER enters Stage Right.)* In
22   the name of all that irritates us, *(To QUEEN)* Mother, you
23   know that we deplore jugglers.
24   QUEEN: We think that they are quite entertaining.
25   KING: Nonsense. *(KING claps and GUARD whacks the JUGGLER*
26   *and removes from stage. CLERK/SERVANT still looks for pen. To*
27   *CLERK/SERVANT)* And why be it that you are still standing
28   here. Is there a problem?
29   CLERK/SERVANT: *(Looking at GUARD)* Uh ... no, no problem.
30   KING: Then be gone with you. *(CUSTOMER 1, getting anxious,*
31   *rings bell.)*
32   CLERK/SERVANT: Yes, Your Majesty. *(CLERK/SERVANT exits*
33   *Stage Right, then enters Stage Left.)* Uh, just one minute please.
34   *(Grabs a pencil, begins writing the KING's message.)* Turmoil ...
35   devastation ... two nights forthwith ... Lord Cuvington III.

1   *(Puts on apron.)* **Yes, I'm sorry about that, Benny. Here ya go.**
2   *(Hands CUSTOMER 1 meal worms and crickets with spoon still*
3   *in it. CUSTOMER 1 exits Stage Left. CUSTOMER 2 enters Stage*
4   *Left. To CUSTOMER 2)* **Yes, can I help you?**
5   **CUSTOMER 2: I have a question. My dog seems to have a bit of a**
6   **flea problem in his ears. They're all red, and he keeps scratching**
7   **them. Do you have anything I could give him for that?**
8   **CLERK/SERVANT: Sure.** *(Grabs bottle, writes on paper as he*
9   *speaks.)* **This is flea-rid. What you want to do is put two to three**
10   **drops in his ears once a day for a couple days until it clears and**
11   **I don't think you'll have …** *(KING rings bell.)* **Excuse me for**
12   **just a second.** *(CLERK/SERVANT exits Stage Left.)*
13   **KING: Servant?** *(CLERK/SERVANT enters Stage Right, out of*
14   *breath.)*
15   **CLERK/SERVANT: Yes, Sire?**
16   **KING: Is that King Ali Quippa's response?**
17   **CLERK/SERVANT: Uh …**
18   **KING: Give it here.** *(CLERK/SERVANT reluctantly hands over note.*
19   *LAWYER enters Stage Right.)* **In the name of all that irritates**
20   **us,** *(To QUEEN)* **you know that we deplore lawyers.** *(KING*
21   *claps and GUARD whacks the LAWYER. LAWYER just staggers.)*
22   **QUEEN: You know you're quite right.** *(QUEEN claps and GUARD*
23   *whacks the LAWYER again. LAWYER falls. GUARD removes*
24   *from stage.)*
25   **KING:** *(Reading note)* **Stick it in my ear?! He is a fool to believe he**
26   **can defy us. Unleash the dragon.** *(CUSTOMER 3 enters Stage*
27   *Left, rings bell.)*
28   **CLERK/SERVANT: Yes, Your Majesty.** *(CLERK/SERVANT exits*
29   *Stage Right, then enters back Center Stage, out of breath, makes*
30   *his way to counter.)* **Can I help you?**
31   **CUSTOMER 3: Yes, my iguana seems sick.** *(Holds up "iguana" to*
32   *CLERK/SERVANT.)*
33   **CLERK/SERVANT: I see. He does look a little green. I think the**
34   **poor guy just needs some vitamins.** *(KING rings bell.)* **I have just**
35   **the thing for him, I'll be right back.** *(CLERK/SERVANT exits*

1   *Stage Left, enters Stage Right still holding "iguana.")* **What!?**
2   **KING: Did you release ...** *(Spots "iguana.")* ***The dragon!*** *(Takes*
3   *"iguana.")* **You shrunk the dragon?**
4   **CLERK/SERVANT: Well, you see, I ... uh ...**
5   **KING: King Ali Quippa must have had a spell cast upon us.**
6   **Quickly, call for the royal magician.** *(CUSTOMER 3 rings bell.)*
7   **CLERK/SERVANT:** *(Reaching for the "iguana")* **Can I have the ...**
8   **KING: Quickly. The royal magician.** *(CUSTOMER 3 rings bell.*
9   *CLERK/SERVANT exits Stage Right, enters Stage Left.)*
10   **CLERK/SERVANT: OK, thank you.**
11   **CUSTOMER 3: My iguana?**
12   **CLERK/SERVANT: Yes, he'll be fine. Next?**
13   **CUSTOMER 3: But you still have him. My iguana.**
14   **CLERK/SERVANT: Yeah, well, he ...** *(DRAGON enters. CUSTOMER*
15   *3 gets scared.)*
16   **CLERK/SERVANT:** *(Disgusted)* **I quit!**
17
18   *Curtain*
19
20
21
22
23
24
25
26
27
28
29
30
31
32
33
34
35

Sound Off

Premise: The sound effects machine is broken, so the audience is asked to supply the sound effects, via cue cards, to the scene. The scene is two bank robbers returning to their hideout after the heist. All goes well until the cue cards are accidentally shuffled.

Cast: Barney — Paranoid robber.
Terrance — A simple-minded robber.
Eddie — Honest gas station attendant.
Mailman — Just delivers a package.
Cue Card Holder — Just holds cards, until they're knocked down.
Director — Explains to audience about the sound effects machine.

Props: Phone, two guns, a package, a bag for stolen money, sound cue cards. Note: The sound cue cards after they are shuffled can be any sound effects. Some suggestions are given but feel free to be creative and have fun with the audience.

Scene: Inside of a hotel room. There is a phone on a table near Center Stage.

1   **DIRECTOR: Hello, ladies and gentlemen. Please excuse this brief**
2   **interruption, but our sound effects machine seems to not be**
3   **working. So we would like you, the audience, to help us with**
4   **our sound effects. The cards will be on an easel so you can see**
5   **what sound is coming up. When it is time for a sound, the cue**
6   **card holder will hold up the card. Let's try one.** *(CUE CARD*
7   *HOLDER holds up [TIRES SCREECHING]. Audience makes*
8   *sound.) (Note: The sound effects are in brackets, and placed in the*
9   *script when they should be held up to the audience.) [TIRES*
10   *SCREECHING] [CAR DOOR SLAMMING] [CAR DOOR*
11   *SLAMMING] (BARNEY and TERRANCE enter hyped from*
12   *robbery, unpacking guns, etc.)*
13   **BARNEY: Shut the door, Terrance.**
14   **TERRANCE: Yeah, sure Barney.** *(TERRANCE closes door.) [DOOR*
15   *CLOSING]*
16   **BARNEY: Wow. That was a close one.**
17   **TERRANCE: You're not kidding. Did you see the look on that**
18   **teller's face when you handed her the note?**
19   **BARNEY:** *(Imitating teller)* **I'm sorry sir, withdrawals are two**
20   **windows down. What a ditz.**
21   **TERRANCE: Yeah, what a ditz.**
22   **BARNEY: All right Terrance; let's see what the take was.**
23   **TERRANCE:** *(Looking sheepish)* **Uh …**
24   **BARNEY: Terrance!**
25   **TERRANCE: I … ah …**
26   **BARNEY: Terrance, where's the money?**
27   **TERRANCE: I thought you had it.**
28   **BARNEY: Aww, Terrance!! What did I tell you? One job. That's**
29   **all you had to do, just one job. You big dummy!**
30   **TERRANCE:** *(Breaking down)* **I'm sorry Barney. In all the excitement**
31   **I lost track of it. I didn't mean to. It was just that I wasn't**
32   **expecting …** *(BARNEY slaps TERRANCE to settle him.) [SLAP]*
33   **BARNEY: Settle down.**
34   **TERRANCE: Sorry Barney, but don't worry. We'll get our money.**
35   **BARNEY: Don't worry?**

1   **TERRANCE:** Yeah, I put my wallet in that sack just in case this
2   kinda thing happened.
3   **BARNEY:** So, tell me Terrance, why shouldn't I worry?
4   **TERRANCE:** Well, if someone finds it, they'll return it with the
5   money.
6   **BARNEY:** Great!
7   **TERRANCE:** Thank you. See, I'm not as dumb as you say I am.
8   **BARNEY:** Terrence, I didn't mean *great great*, I meant *great*, as in
9   great! *(TERRANCE looks confused.)* **Do you honestly think if**
10   someone finds a sack of money that was just stolen from First
11   National, which has probably been broadcast on every TV and
12   radio station by now, and they don't go straight to the cops,
13   they're going to give it back to you?
14   **TERRANCE:** Sure.
15   **BARNEY:** They're going to keep it for themselves, you dolt.
16   **TERRANCE:** I don't think so. Life is full of surprises. There's still
17   a lot of honest folks out there, just like us.
18   **BARNEY:** *We just robbed a bank!* It's just a matter of time ...
19   *[SIREN]* before the cops track us down. *[TIRES SCREECHING]*
20   **TERRANCE:** Maybe they're here to return our money.
21   **BARNEY:** Oh, yeah right, and Ed McMahon is here to tell us we're
22   grand prize winners.
23   **TERRANCE:** *(Excited)* **Really?**
24   **BARNEY:** No, not really!! They're here to take us to jail.
25   **TERRANCE:** *(Still excited)* **Really?**
26   **BARNEY:** Really.
27   **TERRANCE:** Cool. I love that show.
28   **BARNEY:** Huh?
29   **TERRANCE:** *(Singing)* **"Bad boys, bad boys, what ya going to**
30   do ... " *(BARNEY slaps TERRANCE.)* *[SLAP]*
31   **BARNEY:** Listen, and listen good. I'm not going back to the slammer,
32   no matter what! Grab your piece. *(BARNEY breaks window.)*
33   *[GLASS BREAKING]* I'll take the front, you take the back.
34   **TERRANCE:** But I don't want to shoot no one.
35   **BARNEY:** Either you shoot them or I shoot you. Got it?

1   **TERRANCE: I got it.** *(TERRANCE turns frightened and knocks over*
2   *easel holding cue cards. TERRANCE and CUE CARD HOLDER*
3   *gather cards and continue scene. Note: The proper sound appears*
4   *first in brackets and a suggested sound is given after. The proper*
5   *sound should not be given from here on out.)* [PHONE RINGS —
6   CAT MEOW]
7   *(Note: Most times actors are told never to break character, but*
8   *this time "breaking" is part of the joke. Everyone can break to*
9   *laugh at the mishap, and periodically when the wrong sound is*
10   *given the actor can become befuddled "out-of-character.")*
11   **TERRANCE: What's that?**
12   **BARNEY:** *(Recovering)* **It's no doubt, the cops wanting our**
13   **surrender. I'll take care of this.** *(BARNEY answers phone.)*
14   **Hello? ... Uh, yes. Just a minute.** *(To TERRANCE)* **It's for you.**
15   *(Hands TERRANCE the phone.)*
16   **TERRANCE: Hello? ... Yes, this is Terrance Peterson. ... Why, yes**
17   **I did. ... Well, now may not be such a good time. ... Sure.**
18   **That sounds great. Thank you.** *(TERRANCE hangs up the*
19   *phone and goes about his business prepping his gun.)*
20   **BARNEY: So?**
21   **TERRANCE: I guess I got no choice. But I'm only shootin' if they**
22   **shoot at me first.**
23   **BARNEY: No! What'd the cops want?**
24   **TERRANCE: How am I supposed to know?**
25   **BARNEY: The phone call?**
26   **TERRANCE: Oh, no. That wasn't the cops. That was Eddie.**
27   **BARNEY: And who is Eddie?**
28   **TERRANCE: He's the attendant at the station we stopped at for**
29   **gas. He found the money and wants to return it to me.**
30   **BARNEY: You gotta be kidding me.** [KNOCK AT DOOR —
31   AIRPLANE]
32   **TERRANCE: What's that?**
33   **BARNEY: Uh ... sounds like someone's at the door.** *(Moves to door,*
34   *readies gun.)* **Who is it?**
35   **MAILMAN:** *(Off-stage)* **I got a package here for a Terrance**

1   **Peterson.** *(BARNEY carefully lets MAILMAN in.)* **I need a**
2   **signature.** *(TERRANCE grabs for pen, pen drops.)* *[PEN*
3   *HITTING FLOOR — EXPLOSION] (ALL react to explosion.)*
4   **Thanks.** *(MAILMAN exits.)*
5   **TERRANCE: Wonder what this is.** *(Begins to open package.)*
6   **BARNEY:** *No!* **It could be a trap. Listen.** *(BARNEY and TERRANCE*
7   *listen to package)* *[TICKING — DOG BARKING]* **It's some kind of**
8   **bomb!** *(BOTH react.)* **Quick, throw it out the window.** *(BARNEY*
9   *and TERRANCE play "hot potato" with it, then TERRANCE throws*
10   *the package out the window.)* *[CRASH — BOING]* **Ha! So there!**
11   *[KNOCK AT DOOR — DRIPPING WATER]*
12   **TERRANCE: And that would be … ?**
13   **BARNEY: Someone else at the door.** *(Moves to door, readies gun.)*
14   **Who is it?**
15   **EDDIE:** *(Off-stage)* **Eddie Grimmle. I found your money.** *(BARNEY*
16   *carefully lets EDDIE in. EDDIE shows wallet ID to BARNEY,*
17   *then TERRANCE.)* **Terrance Peterson I take it?**
18   **TERRANCE: Yep.**
19   **EDDIE: Here you go. Would have been here sooner but the cops**
20   **have a big speed trap set up right down the street. Well, gotta**
21   **be getting home to the little lady.**
22   **TERRANCE: Thanks a lot, Eddie. Here.** *(TERRANCE hands*
23   *EDDIE some money from the bag)*
24   **EDDIE: Isn't life just full of surprises. It's me and the little lady's**
25   **anniversary today. Didn't get a chance to pick her up**
26   **anything, but somebody was throwing away this perfectly fine**
27   **clock.** *(Shows package that TERRANCE threw out the window.)*
28   **See you fellas later.**
29   **TERRANCE: See ya, Eddie.** *(EDDIE exits.)* *[DOOR CLOSES —*
30   *TARZAN YELL] (BARNEY is startled.)* **Life is full of surprises.**
31   **BARNEY: Shut up!**
32
33   *Curtain*
34
35

Stuntman

Premise: An overeager stagehand suddenly gets promoted to stuntman. He spends the rest of the filming getting punched, hit, and finally blown up.

Cast: Director — Very demanding and convincing Hollywood type.
Woman — Pampered, cheesy overactor.
Hero — Pampered, cheesy overactor.
Crook — Stereotypical movie bad guy.
Assistant — Gung-ho stagehand who gets promoted to stuntman.
Two to four make-up/prop extras — People on the set helping to change props and pamper the "stars."

Props: Clapper board, suitcase, gun, stick, picnic basket, blanket.

Costumes: Wig for stuntman, dress similar to Woman's also for stuntman.

Scene: The set of a movie, the make-up people are helping the stars get ready for the next scene. Enter Director with Assistant following directly behind.

1   DIRECTOR: All right. Everybody quiet on the set.

2   ASSISTANT: Quiet!

3   DIRECTOR: We're going to take it from page eighty-two. Our

4   hero and the damsel are in the train station.

5   ASSISTANT: You heard him. Everybody places.

6   DIRECTOR: Marker.

7   ASSISTANT: *The Man That Couldn't Die,* scene three, take one.

8   DIRECTOR: Roll 'em. And action.

9   WOMAN: Running isn't the answer, you know. They'll still find

10   you.

11   HERO: But if I stay here, I put us both in danger. And if anything

12   would ever happen to you … well … I wouldn't be able to live

13   with myself without you living with me. I must go. *(CROOK*

14   *enters with gun drawn.)*

15   CROOK: Not so fast, Jim Bob. So, we're planning a little trip, are

16   we? And without even telling me. *(Looking at WOMAN)* And

17   who do we have here?

18   HERO: Leave her out of this. *(HERO steps between WOMAN and*

19   *CROOK in very heroic fashion.)* This is between me and you.

20   CROOK: I thought I finished you off in Topeka. You sure are one

21   slimy little tadpole.

22   HERO: So you're going to shoot an unarmed man? *(CROOK puts*

23   *gun away.)*

24   CROOK: I don't need no gun to finish a slug like you. Let's go.

25   *(CROOK and HERO begin sparring. CROOK winds up to throw*

26   *punch.)*

27   DIRECTOR: Cut! Stuntman! … Stuntman?!

28   ASSISTANT: Uh … I don't think he showed today.

29   DIRECTOR: He didn't? That's it. He's fired.

30   ASSISTANT: Actually, I think he quit.

31   DIRECTOR: Well he's fired too. *(Thinking, then looking at*

32   *ASSISTANT)* You, get in there.

33   ASSISTANT: Excuse me?

34   DIRECTOR: Get in there. The clock's ticking. I need a stuntman.

35   ASSISTANT: But I'm just a stagehand, I don't have the experience …

1	DIRECTOR: Experience, humphhhh. You'll get a hundred fifty
2	bucks an hour just to stand there. How tough can that be?
3	ASSISTANT: Just to stand there?
4	DIRECTOR: Just stand there. Let's go. Clock's ticking.
5	ASSISTANT: OK. What do I do?
6	DIRECTOR: Just stand right here. *(DIRECTOR positions*
7	*ASSISTANT where HERO ended.)*
8	ASSISTANT: This ain't so bad.
9	DIRECTOR: Action! *(CROOK finishes punch on ASSISTANT.)*
10	DIRECTOR: Cut. Beautiful!
11	ASSISTANT: Ow. That hurt.
12	DIRECTOR: You're a natural, kid.
13	ASSISTANT: Yeah, but it really ... Really?
14	DIRECTOR: Really. *(To crew)* Places. *(HERO takes ASSISTANT's*
15	*place.)*
16	ASSISTANT: *(Smugly to other actors and extras)* A natural.
17	DIRECTOR: Roll 'em. Action!
18	HERO: That's all you got?
19	WOMAN: Be careful!
20	HERO: Come on. *(CROOK looks around, picks up stick, pulls back to*
21	*swing.)*
22	DIRECTOR: Cut! Stuntman. *(ASSISTANT not paying attention)*
23	Stuntman!
24	ASSISTANT: *(Realizes DIRECTOR means him.)* Ooo. Sorry.
25	*(ASSISTANT takes place.)* The natural's ready.
26	DIRECTOR: Good ... Action! *(CROOK swings and hits ASSISTANT.)*
27	ASSISTANT: Yiiiiiiiowwww!
28	DIRECTOR: Cut. Perfect.
29	ASSISTANT: Perfect my butt. He nearly knocked me into next
30	week.
31	DIRECTOR: And you took it like a pro. Are you sure you never
32	did anything like this before?
33	ASSISTANT: What? Get beat with a stick? Well, there was that
34	one girl I dated back ... No, wait. That really hurt.
35	DIRECTOR: Don't disappoint me, natural.

1 ASSISTANT: Natural. Yeah. Sorry, it's just that I never ...
2 DIRECTOR: You're OK?
3 ASSISTANT: I'm OK.
4 DIRECTOR: I can count on you?
5 ASSISTANT: Sure.
6 DIRECTOR: Great. Let's try that shot again with a little more
7   surprise.
8 ASSISTANT: What?
9 DIRECTOR: Action! *(CROOK swings and hits ASSISTANT.)* Cut.
10   Perfect!
11 ASSISTANT: *Motherless pearl-sucking pig!*
12 DIRECTOR: *(To ASSISTANT)* I tell you what. You're about the best
13   I've ever seen.
14 ASSISTANT: At what?!
15 DIRECTOR: At acting like you're getting hit.
16 ASSISTANT: I *am* getting hit, and I don't think my insurance
17   covers ...
18 DIRECTOR: I'd like to give you a promotion.
19 ASSISTANT: Promotion?
20 DIRECTOR: You deserve it. I've never seen anyone get hit with so
21   much believability in my entire career.
22 ASSISTANT: But those sticks hurt.
23 DIRECTOR: No more sticks. I promise.
24 ASSISTANT: No sticks?
25 DIRECTOR: No sticks. You can help me out with one more scene.
26 ASSISTANT: I guess.
27 DIRECTOR: Great! Everybody, scene thirty-two. *(To ASSISTANT)*
28   I'm promoting you to stuntwoman.
29 ASSISTANT: Stuntwoman?
30 DIRECTOR: Yep.
31 ASSISTANT: But I don't think I can play a woman. *(EXTRAS enter*
32   *and begin dressing ASSISTANT to look somewhat like WOMAN as*
33   *DIRECTOR tries to convince him to be the stuntwoman.)*
34 DIRECTOR: Sure, you can handle it. One more little girlie part.
35 ASSISTANT: Well ... I ...

1	DIRECTOR: This is it. We finish this scene, and it's a wrap. Then
2	you can come to the producer's party with me.
3	ASSISTANT: Me?
4	DIRECTOR: Hey, you're the real star of the show. What do you
5	say? A simple little picnic scene? You can handle it, can't you?
6	ASSISTANT: Sure.
7	DIRECTOR: Places. Let's try to get this in one take, people. Picnic
8	scene. Roll 'em. And action.
9	HERO: Oh, I love you.
10	WOMAN: And I, you. *(WOMAN and HERO ogle, ASSISTANT shows*
11	*concern to DIRECTOR.)*
12	ASSISTANT: *(In a loud whisper to DIRECTOR)* I'm not kissing that
13	guy!
14	DIRECTOR: Quiet!
15	HERO: Maybe we should be going. Looks like a storm's brewing.
16	I'll go get the car.
17	WOMAN: Hurry, my love. *(HERO exits. WOMAN begins to gather*
18	*picnic items.)*
19	DIRECTOR: Cut. Stuntma … stuntwoman. Places. *(ASSISTANT*
20	*takes place.)*
21	ASSISTANT: There's not even anyone here to hit me.
22	DIRECTOR: OK. Here's where the woman gets hit by lightning.
23	Roll 'em …
24	ASSISTANT: Hit by what?!
25	DIRECTOR: … Action. *(A flash of light, loud thunder sound, darkness*
26	*On-stage, and the loud scream of pain from ASSISTANT)*
27	*(Note: When first performed, the person who played the*
28	*ASSISTANT spent the rest of the show with burn marks and hair*
29	*standing up like he'd really been hit by lightning.)*
30	
31	*Curtain*
32	
33	
34	
35	

Sworn In

Premise: A group of immigrants are taking citizenship classes and get a little bit more than a regular history lesson.

Cast: Teacher — Gets fed up with the way things are.
Bonualo — Spanish immigrant.
McDougle — Irish immigrant.
Tootie — Pakistani immigrant.
Deedle — Middle European immigrant.

Props: Four chairs.

Scene: The four immigrants are talking amongst themselves when Teacher enters.

1   TEACHER: Hello, class. I'd like to welcome any new people to
2   class and congratulate you for showing interest in becoming
3   U.S. citizens. This is not only a great privilege, but also a great
4   responsibility. You will represent the people of this great
5   country of free enterprise and opportunity. Where you can be
6   anything you want to be. For those of you who weren't with
7   us last week, I'd like to review what we've been going over.
8   Bonualo? *(BONUALO stands.)*
9   BONUALO: Si?
10   TEACHER: Say you got a job on a loading dock.
11   BONUALO: I got a job on a loading dock.
12   TEACHER: OK. You got a job on a loading dock.
13   BONUALO: *(Very excited)* Gracias, amigo! *(Shakes TEACHER's*
14   *hand.)*
15   TEACHER: No, no, no. You don't really have a job. It's just a
16   hypothetical situation. *(BONUALO looks confused.)* I just
17   made it up to help you understand the way things work here.
18   BONUALO: Oh, señor. So Bonualo, es no ... no ...
19   TEACHER: No job.
20   BONUALO: Heccchhno zshob?
21   TEACHER: No ... I mean yes. That's correct. No job. Bonualo es
22   no chob ... We're just pretending. *(BONUALO looks confused.)*
23   We were pretending! ... Pretendato. Comprende?
24   BONUALO: Bonualo, heccchhno zshob?
25   TEACHER: That's correct. Si.
26   BONUALO: *(Suddenly excited)* Bonualo get welfare. Gracias.
27   *(BONUALO sits.)*
28   TEACHER: No. No. You only get welfare if you are somehow
29   unable to work and need assistance from the government. You
30   understand?
31   BONUALO: Bonualo es unable to work.
32   TEACHER: You're unable to work?
33   BONUALO: Si. Bonualo es ... creeple.
34   TEACHER: You're not crippled! You were just standing up here a
35   second ago.

1 BONUALO: Bonualo hypodermical speaking. I pretendato and get
2   assistant from govermante.
3 TEACHER: Uh … Let me try this a different way. McDougle.
4   Would you please come up here? *(MCDOUGLE stands.)*
5 TEACHER: OK Micky D …
6 MCDOUGLE: Dat's Tarn L. Meeham McDougle from the clan
7   McDougle in Langsheer. I'll pin you boggs tween your ears
8   ifin slack me back.
9 TEACHER: Uh … OK. So, suppose you go and apply for a job.
10   You walk in and the boss asks you why you feel you should get
11   the job. What do you tell him?
12 MCDOUGLE: Dare me not finny if me wench and I are not above
13   the squalor. Once in too many gone by, I too can hear the
14   wailin' of the hungry.
15 TEACHER: *(Confused)* And you would get the job, why?
16 MCDOUGLE: Ifin he nigs, I'll crush his skull.
17 TEACHER: No! You can't just go around crushing people's skulls.
18 MCDOUGLE: Why not?
19 TEACHER: You just can't. What kind of a job do you expect to get
20   if you go around pounding on people?
21 MCDOUGLE: The mob.
22 TEACHER: *(Pause)* Sit down. *(MCDOUGLE sits.)* Let's pretend we
23   all have jobs. Once you find a job …
24 TOOTIE: What kind a job do I have?
25 TEACHER: Anything. It doesn't matter. This is the land of
26   opportunity.
27 TOOTIE: I want to be the president.
28 TEACHER: Umm … that might be a little much.
29 TOOTIE: You told me anything.
30 TEACHER: Yes, I did, but you can't be the president. Anything
31   else.
32 TOOTIE: All right then, I'll be George Washington.
33 TEACHER: George Washington?
34 TOOTIE: He was a president, wasn't he?
35 TEACHER: Well, yes he was, and now he's dead.

1   TOOTIE: All right then … I'll be the Dairy Queen. I always
2   wanted to be royalty.
3   TEACHER: You can't … OK, you're the Dairy Queen.
4   Congratulations. *(To class)* When you work, you make a
5   certain amount of money for what you do. Then, the local,
6   state and federal governments all take taxes.
7   DEEDLE: Taxes?
8   TEACHER: Yes, taxes. A share of your money. They all take a
9   share of your money.
10   DEEDLE: Oh, then they help me work?
11   TEACHER: Umm. No.
12   DEEDLE: But I give them my money I got for working?
13   TEACHER: Yes. They need the money. They use the money to help
14   run the country and take care of you. *(Deedle looks confused.)*
15   They use it to pay for government jobs so they can keep track
16   of all our money and hire people to collect it. It pays for roads
17   so we can get to and from work easier. It pays for prisons.
18   That kind of thing.
19   DEEDLE: They take care of me?
20   TEACHER: Yes. With the money you give them. The taxes.
21   DEEDLE: If I am sick, they pay for the doctor?
22   TEACHER: No. That's something different. That's health care.
23   That comes out of your pay, too, but your employer will
24   explain that.
25   DEEDLE: And if I don't pay them taxes?
26   TEACHER: Well, then they could take your house or throw you in
27   jail.
28   DEEDLE: The house I paid for with money I made working.
29   TEACHER: Yeah.
30   DEEDLE: And throw me in a prison that I pay for.
31   TEACHER: That's correct.
32   DEEDLE: *(Thinking)* Then I don't want a job.
33   TEACHER: But you need a job.
34   DEEDLE: Why?
35   TEACHER: To make money.

1   **DEEDLE:** To give to the government.
2   **TEACHER:** Yes ... I mean no. Not just to give to the government.
3   You need it for ... for things. Like a car, so you can get to
4   work. You'll need gas for your car. Then you'll need insurance
5   for the car in case you wreck.
6   **DEEDLE:** And if I don't wreck?
7   **TEACHER:** It doesn't matter, you still need insurance, just in case.
8   This is America. And you'll need clothes to wear to work ...
9   and ... things.
10   **DEEDLE:** Let me get this straight: To work, I need a car to get to
11   work, gas to run the car, insurance to drive the car, clothes to
12   work in. I pay for roads I need to get to work and help pay for
13   prison they throw me in if I don't pay taxes.
14   **TEACHER:** That's right.
15   **DEEDLE:** If I have job, I have to pay government. If I don't have
16   job, government pays me. No, I just won't work. I will welfare
17   with Bonualo.
18   **BONUALO:** We could room together.
19   **DEEDLE:** Save money.
20   **TEACHER:** No, you can't do that!
21   **BONUALO:** It is our welfare, we do what we want!
22   **TEACHER:** *(Perplexed)* No. I mean you can't just *not* work. If
23   everyone decided they were going to fend for themselves and
24   weren't going to work or pay taxes, the government would
25   just collapse. *(Pause. ALL looked perplexed.)* This is the United
26   States of America. The land of the free, the home of the brave.
27   The land where our forefathers brought forth democracy — a
28   new form of government that allows, we, the people, the
29   opportunity to elect which corrupt politicians will be making
30   a career at telling us how they're going to spend our money
31   and telling us what we can and cannot do. *(ALL start humming*
32   *"Oh Beautiful.")*
33   This is the United States of America, the land of taxes and
34   government bureaucracy. A land where every citizen,
35   regardless of race, creed, or color has the right to vote — but

1   doesn't, because we're free and we don't have to. The United
2   States of America, where we are fortunate enough to not be
3   inundated with the real problems that face this great country
4   of ours. Fortunate enough to have secret government
5   departments that save us from dealing with the truly
6   important issues that guide our lives. Fortunate enough to
7   have people with great smiles doing our thinking for us. The
8   United States of America, sure, maybe it's a land of taxes and
9   laws that restrict us, but it's a country founded on principles,
10   founded by people brave enough to die for what they believed
11   in. People who knew what it meant to be free. So they took the
12   tea and threw it in the harbor, picked up their guns and took
13   the shot heard 'round the world because they were fed up
14   with high taxes and fed up with being told what they can and
15   cannot do. So that's why you have to get a job and pay taxes,
16   because this is America.
17
18   *Curtain*
19
20
21
22
23
24
25
26
27
28
29
30
31
32
33
34
35

Talk Show Restaurant

Premise: Dot is meeting her new boyfriend and her mother at a local restaurant. During their meeting the waitress begins acting like a talk show host and takes questions from the other customers.

Cast: Mom — Really wants her daughter to get married, but doesn't like any of the men she dates.

Dot — Late-twenty-something girl who doesn't like introducing her boyfriends to her mom.

Waitress — The host of a talk show.

Customer One — Restaurant customer and audience member.

Customer Two — Restaurant customer and audience member.

Customer Three — Restaurant customer and audience member.

Dr. Hatly — Specialist in relationships.

Joel — Dot's date.

Customers/Extras — Other customers and audience.

Busboys

Props: Tables, chairs.

Scene: Inside a restaurant. Mom and Dot are sitting at a table. There are other customers in the restaurant.

1   MOM: So where is he?

2   DOT: He should be here any minute. And this time try not to

3   embarrass me.

4   MOM: Embarrass you? Embarrass you?! You have no idea what

5   it's like when I get together with Edna and the girls to play

6   cards. Everyone asking me, "So is your Dot married yet?"

7   and telling me all about, "My Anna and her doctor husband

8   this," "My son-in-law the lawyer that." It's downright

9   embarrassing. I'm running out of excuses.

10   DOT: Who cares? You don't have to make excuses for me. And

11   besides, if you wouldn't keep scaring away the guys I bring

12   around, maybe I would be married by now. It's getting to the

13   point where I'm afraid to bring them around. *(WAITRESS*

14   *enters.)*

15   MOM: Oh. Ashamed of your mother, huh? *(Begins sobbing.)*

16   DOT: Oh, this is just like you. Twisting everything around to make

17   me look like the bad guy.

18   WAITRESS: More coffee?

19   DOT: Yes, please.

20   WAITRESS: Forgive me for intruding, but I couldn't help

21   overhearing your conversation. *(To DOT)* I have a daughter

22   about your age. So, you're ashamed of your mother?

23   DOT: No, that's not what I was saying. There's just no pleasing her.

24   MOM: I'm easy to please.

25   DOT: Then what about Marcus?

26   MOM: That was different. *(To WAITRESS)* He was left-handed. *(To*

27   *DOT)* I'm just watching out for you.

28   WAITRESS: *(To MOM)* Maybe it's time to cut the apron strings

29   and let her go.

30   DOT: Can't you just accept me the way I am, instead of trying to

31   control everything?

32   MOM: Oh, now I control you? *(To WAITRESS)* She thinks I control

33   her.

34   DOT: You do! I mean you try to. Like the other day when we went

35   shopping ...

1   **CUSTOMER ONE: Waitress?** *(From here on out everyone acts like*
2   *they are on a talk show.)*
3   **WAITRESS: I'm sorry. I have to take a quick break, but we will**
4   **return in a moment.** *(WAITRESS crosses to wait on CUSTOMER*
5   *ONE. MOM and DOT just wait. WAITRESS returns.)* **All right,**
6   **I'm back with a daughter and the mother that controls her.** *(To*
7   *DOT)* **You were talking about shopping the other day.**
8   **DOT: Yes. It was Wednesday. I picked her up for our weekly**
9   **shopping outing and all I heard was one thing after another**
10   **about how I looked like I just rolled out of bed.**
11   **CUSTOMER ONE: Excuse me, I have a question.**
12   **WAITRESS: Yes.**
13   **CUSTOMER ONE: I don't know your name, the lady on the left.**
14   **DOT: Dorothy.**
15   **CUSTOMER ONE: Dorothy. You said you pick her up every week?**
16   **Maybe you should count your blessings. At least you spend**
17   **time with your mom. My mother lives out of town, and I'm**
18   **lucky if I see her twice a year.** *(EXTRAS react.)*
19   **DOT: It's not like that. I'm just saying that she's a little**
20   **overprotective sometimes.**
21   **CUSTOMER THREE: I have a question for the mother. My**
22   **daughter thought she was all that. The little witch. That's the**
23   **problem with kids today. All this time-out stuff. Not enough**
24   **whooping.**
25   **WAITRESS: You whip your kids?**
26   **CUSTOMER THREE: Darn straight. All that** *time-out* **stuff does is**
27   **teach a kid to bide their time until they make parole. Next**
28   **thing you know, they're back knocking off convenience stores**
29   **for drug money. And if they do get sent to the slammer, it's like**
30   **summer camp. They catch up with all their old friends and**
31   **their contacts; they have a place to sleep with three square**
32   **meals a day and they have more rights than the poor schmoe**
33   **on the street.** *(EXTRAS react.)*
34   **CUSTOMER ONE: That's bull! Children inherit their anger and**
35   **hostilities from their parents. Parents have to lead by example.**

1   CUSTOMER THREE: I do lead by example. My belt is my
2   example.
3   CUSTOMER ONE: I was never spanked when I was growing up
4   and I turned out fine. What you do should be outlawed.
5   CUSTOMER THREE: Oh, yeah. And while we're at it why don't
6   you make it against the law to be stupid. You'd have a life
7   sentence.
8   CUSTOMER ONE: You're a moron!
9   CUSTOMER THREE: Jerk!
10   CUSTOMER ONE: Oh yeah?
11   CUSTOMER THREE: Yeah! *(CUSTOMER ONE and CUSTOMER*
12   *THREE begin fighting, and the BUSBOYS jump in to break it up.)*
13   WAITRESS: I apologize for that interruption. Now, I'd like
14   everyone to meet a special customer at table two. He's a
15   therapist who specializes in women's issues. He's written the
16   book *Women Are Weird.* Please welcome Dr. Geo Hatly.
17   *(EXTRAS and CUSTOMERS respond.)*
18   WAITRESS: Dr. Hatly, can you tell us what's wrong here at table
19   five?
20   HATLY: Well, first of all, I can tell the daughter has a problem
21   dealing with her father's drinking problem and hates her new
22   haircut. The mother is subconsciously getting back at her
23   daughter for the twelve hours of labor she had giving her
24   birth.
25   DOT: Mom, is that true?
26   MOM: No! It's not true.
27   WAITRESS: Thank you Dr. Hatly. *(CUSTOMER/EXTRA enters.)*
28   For those of you just joining us, we're here today talking with
29   a daughter and the mother who controls her. Now, where were
30   we?
31   MOM: My daughter was telling the world how she wants nothing
32   to do with me anymore.
33   DOT: That's not true. All I'm saying is I need some space. I'm a big
34   girl and can pick my own men.
35   WAITRESS: Speaking of which, I'd like to introduce the third

1	party for table five. Everybody, please give a warm round of
2	applause to Joel. *(EXTRAS and CUSTOMERS react.)*
3	WAITRESS: Welcome to the restaurant, Joel. You're meeting your
4	date's mother for the first time. Are you nervous?
5	JOEL: No, not really. I'm sure if she raised Dorothy, she has to be
6	wonderful.
7	MOM: Suck up.
8	DOT: Mother!
9	MOM: So, Joel?
10	JOEL: Yes, ma'am?
11	MOM: What do you do for a living? *(EXTRAS and CUSTOMERS*
12	*react.)*
13	DOT: Mom! *(EXTRAS and CUSTOMERS react.)*
14	JOEL: *(To DOT)* It's OK. I'm a doctor.
15	WAITRESS: A doctor. Audience? *(EXTRAS and CUSTOMERS*
16	*applaud.)*
17	MOM: A doctor? How wonderful. Surgeon? Podiatrist?
18	DOT: Mom. What difference does it make?
19	MOM: Just curious. Chiropractor?
20	DOT: Just a regular doctor.
21	MOM: Let the handsome young man speak for himself, dear.
22	Psychiatrist?
23	JOEL: I'm a Hydrogeologist.
24	MOM: A Hydro ... And what would that be? I never heard of that
25	before.
26	DOT: Mom, did I tell you that Joel is taking me to the opera
27	tonight?
28	JOEL: I'm the only one as far as I know.
29	MOM: Oooooo. A specialist.
30	DOT: Joel, shouldn't we be going now?
31	JOEL: I think there may be one on Jupiter, but I am definitely the
32	only one here on Earth. Just a minute ... *(Begins talking to*
33	*voices.)* Yes, the great Joojoo says I'm the only one in this
34	quadrant.
35	MOM: Heh?

212

1   **DOT: Uh, gotta go. Come on, Joel.**
2   **JOEL: Call me Karack of Fareena.**
3   **DOT: Whatever. Let's go.** *(Pulls JOEL Off-stage.)*
4   **MOM: Dorothy! You get back here this minute. Stick me with the**
5   **bill will ya. Kids! I never will understand them. Jupiter?**
6   **What's that all about?** *(MOM throws money on table and exits.)*
7   **WAITRESS: That's our show. Thank you for tuning in. Join us**
8   **next meal for "My Daughter Is Dating a Doctor ... from**
9   **Venus." Until then, enjoy your meal.**
10
11   *Curtain*
12
13
14
15
16
17
18
19
20
21
22
23
24
25
26
27
28
29
30
31
32
33
34
35

Teacher Parent Conference

Premise: Martin returns to his old classroom for a parent/teacher conference to discover that not only is his son doing badly, but Martin himself never graduated from high school.

Cast: Martin — An ex-student with attention problems.
Teacher — A concerned teacher.

Props: Flashcards, computer, dry-erase board, Martin's permanent record.

Scene: Teacher is in a classroom, seated at her desk working.

1   *(MARTIN enters. Looks around briefly.)*
2   MARTIN: Hey, Ms. Johnson, this is the same classroom I had you
3   in.
4   TEACHER: Yes, I remember. Now your son is in my class, which
5   is why I called you in.
6   MARTIN: Right, yeah, he's a great kid isn't he?
7   TEACHER: Yes, he's great except at algebra.
8   MARTIN: Takes after his old man. Are those flashcards? *(Moves to*
9   *look at cards.)*
10   TEACHER: Maybe a little too much.
11   MARTIN: I used to hate these things; they drove me nuts.
12   TEACHER: But they are a very useful tool for learning the times
13   tables.
14   MARTIN: When will you need *that* in real life?
15   TEACHER: Mr. Freeman, you use math everyday in life, for
16   figuring out your banking to calculating how much lunchmeat
17   costs.
18   MARTIN: Yeah, right. Machines do that for you. I wasn't very
19   good at math myself. *(Moves to computer.)* Can you get the
20   Internet on this?
21   TEACHER: Yes, actually there are some very good websites that
22   are math related.
23   MARTIN: Look! There's porn on here!
24   TEACHER: Please, Mr. Freeman, we can't have that in schools!
25   *(They struggle for the mouse.)*
26   TEACHER: Don't you have a computer at home? *(MARTIN moves*
27   *away from computer.)*
28   MARTIN: No, when will you need one of those in real life?
29   TEACHER: Well, every day ... just like math. Everywhere you go,
30   everywhere you work there are computers involved. Can I ask
31   where you work?
32   MARTIN: Sure. *(Pause)*
33   TEACHER: Where do you work?
34   MARTIN: Simon and Simon Attorneys-at-Law.
35   TEACHER: Really? That's very surprising for someone with

1   your ... background.

2   MARTIN: Someone has to clean up after those lawyers.

3   TEACHER: Oh, you're a janitor.

4   MARTIN: No ... paper shredder ... but you sure can learn a lot
5   about the law that way.

6   TEACHER: Right, but back to the reason we're here. Martin
7   Junior is failing algebra.

8   MARTIN: Failing? *(TEACHER thinks MARTIN is paying attention*
9   *and turns away from him. MARTIN moves away.)*

10   TEACHER: Yes, he's just not getting it. He doesn't seem to be able
11   to pay attention to ... Mr. Freeman?

12   MARTIN: Is this a dry-erase board?

13   TEACHER: Yes, but ...

14   MARTIN: How do you think these work? I mean back in my day
15   they had markers but if you wrote on something it stayed.
16   Now just whoosh ... wipes right off.

17   TEACHER: *(Getting angry)* Mr. Freeman, your son is failing
18   school. He is going to have to retake the ninth grade if he
19   doesn't get a drastic turn around soon.

20   MARTIN: Really?

21   TEACHER: Really. I think he's a bright kid, but he just needs to
22   focus. His attention span is really short.

23   MARTIN: He gets that from his mother ... look when I scrunch my
24   hands up my lifeline looks like ... that guy ... you know, the
25   first president.

26   TEACHER: Washington?

27   MARTIN: *Yes!* Look, you can see his pointy beard and stovepipe hat.

28   TEACHER: Mr. Freeman, your son.

29   MARTIN: Right. What should we do?

30   TEACHER: He is going to have to retake the class at least and
31   maybe the whole grade.

32   MARTIN: The whole grade? That'll ruin his life.

33   TEACHER: Please, you're exaggerating; this will help him by
34   giving him a chance to really grasp what's going on in math.
35   But he'll need help. You need to be involved in this.

1   MARTIN: Me?
2   TEACHER: Yes, teaching kids is not just the job of schools.
3   MARTIN: Then whose is it?
4   TEACHER: Parents, too.
5   MARTIN: Then why do I pay taxes?
6   TEACHER: Parents need to take some responsibility in their
7   children's education. You need to spend a little more time at
8   home teaching him good habits.
9   MARTIN: But I'm not a teacher.
10   TEACHER: Parents are a child's first teacher. And frankly, you're
11   failing.
12   MARTIN: I'm failing? *(TEACHER gets out permanent record.)*
13   TEACHER: Yes. Math isn't the only subject he's doing badly in,
14   look at his record. Failing math, science, and English.
15   MARTIN: Getting an A in auto shop though.
16   TEACHER: But when will you use that in real life?
17   MARTIN: *(Suddenly realizing)* This isn't my son's record.
18   TEACHER: Yes, it is.
19   MARTIN: No, no. See, no Junior. This is my record.
20   TEACHER: *(Confused)* Well, I must have pulled yours out by
21   mistake. But why was your record in the active student files?
22   MARTIN: I don't know.
23   TEACHER: *(Realizes.)* There's only one explanation — you never
24   graduated.
25   MARTIN: Yes, I did; my picture's in the yearbook.
26   TEACHER: But you shouldn't have graduated. According to these
27   records, you failed.
28   MARTIN: *(Looking at record)* But I got a diploma and I ... Hey, I
29   got a detention in eighth grade for smoking. This is my
30   permanent record. I always wondered what this looked like.
31   TEACHER: There's really only one thing to do. You're going to
32   have to retake the ninth grade.
33   MARTIN: What?
34   TEACHER: You failed, and the only answer is to retake it.
35   MARTIN: I can't do that. I'd be in the same grade as my son.

1 TEACHER: Not if he passes.

2 MARTIN: But you said he was failing! Of course, someone could

3 send him on anyway. I mean I failed but I went on and that's

4 not the only time that's ever happened. I shredded some

5 papers once down at Simon and Simon on a big case where

6 someone was suing a school district for letting kids pass even

7 though they didn't ... Hey, maybe that's what I'll do.

8 TEACHER: Sue?

9 MARTIN: Why not? You people let me out into the real world

10 without really passing.

11 TEACHER: *(Very nervous)* Yes, but you can't sue us ... I mean, it

12 was a mistake.

13 MARTIN: People sue for mistakes all the time, I'll get some of my

14 lawyer buddies together and sue. They live for stuff like this.

15 Schools have a certain responsibility to their students and the

16 community as a whole, and one of those responsibilities is that

17 the student learns what he's given credit for learning.

18 TEACHER: So many kids pass through these doors every year,

19 some are bound to slip through the cracks.

20 MARTIN: What if I had failed auto mechanics?

21 TEACHER: But you didn't. You got an A.

22 MARTIN: I could have worked on a car, the brakes could have

23 gone bad, and someone could have died.

24 TEACHER: But that's all just conjecture.

25 MARTIN: Conjecture could be worth a lot of money. With this

26 evidence *(Holds up files)* I'll sue for hundreds of thousands of

27 dollars. I'll pay someone else to do the math on my banking

28 stuff. Me and my kid will be set for life.

29 TEACHER: You can't. I'll lose my job!

30 MARTIN: You should have thought of that before you passed me!

31 TEACHER: Give me those files! *(TEACHER chases MARTIN around*

32 *briefly and then stops at the computer.)* **Look ... Pam Anderson.**

33 *(MARTIN goes to computer as TEACHER takes files back.)*

34

35 *Curtain*

Testosterone Challenge

Premise: A television game show decides who the real men are, but today equal opportunity lets a woman on the show.

Cast: Fuzzy — Television game show host.
Butch — Construction worker with compassion and feelings.
Ishdaheem — Ruthless king of a small country.
Matilda — Extreme feminist.
Butch's girl — Sitting in audience.

Props: Buzzers, two beer cans, two television remotes, two containers with chicken wings.

Scene: Game show set with places for three contestants. An obstacle course is on the side of the stage.

Notes: Each buzzer should make a disgusting man noise instead of the regular buzz or beep.

1   *(FUZZY enters.)*
2   FUZZY: Hello everyone, I'm Fuzzy Hardbuckle. Welcome to the
3   *Testosterone Challenge.* The game show where we find out who
4   the real men are. I'd like you to meet our contestants for
5   today's game. First we have a construction worker from
6   Pittsburgh. Everyone please welcome Butch Harper. *(BUTCH*
7   *enters.)* Hello, Butch. Welcome to the show.
8   BUTCH: Hello, Fuzzy. Good to be here.
9   FUZZY: Next we have a gentlman from Minapoo. He's king of the
10   southwestern region and is married to eighteen wives and is
11   father to fifty-three children. Please welcome Minumummie
12   Ishdaheem Klatubarimba. *(ISHDAHEEM enters.)* Good to
13   have you here with us Mr. Klatubarimba.
14   ISHDAHEEM: Oooo. Ya, ya, ya, ya. Salutate me as Ishdaheem.
15   FUZZY: OK, Ishdaheem. Our next contestant is an ex-marine, now
16   a cabbie from Cleveland, who enjoys collecting beer cans.
17   Please welcome ... This can't be right. *(Confers with judges.)*
18   All right. Apparently to pacify some protesters we've modified
19   our contestant guidelines. Next we have Matilda Blanarski.
20   *(MATILDA enters. BUTCH pulls chair out for her. MATILDA*
21   *objects.)*
22   MATILDA: I got it, fella.
23   FUZZY: Welcome, Matilda.
24   MATILDA: Call me, Mat. And that's just beer.
25   FUZZY: Excuse me?
26   MATILDA: I collect beer. Forget the cans. *(Burp.)*
27   FUZZY: I see. Very good. You all know how the game is played. I
28   ask a question, you buzz in with your answer. Each correct
29   answer gets ten macho points. At the end of the round, scores
30   are tallied, and the two highest scores go on to the bonus
31   round. Everyone ready? Here we go. First question.
32   Humanity's greatest invention is? *(BUTCH's buzzer sounds.)*
33   Butch.
34   BUTCH: The computer?
35   FUZZY: No, I'm sorry that's wrong. *(ISHDAHEEM's buzzer*

1   *sounds.)* **Ishdaheem?**

2   **ISHDAHEEM: The MCP-11 automatic nuclear missile with**

3   **harrier tracking capabilities and chemical warfare retrofits.**

4   **FUZZY: No.** *(MATILDA's buzzer sounds.)* **Mat?**

5   **MATILDA: The remote.**

6   **FUZZY: That's correct. That's good for ten macho points. Next**

7   **question. Who is the machoest man in the world?**

8   *(ISHDAHEEM's buzzer)* **Ishdaheem?**

9   **ISHDAHEEM: John Travolta.**

10   **FUZZY: I'm afraid not.** *(BUTCH's buzzer)* **Butch?**

11   **BUTCH: It's all in the eye of the beholder.**

12   **FUZZY: No.** *(MAT's buzzer)* **Mat?**

13   **MATILDA: Me.**

14   **FUZZY: Judges?** *(Confers with judges.)* **Yes! I guess, it's always**

15   **yourself unless your in Vern's Tavern, in that case it's**

16   **whoever says "What are you lookin' at punk?" That will be**

17   **another ten macho points for Mat. Next question. What's the**

18   **best thing to get your partner for her birthday?** *(BUTCH's*

19   *buzzer)* **Butch?**

20   **BUTCH: Flowers, chocolates, and take her out to dinner.**

21   **FUZZY: No, nice try.**

22   **BUTCH: … Or perhaps buy her a nice piece of jewelery.**

23   **FUZZY: No, I'm sorry.**

24   **BUTCH: … A love note taped to the bathroom mirror.**

25   **FUZZY: No, I'm sorry it's …**

26   **BUTCH: A new car, or …**

27   **FUZZY: No! Anyone else?** *(ISHDAHEEM's buzzer)* **Ishadaheem?**

28   **ISHDAHEEM: Which wife?**

29   **FUZZY: It doesn't matter.**

30   **ISHDAHEEM: Does matter.**

31   **FUZZY: I need an answer.**

32   **ISHADAHEEM: A small third-world country?**

33   **FUZZY: No, I'm sorry.** *(MATILDA's buzzer)* **Mat?**

34   **MAT: An I'm-sorry-I-forgot-your-birthday card and four months**

35   **of groveling and begging for forgiveness.**

1   FUZZY: That's correct, for ten macho points. Next question. What
2   is the best way to propose to your sweetie? *(ISHDAHEEM's*
3   *buzzer)* Ishdaheem.
4   ISHDAHEEM: Kill her father and take over his country.
5   FUZZY: No. *(MATILDA's buzzer)* Mat?
6   MATILDA: When's the baby due?
7   FUZZY: No, I'm sorry. *(BUTCH's buzzer)* Butch?
8   BUTCH: Excuse me, Fuzzy. *(BUTCH moves into audience.)* Sweetie, I
9   am so happy to be with you and I just want to say, the last two
10   years of my life have been the best any man could ever hope for.
11   You are the most beautiful, compassionate person I've ever
12   known, and I would be honored if you would become my wife.
13   *(BUTCH and GIRL embrace. BUTCH returns to position.)*
14   FUZZY: Did she say yes?
15   BUTCH: Yes, she did.
16   FUZZY: Then that's correct. *(Buzzer sounds.)* Ooo. There we have
17   it. That means it's the end of the round. We have forty for
18   Mat, ten macho points for Butch, and I'm sorry Ishdaheem,
19   you have zero points, so it looks like Butch and Mat go on to
20   the bonus round. *(Ishdaheem exits.)*
21   The bonus round of the *Testosterone Challenge* is a small
22   relay consisting of four segments. The first contestant to make
23   it through the *Chug-a-lug-a-remote-scarf-a-burp-athon* wins
24   the game. We begin with chugging eight ounces of beer. Then,
25   moving to the televisions and using the remote, you must find
26   a televised football game. Once you find a football game, you
27   consume as many wings as you can and burp before the sound
28   of the final buzzer. OK?
29   BUTCH: Yes.
30   MAT: As long as it ain't none of that light beer. Light beer's for
31   sissies.
32   FUZZY: No. It's not light beer. Ready?
33   MAT and BUTCH: Ready.
34   FUZZY: Go. *(BUTCH and MAT begin relay. BUTCH offers seat,*
35   *offers food to MAT. MAT can't find remote, BUTCH offers his,*

1 *and then MAT ends up winning.)*
2 **FUZZY: There you have it. A new *Testosterone Challenge* champ,**
3 **Matilda, uh … Mat Blanarski. Please join us next time on the**
4 ***Testosterone/Estrogen Challenge.***
5
6 *Curtain*
7
8
9
10
11
12
13
14
15
16
17
18
19
20
21
22
23
24
25
26
27
28
29
30
31
32
33
34
35

Theater (Medium Rare)

Premise: An ex-boyfriend and girlfriend meet by chance at a movie theater while both are on dates. It is apparent that the two belong with each other, but will they get back together?

Cast: Myra — Talkative, complainer, on a date with Allen.
Allen — Myra's date, just trying to make the best of it.
Manager — Young person, tries to please the customers.
Clayton — Nerd, Myra's ex-boyfriend and Nina's date.
Nina — Clayton's date, just trying to survive the night.
Two theater patrons — No lines.

Props: Popcorn bucket, candy, pop, two movie passes, flashlight.

Scene: Movie theater. Two customers are awaiting the start as Myra and Allen enter. Allen is loaded up with popcorn, candy, and pop.

1   MYRA: I love Don Amillio. He's my favorite actor of all time. I saw
2   this movie seven times.
3   ALLEN: We can go see a different movie.
4   MYRA: No, this is fine. And the twist ending is great. You'd never
5   expect the lawyer to be the killer. *(Two PATRONS stand, give*
6   *MYRA a dirty look and exit.)*
7   ALLEN: Oh, that's nice.
8   MYRA: And the way he killed his wife. Who would have thought
9   he ...
10   ALLEN: *(Interrupting)* Where do you want to sit?
11   MYRA: I don't care. Wherever you want is fine.
12   ALLEN: Right here then?
13   MYRA: Ooo. I didn't bring my glasses. Do you mind if we sit closer?
14   ALLEN: No. Not at all. How's this?
15   MYRA: My neck always ends up sore if I sit this close.
16   ALLEN: Fine. Then how about here?
17   MYRA: Wherever you want is fine with me. I don't want to be a
18   pain.
19   ALLEN: Ladies first. *(MYRA and ALLEN sit.)*
20   MYRA: Actually, I'd prefer the aisle seat, if you don't mind.
21   ALLEN: No, I don't mind. *(They exchange seats clumsily,*
22   *exchanging popcorn, candy, drinks, etc. MYRA should end up*
23   *with popcorn. She eats periodically as she talks.)*
24   MYRA: I never in a million years would have imagined finding
25   someone like you with Selective Singles. Usually I end up with
26   the losers. But you seem pretty normal. I mean, as far as I can
27   tell. I'm sorry about dinner.
28   ALLEN: That's OK.
29   MYRA: I asked for medium rare, and what do they do? Give me
30   medium. No sense eating something you're not happy with.
31   Right?
32   ALLEN: Right.
33   MYRA: And I wouldn't have even said anything, but my
34   vegetables were touching my potatoes. I specifically asked
35   them to keep them separated. You heard me.

1   **ALLEN:** I heard you.

2   **MYRA:** I said I didn't want my food touching. And he looked at me

3   like I was a moron when I showed him the spots on my glass.

4   You saw them. As big a my thumb. And who washes their

5   silverware? Two year olds? I just couldn't stand for it.

6   **ALLEN:** Yep. You sure gave them a piece of your mind. *(Under his*

7   *breath)* Like you can afford it.

8   **MYRA:** And the prices! I'm surprised they stay in business.

9   **ALLEN:** It's one of the best four-stars around.

10   **MYRA:** Well, all I have to say is ... *(Starts choking on a popcorn*

11   *kernel. Another clumsy exchange of the popcorn bucket and*

12   *drink.)*

13   **ALLEN:** You're OK, then?

14   **MYRA:** I could have choked to death. I want to speak to the

15   manager.

16   **ALLEN:** It was just a popcorn kernel.

17   **MYRA:** The size of my fist! Excuse me, usher?

18   **ALLEN:** Myra, really. No harm done.

19   **MYRA:** No harm done this time! What about next time! *Usher!*

20   *(MANAGER enters.)*

21   **MANAGER:** May I help you?

22   **MYRA:** I nearly choked to death on your popcorn. I demand to see

23   your manager.

24   **MANAGER:** I am the manager, ma'am.

25   **MYRA:** You're just a kid. No wonder this place is run like it is.

26   **MANAGER:** I'm really sorry for the inconvenience, ma'am. I

27   would gladly replace your popcorn.

28   **MYRA:** So I can choke on the next batch? No thanks.

29   **ALLEN:** Let's just try to enjoy the movie.

30   **MANAGER:** *(Handing MYRA passes)* Here you go, ma'am. Two

31   complimentary passes for your next visit.

32   **MYRA:** *(Grabbing tickets)* Like I'll be coming back here. I don't

33   think so. You're lucky I don't sue.

34   **ALLEN:** Please, Myra.

35   **MYRA:** I don't want to spoil this evening for this fine young man

1	who spent his good, hard-earned money on that *bucket of*
2	*death*. *(MYRA shoves popcorn at MANAGER who falls into the*
3	*seats.)* You're lucky this time! *(MANAGER exits.)* Do you
4	believe this place? And these seats. They feel like I'm sitting
5	on cement. *(NINA and CLAYTON enter.)* Oh my goodness
6	gracious. *(MYRA slinks down.)*
7	ALLEN: What's the matter?
8	MYRA: Shhhh. *(Pulls ALLEN down.)* It's Clayton. I might have
9	mentioned him over dinner.
10	ALLEN: That's all you talked about.
11	MYRA: Just look at him. *(ALLEN goes to look.)* Don't look, he'll see
12	you. Just look at that hussy he's with. *(ALLEN goes to look*
13	*again. MYRA pulls him back again.)* I don't believe he's dating
14	already.
15	ALLEN: I thought you said you broke up last year?
16	MYRA: Yeah, well, he should still be grieving.
17	ALLEN: *You're* on a date. Do you want to leave?
18	MYRA: No. He's not running my life. We're here to enjoy
19	ourselves, let's just forget he's here. *(ALLEN and MYRA sit up*
20	*in seats. MYRA then proceeds to be very noticeable.)*
21	CLAYTON: *(Finally noticing MYRA)* Myra? Is that you?
22	MYRA: Oh. Clayton. I didn't see you. What a pleasant surprise.
23	This is my *(Decides to lie)* ... fiancé, Dr. Allen.
24	ALLEN: *(Confused)* Doctor? *(MYRA elbows ALLEN knocking him off*
25	*the chair.)*
26	CLAYTON: Oh. How nice. This is my ... *(CLAYTON tries to put*
27	*arm around NINA.)*
28	NINA: Don't even think it!
29	CLAYTON: This is Nina. *(Lights dim, movie starts. To NINA)* This
30	opening is great. Watch the red car. It's going to run right off
31	the bridge. *(Pause)*
32	MYRA: *(To ALLEN)* Here's where Don Amillio jumps in the river
33	and saves her.
34	CLAYTON: See, you don't know it yet. But she's actually a spy ...
35	MYRA and CLAYTON: ... and he doesn't know that it was *her*

1 **brother that he killed in Vienna.**

2 **NINA and ALLEN:** *(To respective dates)* **Do you mind?**

3 **MYRA and CLAYTON: Sorry.** *(Pause)*

4 **MYRA: Now she falls for his lies. He never loved her.**

5 **CLAYTON: She refuses to believe him.**

6 **MYRA: If he gave her a reason to believe him, maybe she would.**

7 **CLAYTON: She's all that ever mattered to him.**

8 **MYRA: Then why'd he dump her?**

9 **CLAYTON: He didn't. She dumped him.**

10 **MYRA: She knew he was just going to crush her and wanted to**

11   **beat him to the punch.**

12 **NINA and ALLEN: Please!** *(Pause)*

13 **CLAYTON: I'd never crush you, Myra.** *(Pause)* **I miss you.**

14 **MYRA: I miss you, too.**

15 **CLAYTON:** *(Turns to NINA.)* **Look. I was wondering ...**

16 **NINA: Go.** *(CLAYTON gets up, moves to MYRA, holds out hand.*

17   *MYRA jumps up, moves to CLAYTON.)*

18 **CLAYTON: What about your fiancé?**

19 **MYRA: Who? Oh, yeah. Uh, maybe you should give me a minute**

20   **to let him down softly.**

21 **CLAYTON: Sure.**

22 **MYRA: Allen? I'm really sorry about this. I hope you don't take**

23   **this too hard, but, well, Clayton and I ...**

24 **ALLEN: Please. Go right ahead.**

25 **MYRA: Don't worry, you'll find someone else. Thanks for the**

26   **great time.** *(MYRA and CLAYTON exit.)*

27 **NINA and ALLEN: Thank goodness.** *(Chuckle)*

28 **ALLEN: Hey, seeing that apparently we both just got dumped, I**

29   **was wondering if you'd like to maybe grab something to eat?**

30 **NINA: I would love to. My date kept sending back our food.**

31 **ALLEN: Medium instead of medium rare, huh?**

32 **NINA: How'd you know?**

33

34   *Curtain*

35

Time Lapse — The Artist's Model

Premise: This skit about an artist and his model falling in love takes place over a span of ten years. Periodically, a card holder crosses the stage to inform the audience of how much time is elapsing while the stage crew updates the scene and props.

Cast: Artist — Portrait artist hired to paint model.
Model — Posing for a picture.
Child — Nine years old.
Time Card Holder — Crosses the stage with time lapse cards.
Stage Crew — Two to four people who change the set during the time lapse.
Announcer — Just a voice on the radio.
Preacher — Marries the couple.

Props: Time lapse cards — 15 minutes, 10 minutes, 1 hour, 2 minutes, 2 hours, 3 days, 1 year, 9 minutes, 9 months, 10 years. Two glasses, shaving razor, easel, empty canvas, canvas with painting, partially built house of cards, completed house of cards, portfolio (collection of paintings), juice, bread, toaster, phone, coat for model, TV remote, clothes or other clutter to mess apartment, broom, bag of groceries, umbrella, pot, spoon, oven mitts, money, take-out order, table setting, video tapes or DVD cases, bridal veil and dress, tux and tie, pillow or stuffing, sketch pad and pencil.

Note: Some creative thinking in prop preparation can add to the efficiency and impact of the skit. The tux could be an open-back jacket with the shirt and tie sewn into the front opening; tape together the card houses for quick set up; a loose fitting white gown for the bride can quickly be rolled up to stuff in the model's shirt for the pregnant scene; the blank canvas can be used for the finished painting as long as it faces away from the audience, etc.

Scene: A small apartment with a kitchenette and living room area. Artist is sleeping on couch.

Notes: A light change, some ambient music, and the actors freezing while the card holder crosses and stage crew update the scene would make the skit more effective. This should happen as fast as possible.

1   (*Alarm sounds. ARTIST wakes and moves to sink. He rinses*
2   *mouth then grabs a razor to shave.*)
3   **TIME LAPSE — 15 minutes**
4   (*STAGE CREW — Applies tissue patches on ARTIST's face,*
5   *dresses him. ARTIST moves to kitchen, turns on radio broadcast*
6   *or song begins. ANNOUNCER says time. ARTIST puts bread in*
7   *toaster, pours some juice, and starts to set up easel and painting*
8   *supplies.*)
9   **TIME LAPSE — 10 minutes**
10 (*STAGE CREW — Drinks ARTIST's juice, eats toast, and finishes*
11 *setting up studio. Broadcast or song finishes. ANNOUNCER says*
12 *time. The phone rings and ARTIST answers.*)
13 **ARTIST: Hello? Yes. Noon? Sure. I will see you then.** (*ARTIST*
14 *hangs up and picks up remote and sits to watch TV.*)
15 **TIME LAPSE — 1 hour**
16 (*No change*)
17 **TIME LAPSE — 1 hour.**
18 (*STAGE CREW — Place partial house of cards on end table.*
19 *ARTIST is building house of cards.*)
20 **TIME LAPSE — 1 hour**
21 (*STAGE CREW — Updates house of cards on end table. ARTIST*
22 *is watching TV and there is a knock at the door.*)
23 **ARTIST:** (*Answers the door. MODEL enters.*) **Hello, you must be Ms.**
24 **Harquain?**
25 **MODEL: Yes.**
26 **ARTIST: Come on in.**
27 **MODEL: Thank you so much for squeezing me in like this.**
28 **ARTIST: No problem. Why don't you make yourself comfortable.**
29 **Can I get you something to drink?**
30 **MODEL: A glass of water would be great.**
31 **TIME LAPSE — 2 minutes**
32 (*STAGE CREW — Takes off MODEL's coat. Gives ARTIST and*
33 *MODEL drinks. Sets out ARTIST's portfolio. ARTIST and*
34 *MODEL move to sit on couch.*)
35 **ARTIST: ... and this is an oil I did for a coffee ad in *Mocha***

1   *Magazine.*
2   MODEL: They're all wonderful. You're very talented.
3   ARTIST: Thank you. Shall we get started then?
4   MODEL: Sure. I'm a little nervous. I've never done anything like
5   this before.
6   ARTIST: I understand. No need to be. The human body is nothing
7   to be ashamed of. Take your time. Whenever you're ready, you
8   can hang your clothes over there. You'll be posing over here.
9   *(MODEL begins to undress.)*
10 TIME LAPSE — 2 hours
11   *(STAGE CREW — Removes empty canvas and replaces with*
12   *finished painting. MODEL finishes dressing.)*
13 MODEL: Thank you so much.
14 ARTIST: You're quite welcome. I hope your husband likes it.
15 MODEL: Oh, I'm not married.
16 ARTIST: You're not? Then the portrait is for ...
17 MODEL: My portfolio. I'm have an audition with Flavio
18   Darnelion on Monday. He's casting for the artist's model in
19   his new movie and I thought it would be a nice touch if I had
20   an actual portrait in my portfolio. Competition nowadays, a
21   girl can use all the help she can get.
22 ARTIST: Well, good luck.
23 MODEL: Thank you. Here you go. I'll have the rest for you next
24   week. You deserve so much more. It turned out fabulous.
25 ARTIST: It's easy when the subject is as pretty as you. *(MODEL*
26   *goes to exit.)* Excuse me, Rachel?
27 MODEL: Yes?
28 ARTIST: I was wondering, if you wouldn't mind maybe having
29   dinner or something sometime?
30 TIME LAPSE — 3 days
31   *(STAGE CREW — Throws clothes, glasses, magazines, etc.*
32   *around apartment to make a mess. MODEL exits and ARTIST is*
33   *sleeping on couch. ARTIST wakes, rinses mouth, then begins to*
34   *clean apartment.)*
35 TIME LAPSE — 1 hour

1	*(STAGE CREW — Cleans apartment, hands ARTIST broom.*
2	*ARTIST notices time, puts broom away, and hurriedly exits.*
3	*OPTION: ARTIST could look out window and grab umbrella then*
4	*exit to return wet after next time lapse.)*
5	**TIME LAPSE — 1 hour**
6	*(ARTIST enters with groceries and begins to unpack them.)*
7	**TIME LAPSE — 15 minutes**
8	*(STAGE CREW — Unpacks groceries, sets pot on table and*
9	*hands ARTIST box. ARTIST is stirring pot.)*
10	**ARTIST:** *(Reading directions on box)* **Then cook at three fifty for**
11	**one hour.** *(ARTIST grabs pot and turns towards oven.)*
12	**TIME LAPSE — 1 hour**
13	*(STAGE CREW — Puts oven mitts on ARTIST. ARTIST turns back*
14	*and places pot on table, then takes a taste a with spoon. ARTIST*
15	*grimaces then spits. He then grabs the phone book, looks up a*
16	*number, and dials phone.)*
17	**TIME LAPSE — 1 hour**
18	*(STAGE CREW — Cleans kitchen and sets table. Hands ARTIST*
19	*money and take-out menu.)*
20	**TIME LAPSE — 15 minutes**
21	**ARTIST:** *(ARTIST at open door)* **Here you go. Keep the change.**
22	*(ARTIST unpacks the food onto the table. There is a knock at the*
23	*door. ARTIST disposes of the bag and answers the door.)* **Hello.**
24	*(MODEL enters.)*
25	**MODEL: Hi. I got the part.**
26	**ARTIST: Great.**
27	**MODEL: Thanks to you. Ooo. Something smells wonderful.**
28	**ARTIST: I hope you're hungry.** *(ARTIST escorts MODEL to table.*
29	*Both sit.)*
30	**TIME LAPSE — 1 hour**
31	*(STAGE CREW — Clears dinner.)*
32	**MODEL: That was delicious. I couldn't eat another bite.**
33	**ARTIST: Would you like to retire to the living room? I rented a few**
34	**movies.** *(ARTIST grabs movies. MODEL crosses to look at*
35	*selection.)*

1   MODEL: What did you get? *(ARTIST and MODEL move to couch.)*
2   TIME LAPSE — 1 year
3   *(STAGE CREW — Puts veil and bridal dress on MODEL and tux*
4   *on ARTIST.)*
5   MODEL: I do.
6   PREACHER: Do you, Arthur, take Rachel to be your wife?
7   ARTIST: I do.
8   PREACHER: You may now kiss the bride.
9   TIME LAPSE — 9 months
10   *(STAGE CREW — Takes veil, dress and tux. Gives MODEL pillow*
11   *or stuffing for stomach to look pregnant. Note: MODEL should*
12   *face away from audience or be seated to try to conceal the*
13   *stomach.)*
14   ARTIST: Would you like to retire to the living room? I rented a few
15   movies.
16   MODEL: Sure. *(MODEL stands to expose belly.)*
17   TIME LAPSE — 10 years
18   *(STAGE CREW — Takes pillow. CHILD sits on floor with crayons*
19   *and paper.)*
20   CHILD: *(Giving MODEL picture.)* Look Mom, look what I drew.
21   It's a picture of you.
22   MODEL: That's fabulous. Look, honey. *(Shows ARTIST.)*
23   ARTIST: It's easy when the subject is as pretty as you. *(ARTIST and*
24   *MODEL hug.)*
25
26   *Curtain*
27
28
29
30
31
32
33
34
35

Work/School Day

Premise: Stereotypical schoolgirls working in the real world. A substitute boss arrives and mayhem breaks out.

Cast: Margaret — The school bully.
Lisa — Panicky, unorganized, and gets picked on a lot.
Alice — Brainiac, timid, also gets picked on.
Nancy — Snobby girl.
Dee — Another snobby girl.
Fillenbrecker — The substitute boss.

Props: Five chairs and desks (or table space), a dry-erase board to write on, papers and office supplies, backpack full of files and organized papers, two reports, five lunches (no real food).

Scene: Margaret and Lisa are standing in an office with five desks.

1   MARGARET: Back to the old grind.

2   LISA: Yep. I hate Mondays. A nice long weekend, then ...

3   MARGARET: Back to the old grind.

4   LISA: Exactly. Hey, did you hear about Peterson?

5   MARGARET: No. What's up?

6   LISA: A car accident. Heard she won't be back for at least a week.

7   MARGARET: A week? All right! While the boss is away ... *(ALICE*
8   *enters and reads name cards on desks.)*

9   ALICE: Morgan, Talbert, *(MARGARET crumples a piece of paper*
10   *and tosses it at ALICE.)*

11 MARGARET: The rats will pay. *(ALICE looks confused, then continues.)*

12 ALICE: Wallace, Berger ... Here we are. *(ALICE finds hers, then*
13   *sits and begins to unpack her backpack.)* Good morning, ladies.

14 LISA: Morning, Alice.

15 MARGARET: Morning, Booger.

16 ALICE: That's Berger. Are you ladies ready for the big meeting
17   today?

18 LISA: That's today?! *(ALICE pulls a large stack of files and other*
19   *organized papers from her pack.)*

20 ALICE: Sure is. One-thirty in the main conference room. *(LISA*
21   *rushes to her desk beside ALICE and frantically begins to*
22   *prepare. NANCY and DEE enter.)*

23 NANCY: ... And she looked at me like I was the one wearing the
24   gawdawful plaid hip-huggers.

25 DEE: Ewww, like wig me out.

26 NANCY: For real.

27 ALICE: Good morning ladies. *(NANCY and DEE give ALICE a*
28   *bothered look, then resume their conversation.)*

29 NANCY: So, did Robbie in accounting ask you out yet?

30 DEE: No, not yet. But he's going to ask me today. I can feel it. His
31   kids are with his ex this week. *(ALICE catches LISA trying to*
32   *cheat from her.)*

33 ALICE: Hey, eyes on your own files, buster. *(LISA frantically*
34   *resumes preparing for meeting.)*

35 NANCY: Have you heard about Peterson?

1 DEE: I did. A broken nose. Poor girl.

2 NANCY: Like she can afford for it to swell.

3 DEE: Really. But anything would be an improvement.

4 NANCY: You're telling me. *(MARGARET moves to ALICE who is*
5   *busy sorting her files.)*

6 MARGARET: Hey, Booger. I believe you have something for me.

7 ALICE: For the quadrillionth time, it's Berger.

8 MARGARET: Like I said, Booger. You have my share dividend
9   report all ready, right?

10 ALICE: *(Mustering up courage)* Maybe I don't. Maybe it's about
11   time I stand up for myself and you answer for yourself. You
12   know you can't go through your entire life bullying everybody
13   to get what you want.

14 MARGARET: So are you telling me you don't have it?
15   *(MARGARET stares down ALICE. ALICE cracks and pulls the*
16   *report out of her stack.)*

17 ALICE: *(Trembling)* Well, no. Here you go. Sorry about that little
18   unwarranted outburst of insanity. *(ALICE hands MARGARET*
19   *the report.)*

20 MARGARET: I'll remember this when I get promoted.

21 ALICE: Yeah, good luck on that by the way. *(MS. FILLENBRECKER*
22   *enters.)*

23 FILLENBRECKER: Good morning everybody. Your normal boss is
24   not going to be in for a while and I'll be filling in for her. *(ALL*
25   *react.)* Can we all take our seats please? *(FILLENBRECKER*
26   *writes name on a dry-erase board.)* My name is Ms. Fillenbrecker.
27   *(MARGARET chuckles.)* Excuse me Ms. ... ?

28 MARGARET: Demeanor.

29 FILLENBRECKER: Ms. Demeanor. *(MARGARET chuckles again.)*
30   Is there something amusing you would like to share with your
31   co-workers Miss Demeanor?

32 MARGARET: No, Ms. Fillenbrecker.

33 FILLENBRECKER: Are you sure?

34 MARGARET: Yes, Ms. Fillenbrecker.

35 FILLENBRECKER: All right then. Like I was saying ...

1 *(FILLENBRECKER turns and continues to write and draw graphs*
2 *on board as EMPLOYEES act out.)* **I was brought in to economize**
3 **the efficiency of output in all divisions of this office. In the first**
4 **quarter of next year our figures will be at least comparable to**
5 **last year's projected ratios.** *(FILLENBRECKER turns around and*
6 *all employees straighten.)* **Can anyone tell me what our sales**
7 **dividends for next quarter are?** *(ALICE is the only one to raise her*
8 *hand.)* **Yes?**
9 ALICE: **Fourteen percent with a two dollar yield on each packaged**
10 **item.** *(ALICE hands FILLENBRECKER her report.)*
11 FILLENBRECKER: **That's correct.**
12 MARGARET: *(Reading from her report)* **With a gross annual rainfall**
13 **of thirty inches.** *(MARGARET pleased with herself hands*
14 *FILLENBRECKER her report. FILLENBRECKER is confused.)*
15 FILLENBRECKER: **Uh-huh. Thank you Ms. Demeanor.**
16 MARGARET: **Actually, it's Lowder. Margaret Lowder.**
17 FILLENBRECKER: **Right. As I was saying, to accomplish this we**
18 **are going to establish two strategic planning committees. I**
19 **need a volunteer to head up North-Eastern sales ...** *(ALICE*
20 *raises her hand. Pointing to MARGARET)* **Good, and how about**
21 **you, Ms. Lowder, for Southern? Now I have to run to**
22 **packaging for a moment, if you two can please organize your**
23 **committees, I will be right back.** *(FILLENBRECKER exits.)*
24 NANCY: **Gee, with a capital G. Who broke their nose and made**
25 **her boss?**
26 DEE: **Really. And what geriatric closet did she dig that wardrobe**
27 **out of?**
28 MARGARET: **Well, you heard her, I'm in charge now. Morgan,**
29 **Talbert ... you're on my committee.**
30 ALICE: **Not so fast. She said** *we* **were in charge.**
31 MARGARET: *(Frustrated)* **Fine.** *(DEE, NANCY, and LISA [still*
32 *working on report] line up. MARGARET and ALICE play a quick*
33 *hand of rock-paper-scissors to see who picks first. ALICE wins.)*
34 ALICE: *(Contemplating)* **I guess I'll take Morgan.** *(DEE)*
35 MARGARET: **Talbert.** *(NANCY) (Pause as they contemplate LISA.)*

1   You can have Stubans. *(LISA)*
2   ALICE: That's OK, you can have her.
3   MARGARET: No, really. You can.
4   LISA: Look, if it's just the same to you, I'd really just rather finish
5   my report.
6   MARGARET: Ooo, Lisa wants to finish her report.
7   LISA: That's right.
8   MARGARET: Ooo, little report finisher.
9   ALICE: Hey, give it a break.
10   MARGARET: Oh, and now all of the sudden we have a spine. You
11   know what, I think I'm taking Morgan too. *(MARGARET glares*
12   *and motions at DEE. DEE scurries to MARGARET's team.)*
13   ALICE: That's fine with me. You'll need all the help you can get.
14   The report you just handed in was my son's homework from
15   last week. I'm sure Fillenbrecker will have some interesting
16   questions for you regarding next quarter's earnings. *(Bell*
17   *sounds and all grab lunches and head toward door as they*
18   *improvise about lunch. FILLENBRECKER returns.)*
19   FILLENBRECKER: Uh, uh, uh. Not so fast. Be sure you all log off
20   the server before you go, we'll be rebooting it during lunch.
21   And Lowder, can I see you for a moment? *(ALL exit to lunch*
22   *except MARGARET who visually threatens ALICE as she leaves.)*
23   Please, have a seat.
24   MARGARET: Save it. I know what you're going to say. Let me
25   make it easy for you. I quit. I don't need this stinking job
26   anyway. I mean when will I ever use this stuff in the real world?
27   FILLENBRECKER: I'm sorry to hear that, but I understand. Your
28   talents are definitely being wasted here. This report of yours
29   was the most insightful economic analysis I've seen in all my
30   years in this business. Good luck. *(FILLENBRECKER shakes*
31   *MARGARET's hand then exits office. MARGARET is stunned.)*
32
33   *Curtain*
34
35

Wrestlerant

Premise: The world of professional wrestling in a five-star restaurant. The theme restaurant uses referees as maitre d's and wrestlers as waiters. Be careful when you ask for a chair or to see the manager.

Cast: Milton — Husband taking his wife out for their anniversary.
Celia — Wife not amused by the theme restaurant.
Wrestler — Waiter.
Opponent — Wrestler.
Ref — Maitre d' and referee.
Manager — Pro-wrestling manager.

Props: Table, chairs, restaurant settings, and fake furniture (if used in fight).

Costumes: Professional wrestling costumes and a referee costume, a tacky unmatched manager's outfit.

Scene: The inside of a restaurant. Milton and Celia are waiting to be seated.

1 MILTON: This is so cool. *(Sees CELIA not enthused.)* **What's the**
2   **matter, sweetie?**
3 CELIA: Well, I was kind of hoping for something a little more
4   romantic for our anniversary.
5 MILTON: What do you mean? This place is great.
6 CELIA: I just think this whole thing is getting out of hand. The
7   world is violent enough. I really would rather eat my dinner
8   in peace. *(WRESTLER and OPPONENT come brawling in.*
9   *OPPONENT pins WRESTLER. REF comes in and gives a two*
10   *count. WRESTLER gets loose. OPPONENT and WRESTLER*
11   *work their way Off-stage.)*
12 REF: Can I help you folks?
13 MILTON: Yes, we'd like a seat.
14 REF: Booth or ringside?
15 MILTON: Ringside would be great.
16 CELIA: Honey, I'm not sure about ringside.
17 MILTON: Nonsense. It'll be killer.
18 CELIA: That's what I'm afraid of. *(REF seats MILTON and*
19   *CELIA.)*
20 REF: Your heavy waiter will be with you in a moment.
21 MILTON: Thanks. *(REF sees brawl Off-stage.)*
22 REF: Hey! There'll be none of that! You! Put that salad bar down!
23   *(REF exits.)*
24 MILTON: You've been all bent out of shape since "The Body" was
25   elected governor.
26 CELIA: Honestly, a goofy wrestler as governor?
27 MILTON: He's not a goofy wrestler, he's Jessie "The Body"
28   Ventura.
29 CELIA: What's next? A sumo president?
30 MILTON: That would be so awesome! Can you imagine the whole
31   new way foreign affairs would be handled? *(MILTON gets up*
32   *and imitates sumo.)*
33 CELIA: Milton, you're making a fool of yourself.
34 MILTON: Oooosumma Binradin, I take you out. *(CELIA is*
35   *embarrassed. MILTON continues with echo voice.)* **Ladies and**

1   gentlemen. It's the pay-per-view breakfast special brawl. *Let's*

2   *get ready to scramble.*

3   CELIA: Milton, would you please just sit down? *(MILTON sits.)*

4   Wrestlerants. Next thing you know there will be boxing

5   banking.

6   MILTON: You think so?

7   CELIA: Honey, couldn't we just go to LaCassa Domia for a nice

8   little quiet ... ?

9   MILTON: Just give it a chance. The food is supposed to be great.

10   Here, let's see what "The Rock" is cookin'. *(Hands menu to*

11   *CELIA.)* Wow, what a selection.

12   CELIA: Yes, some selection.

13   MILTON: I think I'm going to try the Hulk Hogan Hoagie.

14   CELIA: What is an Apple Turnbuckle? *(WRESTLER comes flying*

15   *On-stage.)*

16   WRESTLER: I'm the Macho Man Waiter and I'm here to take

17   your new world order. Our special today is the Steve Austin

18   Special for three sixteen. It includes our slam burger and the

19   soup-lex of the day.

20   MILTON: I'd like the Hulk Hogan Hoagie with an order of onion

21   ringside.

22   WRESTLER: Would you like that Andre-the-Giant-sized?

23   MILTON: Sure. *(Mic drops from ceiling. WAITER places order.)*

24   WRESTLER: And at this table, ordering in at seven thirty-two

25   p.m., a Hulk Hogan Hoagie with Andre-sized rings.

26   MILTON: That is so cool. What would you like sweetie?

27   CELIA: I'll try the Nelson sandwich.

28   WRESTLER: The whole or half Nelson?

29   CELIA: The half would be ... *(OPPONENT enters and attacks*

30   *WRESTLER. They grapple and then WRESTLER reaches for a tag*

31   *from MILTON. MILTON gets caught up in the action, reaches for*

32   *the tag.)*

33   CELIA: Milton! Milton?! Settle down right now! Milton!

34   MILTON: Call me Mighty "The Meat" Milton! *(MILTON gets*

35   *tagged and joins fight. As they wrestle CELIA gets angry.)*

1   **CELIA:**   **Milton? This is ridiculous.** *(To WRESTLER)* **I want to see**
2   **your manager!** *(MILTON is winning the fight. Enter MANAGER.)*
3   **MANAGER:**   **I'm the manager, what seems to be the trouble?**
4   **CELIA:**   *(Pointing to the brawl)* **This!** *(MANAGER sees the brawl and*
5   *hits MILTON with a fake chair and joins in. CELIA gets mad.)*
6   **Hey, you big thug. Why don't you pick on someone your own**
7   **size? I'm coming Mighty Meat!** *(CELIA climbs on her chair,*
8   *slaps her elbow ...)*
9
10   *Curtain*
11
12
13
14
15
16
17
18
19
20
21
22
23
24
25
26
27
28
29
30
31
32
33
34
35

Easy Reference Guide

A Pile-O-Chips Now 3
Number of Cast: 6
Style: Physical and dialog
Difficulty: Medium
Props: Minimal
Costumes: Extensive
Premise: A group of army ants are in the middle of a battle, on the picnic grounds. The ants discuss their strategy and the fate of an ant wounded by "potato salad" shrapnel.

Back in My Game Day 6
Number of Cast: 3
Style: Dialog and physical
Difficulty: Basic
Props: Minimal
Costumes: Minimal
Premise: Two old men try explaining the beginnings of video games to a young boy who only knows virtual reality helmets. The men begin having "flashbacks" as they explain.

Backwards Bank Robbery 12
Number of Cast: 8 (10)
Style: Physical
Difficulty: Challenging
Props: Minimal
Costumes: Minimal
Premise: The scene is written for part of the first half to seem to be running backwards and the second half to run forward. It seems someone forgot to rewind the scene after the last rehearsal. Lines are not backwards but the order of the lines and the actions are.

Bad Night/Busy Week 17
Number of Cast: 6
Style: Dialog
Difficulty: Basic
Props: Minimal
Costumes: Minimal
Premise: Due to an oversight, an actress is forced to conduct a scene with four fill-in actors playing her husband at the same time.

The Bug Doctor 22
Number of Cast: 6
Style: Physical and dialog
Difficulty: Medium
Props: Medium
Costumes: Extensive
Premise: A doctor for bugs, who is a bug himself, treats an eccentric group of insects.

The Chi-Talian Restaurant 26
Number of Cast: 4
Style: Dialog
Difficulty: Medium
Props: Medium
Costumes: Minimal
Premise: Two local mobsters meet at a neutral site to talk "business." Since one mobster is Chinese and the other is Italian, the neutral site is a combination Chinese and Italian restaurant. A mechanical translator helps the conversation until it's accidentally shot and begins translating in different accents.

The Cookout 31
Number of Cast: 11 (could be done with 9)
Style: Physical
Difficulty: Challenging
Props: Medium
Costumes: Medium
Premise: It's a cookout with a catch. The horizontal hold on the stage is out, making the middle of the stage appear to be the sides. Everything that goes off stage right must immediately enter stage left, including thrown balls, dogs, and people.

Consumer Watchdogs 36
Number of Cast: 2
Style: Dialog and physical
Difficulty: Medium
Props: Minimal
Costumes: Minimal
Premise: In this world of big business and bigger advertising, consumers needs someone to look out for their best interests. Consumer watchdogs fill that role, but they also seem to have their own agendas and their own favorites when it comes to products.

Feen Daning (Fine Dining) 82
Number of Cast: 3
Style: Dialog
Difficulty: Medium
Props: Minimal
Costumes: Minimal
Premise: A married couple finally saves up enough money to go on a honeymoon and has a unique experience ordering breakfast with the locals' native tongue.

The First Dictionary Salesman ... 86
Number of Cast: 5
Style: Dialog
Difficulty: Basic
Props: Minimal
Costumes: Medium
Premise: The man who writes the world's first dictionary tries to peddle it door to door. Unfortunately, the majority of the population is illiterate and has no use for the book.

The Fish Tank 92
Number of Cast: 5
Style: Physical and dialog
Difficulty: Basic
Props: Minimal
Costumes: Medium
Premise: Life inside an aquarium. Fish are swimming around. Wayne, one of the fish, is missing. The police come looking. Nothing really happens. Hey, they're fish, what did you expect?

The Float Attendant .... .96
Number of Cast: 4
Style: Dialog
Difficulty: Basic
Props: Minimal
Costumes: Minimal
Premise: An airplane pilot and a flight attendant are put in charge of a lifeboat. They use their airline skills to keep control of the boat. One passenger is particularly upset.

Halloween Candy 102
Number of Cast: 6
Style: Dialog and physical
Difficulty: Basic
Props: Minimal

Costumes: Medium
Premise: This scene takes place inside a trick-or-treat bag on Halloween. The pieces of candy interact with each other, each with their own personality fitting their name.

Husbands Hypnotized 106
Number of Cast: 6
Style: Dialog and physical
Difficulty: Basic
Props: Minimal
Costumes: Minimal
Premise: A wife can't get her husband to listen to her and in a desperate measure orders the Husband Hypnosis Video. It works but she never knows.

I Done Got Happy 110
Number of Cast: 4
Style: Dialog
Difficulty: Medium
Props: Minimal
Costumes: Minimal
Premise: "Blind Boy" is a blues singer, but he regained his sight and is no longer sad. He arrives at the recording studio but is too cheerful to sing the blues. The producer and his agent try to make him "blue" again, through a series of traumatic events.

The Interview Come-On 114
Number of Cast: 3
Style: Dialog
Difficulty: Basic
Props: Minimal
Costumes: Minimal
Premise: A seemingly self-assured professional interviews a loser for a job, and they end up switching roles.

Keeping Up with the Joneses 119
Number of Cast: 4
Style: Physical
Difficulty: Medium
Props: Extensive
Costumes: Minimal
Premise: Two construction workers try to out do each other in their conversation, which then carries over into their work, until they begin purposefully hurting themselves.

Premise: A man on his lunch break meets a strange man who won't leave him alone until he gets some things off his chest.

Pirate Training 167
Number of Cast: 4
Style: Physical and dialog
Difficulty: Medium
Props: Medium
Costumes: Minimal
Premise: A new baseball player has just come over from the Pirates. Not from Pittsburgh, but from the Caribbean.

The Pizza Audition 173
Number of Cast: 3
Style: Dialog
Difficulty: Basic
Props: Minimal
Costumes: Minimal
Premise: A has-been actor looks for her last big break, and inadvertently lands a pizza delivery job.

Real Job Morale 178
Number of Cast: 3
Style: Dialog
Difficulty: Basic
Props: Minimal
Costumes: Minimal
Premise: An enthusiastic employee gets disillusioned when she finds out the real motivation behind her company's policies.

The Real Scoop 183
Number of Cast: 2
Style: Dialog
Difficulty: Basic
Props: Minimal
Costumes: Minimal
Premise: Two ladies who are neighbors get together and gossip about the local news of their town, which ends up being news about the other neighbors' private lives.

The Royal Pet Store 187
Number of Cast: 8
Style: Physical
Difficulty: Medium
Props: Medium
Costumes: Medium
Premise: Because of technical difficulties

two skits need to be put on at one time; unfortunately, one person is in both skits. See how he handles running from a medieval English castle to a modern day pet store.

Sound Off 192
Number of Cast: 5
Style: Physical and dialog
Difficulty: Medium
Props: Medium
Costumes: Minimal
Premise: The sound effects machine is broken, so the audience is asked to supply the sound effects, via cue cards, to the scene. The scene is two bank robbers returning to their hideout after the heist. All goes well until the cue cards are accidentally shuffled.

Stuntman 197
Number of Cast: 5 (+ extras)
Style: Physical
Difficulty: Basic
Props: Medium
Costumes: Minimal
Premise: An overeager stagehand suddenly gets promoted to stuntman. He spends the rest of the filming getting punched, hit, and finally blown up.

Sworn In 202
Number of Cast: 5
Style: Dialog
Difficulty: Basic
Props: Minimal
Costumes: Minimal
Premise: A group of immigrants are taking citizenship classes and get a little bit more than a regular history lesson.

Talk Show Restaurant 208
Number of Cast: 7 (+ extras)
Style: Dialog
Difficulty: Medium
Props: Medium
Costumes: Minimal
Premise: Dot is meeting her mother and her new boyfriend at a local restaurant. During their meeting the waitress begins acting like a talk show host and takes questions from the other customers.

249

Number of Cast: 2
Style: Dialog
Difficulty: Basic
Props: Minimal
Costumes: Minimal
Premise: Martin returns to his old classroom for a parent/teacher conference to discover that not only is his son doing badly but Martin himself never graduated from high school.

Number of Cast: 5
Style: Physical and dialog
Difficulty: Basic
Props: Medium
Costumes: Minimal
Premise: A television game show decides who the real men are, but today, equal opportunity lets a woman on the show.

Number of Cast: 7
Style: Physical and dialog
Difficulty: Medium
Props: Minimal
Costumes: Minimal
Premise: An ex-boyfriend and girlfriend meet by chance at a movie theater while both are on dates. It is apparent that the two belong with each other, but will they get back together?

Number of Cast: 8
Style: Physical and dialog
Difficulty: Challenging
Props: Extensive
Costumes: Medium
Premise: This skit about an artist and his model falling in love takes place over a span of ten years. Periodically, a card holder crosses the stage to inform the audience of how much time is elapsing while the stage crew updates the scene and props.

Number of Cast: 6
Style: Physical and dialog
Difficulty: Medium
Props: Medium
Costumes: Medium
Premise: Stereotypical schoolgirls working in the real world. A substitute boss arrives and mayhem breaks out.

Number of Cast: 6
Style: Physical and dialog
Difficulty: Challenging
Props: Medium
Costumes: Medium
Premise: The world of professional wrestling in a five-star restaurant. The theme restaurant uses refs as maitre d's and wrestlers as waiters. Be careful when you ask for a chair or to see the manager.

About the Authors

John J. Dessler, artist, musician, performer, filmmaker, teacher, and writer, began performing as a teenager in various bands and community theater productions. He attended The Art Institute of Pittsburgh for Visual Communication and, upon graduating in 1984, was hired as the newsroom artist for *The Beaver County/Allegheny Times*. During his fifteen-year career at the newspaper, he continued to perform and produce shows throughout the Pittsburgh tri-state area. He has won various awards in The Arts including first place for illustration in the Keystone Press Awards, and has freelanced for companies such as GE, NBC, and Heinz. In 1996 he founded The Outlet for Creativity in Rochester, PA. (www.outletforcreativity.org), which became a privately-funded venue to showcase The Arts. In 1999 The Outlet became a non-profit 501(c)(3). John quit his job at the newspaper and began to pursue fostering and supporting The Arts on a full-time basis as President of The Outlet for Creativity, Inc.

Lawrence E. Phillis, writer, performer, and songwriter, has a bachelor's degree in communication and English, graduating cum laude from Slippery Rock University. Larry worked as an editor/writer/designer for the Ellwood City Area Chamber of Commerce and Adult Literacy Action and has won awards for his layouts. In 1993, Larry was working with John's brother, who recruited him to help out with a production. John and Larry have been working together on projects ever since. Larry became Vice President of The Outlet in 1999. He has attended and performed with Second City in Cleveland, OH, and instructs young adults in writing and performing workshops.

Order Form

Meriwether Publishing Ltd.
PO Box 7710
Colorado Springs, CO 80933-7710
Phone: 800-937-5297 Fax: 719-594-9916
Website: www.meriwether.com

Please send me the following books:

_____	**Sketch-O-Frenia #BK-B263** by John Dessler and Lawrence Phillis *Fifty short and witty satirical sketches*	**$19.95**
_____	**Improv Ideas #BK-B283** by Justine Jones and Mary Ann Kelley *A book and CD-rom of games and lists*	**$22.95**
_____	**Drama Games and Improvs #BK-B296** by Justine Jones and Mary Ann Kelley *Games for the classroom and beyond*	**$22.95**
_____	**Theatre Games and Activities #BK-B304** by Lynda A. Topper *Games for building confidence and creativity*	**$17.95**
_____	**Theatre Games for Young Performers #BK-B188** by Maria C. Novelly *Improvisations and exercises for developing acting skills*	**$17.95**
_____	**More Theatre Games for Young Performers #BK-B268** by Suzi Zimmerman *Improvisations and exercises for developing acting skills*	**$17.95**
_____	**112 Acting Games #BK-B277** by Gavin Levy *A comprehensive workbook of theatre games*	**$17.95**

**These and other fine Meriwether Publishing books are available at
your local bookstore or direct from the publisher. Prices subject to
change without notice. Check our website or call for current prices.**

Name: _____ e-mail: _____

Organization name: _____

Address: _____

City: _____ State: _____

Zip: _____ Phone: _____

❑ **Check enclosed**

❑ **Visa / MasterCard / Discover / Am. Express #** _____

Signature: _____ *Expiration
date:* _____ / _____
  (required for credit card orders)

Colorado residents: Please add 3% sales tax.
Shipping: Include $3.95 for the first book and 75¢ for each additional book ordered.

❑ *Please send me a copy of your complete catalog of books and plays.*